Magnificent Milwaukee

Magnificent Milwaukee

Architectural Treasures
1850-1920

H. Russell Zimmermann

Milwaukee Public Museum

This book was typeset by Ken Lefevre
in ITC Berkeley Oldstyle at Parnau Graphics, Inc.
New Berlin, Wisconsin. It was designed by Gregory T. Raab.
Color separations were provided by Mueller Krus, Milwaukee.
The book was printed on Vintage Velvet by Inland Press,
Menomonee Falls, Wisconsin. Binding was done by Lake Book — Cuneo,
Chicago, Illinois. The project was directed by Mary Garity, Editor

Cover: Residence of Joseph E. Uihlein

Endsheets: Prospect Avenue around 1900.
Photographed by Jos. Brown & Son Studio.

Library of Congress Cataloging-in-Publication Data

Zimmermann, H. Russell.
     Magnificient Milwaukee.

Bibliography: p.
     Includes index.
     1. Architecture, Domestic — Wisconsin — Milwaukee.
2. Architecture, Modern — 19th century — Wisconsin —
Milwaukee. 3. Architecture, Modern — 20th century —
Wisconsin — Milwaukee. 4. Milwaukee (Wis.) — Buildings,
structures, etc.   I. Title.
NA7238.M53Z56   1987   728'.09775'95   87-5651

ISBN 0-89326-150-5

Earlier versions of selected stories appeared in *The Milwaukee Journal*

CONTENTS

FOREWORD

In *Magnificent Milwaukee,* H. Russell Zimmermann has produced a major work about a major city. In an entertaining writing style he tells the stories of numerous buildings, their architects and their occupants. Both as a guide and a local architectural primer, *Magnificent Milwaukee* provides the most comprehensive history to date of the buildings featured in this book.

Wisconsin's architectural heritage is extremely rich: Few states can boast the quality and quantity of Wisconsin's architectural treasures — most especially when it comes to ethnic buildings or the work of Frank Lloyd Wright and his disciples. The kind of mansions included by Zimmermann in this book remind us that our architecture of elegance is also worthy of appreciation.

Milwaukee is unique among Wisconsin's communities for the variety of its historic architecture and the opulence of its historic mansions. Its rich ethnic and industrial history gives the Lake Michigan city much of its visual character and sense of community.

The Milwaukee Public Museum, which published this book, is to be commended for its continuing interest in works on Wisconsin architectural subjects. It has published works of the distinguished Milwaukee architect Richard W.E. Perrin, FAIA. The writings of Dick Perrin, Wisconsin's premier architectural historian, are well represented in the Museum's publications *Milwaukee Landmarks* and *Historic Wisconsin Buildings: A Survey of Pioneer Architecture.* Zimmermann's book continues what is now a worthy tradition — one it is hoped the Museum will maintain in the years to come.

Few persons are better qualified to write about the architecture of southeastern Wisconsin than Zimmermann. His *The Heritage Guidebook* (1975), a survey of the state's southeastern architecture, has sold some 8,000 copies — no small statistic for a regional architectural guide. He may be known best, however, for over 100 articles about historic buildings he wrote for the "Home Section" of *The Milwaukee Journal.* This series began in 1967 and led to a merit award from the Milwaukee County Historical Society. The Society also gave him the Marion G. Ogden Prize in 1971 for an article on Milwaukee's famous cream-city brick.

Beyond writing about historic architecture, Zimmermann practices what he preaches. He graduated in 1960 from the Layton School of Art and currently heads Zimmermann Design Consultants. In his professional capacity, he specializes in old buildings, artifacts, and designs. He was involved in the restoration of Milwaukee's Germania Building, Pritzlaff-Gallun mansion, Astor Hotel, and Grain Exchange Room in the Mackie Building. He lives in an historic Wauwatosa house and served for eight years as the chairman of the Wauwatosa Landmarks Commission.

Through his writings and lectures, Zimmermann has been a major force in Milwaukee, spreading knowledge and an awareness of this wonderful city's heritage among its residents and admirers. This new book is an important milestone in Zimmermann's career and suggests that his personal tradition parallels that of the publications program of the Milwaukee Public Museum.

Milwaukee's heritage has been and is being

studied exhaustively by the city's government, using federal grant funds provided by the State Historical Society of Wisconsin under the National Historic Preservation Act. In 1981, this state-and-local partnership resulted in an interim publication, *Built in Milwaukee: An Architectural View of the City,* culminating an intensive two-year survey of the city's architecture. The Milwaukee Historic Preservation Commission, with its full-time staff, has been in operation for some two decades and is now an entrenched part of city government and the local development scene.

However, local, state, and federal governments alone cannot be expected to effectively preserve the city's architectural heritage. Local private historic preservation organizations such as Historic Milwaukee, Inc., and Wisconsin Heritages, Inc., are actively promoting awareness of significant historical and architectural properties. Publications such as *Magnificent Milwaukee* are important in providing information about the quality of local historic architecture and inspiration to citizens to plan for its preservation. In the last analysis, the preservation of Milwaukee's heritage, like Wisconsin's, rests in the hands of its citizens.

Jeff Dean
State Historic Preservation Officer
Division of Historic Preservation
State Historical Society
Madison, Wisconsin

INTRODUCTION

Milwaukee has a very special personality which can be traced — in part — to its topographic features, its unusual ethnic blend, a generous supply of skilled artisans and a single building material. Located in a large natural bay on the western shore of Lake Michigan, Milwaukee was built around the intersection of three rivers which joined here to flow into the lake. Most of the present central city began as a wild rice and tamarack swamp surrounded by high, wooded bluffs. In the early years an almost unbelievable effort made this low-lying estuary into buildable land. Bluffs were shaved down and the resulting soil was used to fill the swamp. The high ground dropped as much as sixty feet in some areas while up to twenty feet of fill was required in the low spots.

Milwaukee's early settlers congregated into three separate communities which were isolated from each other by natural topographic barriers. In the beginning an intense rivalry existed between the three groups as each competed for the steady flow of immigrants. In 1846 the competition ended when these groups decided to incorporate as the city of Milwaukee.

But the early incompatibilities left a never-to-be-forgotten, permanent scar on the city. Since they had no intention of merging, each community had laid out its streets without any regard for the other. In fact Byron Kilbourn (the developer of the western-most settlement) is said to have purposely surveyed his streets so that they would not line up with those on the east side. Later, when it came to connecting these thoroughfares over the river, the bridges had to be set on the diagonals, which survive today.

Into this interesting geographical situation came another key ingredient in Milwaukee's complex personality . . . an unusual blend of American and foreign settlers which combined to create a city with a recognizably unique flavor. A large contingent of "Easterners" from New England and New York State established homesteads on the high ground between the Milwaukee River and Lake Michigan. For decades this tightly-knit neighborhood was nicknamed "Yankee Hill" — a name which still survives in some quarters.

This group, which included a number of shrewd merchants, lawyers, and bankers, built a residential enclave that was considered the city's finest for decades. Milwaukee's "Yankees" included a number of distinguished and scholarly gentlemen such as Professor Milo Parker Jewett. Before moving here in 1867, Jewett planned and organized Vassar College and served as its first president.

A Scotsman, Alexander Mitchell, built banks and railroads and became the wealthiest man in Wisconsin. But it was the Germans who left the biggest mark on Milwaukee. They were present here in the prairie outpost period of the 1830s, but only in small numbers. In the 1840s pamphlets and books describing the area's advantages were widely circulated in Germany. When they read about the low price of land here, Wisconsin's liberal laws, and a climate which resembled their homeland, Germans began to move to this bustling young community.

The first immigrants were largely peasants from the rural areas, but, after the "revolutionary outbreaks" of 1848, intellectuals and student refugees began to flee in large numbers. As Milwaukee's German population grew it became increasingly attractive for would-be immigrants to select this city as the best place in America to become acclimated to the new country. In 1884, Captain Willard Glazier, in his *Peculiarities of American Cities,* observed that, "No one who visits Milwaukee can fail to be struck with the semi-foreign appearance of the city. Breweries are multiplied throughout the streets, lager beer saloons abound, beer gardens, with their flowers and music and tree or arbor-shaded tables, attract the tired and thirsty in various quarters. German music halls, Gasthausen, and restaurants are found everywhere, and German signs are manifest over many doors. One hears German spoken upon the streets quite as often as English."

It has been estimated that by the turn of the

Downtown Milwaukee, looking south on the Milwaukee River. Opposite, the Schlitz Palm Garden,
once called America's grandest saloon. It was
razed in 1964.

x

century, 72% of Milwaukee was German by birth or descent. At that time the Germania Building had the honor of being called the world's largest newspaper building. From that stately structure George Brumder ran a publishing empire which issued America's largest-circulation German language newspaper, the *Germania*.

The Germans turned Milwaukee into the nation's leather tanning capital and established a sausage industry which is still well-known. But it was the brewing of beer which attracted the most attention, built great fortunes and established large and powerful dynasties. In 1972 *Forbes* magazine noted that the Schlitz Brewing Company was still 80% family-owned and that fourteen of its seventeen directors were members of the Uihlein clan. In describing the family stockholders they said, "There are some 420 of them. Think that over! Four hundred and twenty people, each of them — on the average — a millionaire three times over. Can the du Ponts match that?" And this was only one of the city's many brewing families. By 1879 Milwaukee had sixteen breweries and a number of them — Schlitz, Blatz, Miller, and Pabst — grew into exporting giants with world-wide reputations. By the 1890s beer was the city's principal industry and Pabst could claim that it was the largest lager beer brewery in the world.

The power and wealth of the beer barons was evident everywhere. Schlitz built an opera house and a large observatory tower in their north side park. They operated a spectacular indoor Palm Garden which deserved its reputation as America's grandest saloon. Blatz and Pabst owned hotels in the city and all of the breweries built hundreds of romantic and picturesque taverns to dispense their product. Frederick Pabst built a fine theater which still exists, the city's first "skyscraper," and a fine summer resort on the Lake Michigan bluff (the Pabst Whitefish Bay resort).

Nineteenth century tourists would inevitably drive past the impressive brewery works, each of which was a picturesque grouping of ornamental architecture. But the favorite places to take out-of-town guests were the mansion-lined streets where the wealthy lived. These included Prospect Avenue, which ran north along the lake bluff and was nicknamed the "gold coast," Grand Avenue (now Wisconsin Avenue) which ran west from the lake, and Highland Boulevard which was lined with the mansions of so many Germans that it acquired the nickname, "sauerkraut boulevard."

The massive German immigration brought not only the talents for brewing and tanning, but astute political types, scholars and intellectuals, architects and craftsman, and an innate love for music, gardening, and beauty. The impact of this well-organized national culture cannot be overrated. Architects, trained in the fatherland, kept up with the old-world's progress by reading professional periodicals and buying foreign books from local dealers. They felt comfortable designing in European styles because the city was filled with clients who remembered — and appreciated — those buildings.

The German architects had no problem executing their designs since Milwaukee was a natural haven for builders and craftsmen who were familiar with the ways of their homeland. Cyril Colnik, for example, was sent to Chicago by the German government to set up its national wrought iron display for the World Columbian Exposition in 1893. He was encouraged to stay in this country and to move to Milwaukee, where so many people spoke his language and would appreciate his work. Colnik spent the rest of his life here creating some of the finest hand-wrought iron in the country for what seemed to be an inexhaustible list of German (and other) clients.

Robert Machek came to Milwaukee with incomparable wood carving skills and a reputation second to none. A native of Vienna, he had done work for the Hapsburgs and in, 1884, was awarded a silver medal by King Milan I of Serbia for his work on the royal palace in Belgrade.

Leonhard Schmidtner, one of the city's distinguished early architects, was educated in the universities of Warsaw and Munich and had, reportedly, descended from "noble stock." His father is believed to have been the "Royal Architect of Russia."

Erhard Brielmaier began as a woodcarver and altar builder. He later became an important architect whose Milwaukee office produced plans

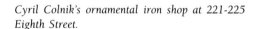

Cyril Colnik's ornamental iron shop at 221-225 Eighth Street.

Original India ink perspective drawing for Milwaukee City Hall by H.C. Koch.

for churches in thirteen states and Canada. His local masterpiece was St. Josaphat's which became the first Polish basilica in the United States and claims to have the sixth largest dome in the world.

Alphons J. Moroder established a Milwaukee branch of his father's wood carving company. Founded in the Austrian Tyrol in 1866, this large family of altar builders and carvers worked out of their Milwaukee and European studios to serve churches throughout the world. They produced catalogs offering their ecclesiastical carvings, statuary and elaborate altars.

The high concentration of European-trained architects and craftsmen could not help but leave a strong imprint on Milwaukee. Many of the city's buildings exhibit strong foreign influence and a few were so specialized and unique that they may well have been the only examples of their style in the country. For example, two local German architects created buildings in the Jugendstil (German version of the Art Nouveau) and German New Renaissance styles.

There is no better example of unique flavor than Milwaukee's spectacular City Hall. Built in the 1890s, this 393-foot-high landmark was designed to fit an odd wedge-shaped lot and is quite unlike any other city hall in America. The

architect, H.C. Koch, borrowed liberally from the Flemish Renaissance style for this ornamental masterpiece in granite, sandstone, brick and terra-cotta. A huge 10-ton bell, once the third largest in the world, hangs in the tower.

Unfortunately, Milwaukee's most spectacular example of German design has been gone for nearly half a century. Before it was razed, Emil Schandein's house could have been the national archetype for beer barons' mansions. Schandein was Captain Frederick Pabst's brother-in-law and a co-owner of the Pabst Brewing Company. The exterior of his incredible palace was an exact duplicate of Villa Gutmann in Baden near Vienna, Austria. It is not known whether he bought a set of plans or had the original architect come to Milwaukee to execute this structure. But one thing is clear from the surviving documentation: the mansion was finished in first-class style with no concern for expense. If Schandein's jewel was still standing today, it would eclipse the remaining mansion of his relative, Fred Pabst, just a few blocks to the east.

Milwaukee's architectural landmarks are interesting, important, and sometimes unique. But a single building material has probably cut a wider swath through American history than any of the

Emil Schandein Mansion.

individual structures. Milwaukee's world-renowned "cream city" brick was the first local feature to attract nationwide attention. The city was formally incorporated in 1846 and already in that year, the country was beginning to read glowing accounts of the pretty yellow brick buildings here.

The New York Courier and Enquirer compared Milwaukee's brick to England's famous Portland stone while a reporter for the *Buffalo Commercial Advertiser* called them "the best bricks I ever met with." It was the subtle pale-straw color which seemed so rare and beautiful that one could not help but be impressed. Street after street was lined with residential, commercial and even factory buildings made of this unusual brick.

Although it was the common material here, it was regarded as a premium or luxury product elsewhere. While Milwaukeeans were building three-course warehouse walls out of it, architects in other cities were importing cream city yellows to use sparingly as a veneer on the front façade of red brick buildings. As early as 1847 local brick yards were shipping south to Chicago and one building going up there prompted the *Chicago Tribune* to claim, "at a little distance (the brick) looks almost as well as marble." (After the great fire in 1871, the *Tribune* specified cream city brick for the re-building of its own offices.)

As years passed it seemed that no travel book, tour guide, or gazeteer would fail to mention Milwaukee's brick, no matter how short the city's paragraph. Captain Glazier observed that the brick "gives to the streets a peculiar light and cheerful aspect. The whole architectural appearance of the city is one of primness rather than grandeur." Milwaukee's yellow brick grew into a large industry and it was widely exported to cities across America for use in special building projects. A number of shipments were even made to customers in Europe.

Milwaukee's image as the city of yellow brick, and later as the center for German immigration, has tended to overpower the fact that this is a wealthy, cosmopolitan metropolis which hosted numerous ethnic groups, fostered countless cultural institutions, and became one of the largest manufacturers of heavy machinery in the nation. In the 1870s Milwaukee was the largest primary wheat market in the world. In the 1890s it could boast the manufacture of the biggest steam engines in the world, the largest tannery, and the largest lager beer brewery in the world.

Balancing these bold claims were such civilized amenities as Lake Park which was created by Frederick Law Olmsted, the world-famous

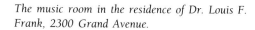

The music room in the residence of Dr. Louis F. Frank, 2300 Grand Avenue.

designer of New York's Central Park. And, in 1892 Milwaukee claimed that it "requires and has fewer policemen-per-capita than any other large city in the world." In 1876 a bold and forward-thinking group of women invited Julia Ward Howe to visit the city to help them organize the Woman's Club of Wisconsin. This group later formed the first stock company of women in the world and built the first clubhouse in America to be owned by a woman's club. Their Athenaeum building attracted a great deal of publicity and inquiries from similar institutions across the country.

In retrospect it seems that Milwaukee has been more conservative and frugal than other cities of its size. It has, accordingly, resisted the temptation to run roughshod over its history in an effort to grow fast. From an architectural viewpoint this has been good news. While there have been tragic losses due to civic shortsightedness and personal greed, the city's predominant attitude followed the European tendency to use buildings until they could no longer be used.

This has resulted in a generous supply of buildings surviving from almost all phases of the city's growth. Today it is still a pleasure to take scenic drives through Milwaukee's fine residential neighborhoods.

The residence of brewer Valentin Blatz on Van Buren Street was razed in 1964.

Magnificent Milwaukee

Architectural Treasures
1850-1920

Tinted lithograph of Alexander Mitchell residence on Grand Avenue. At one time Mitchell was the richest man in Wisconsin. His mansion was later enlarged and still survives, along with the octagonal gazebo, as a clubhouse. Following pages, a view of Milwaukee drawn by C.J. Pauli in 1876.

MILWAUKEE LITH. & ENG. CO.

*Mottled white and gray marble fireplace mantel in
the parlor of the south half.*

"Brown's Folly" was the home of Milwaukee's eleventh mayor. Built on the highest ground in the historic "Yankee Hill" district, this brick double-house, at 1122 North Astor Street, is one of the oldest structures in the city. In its more than 130 year existence, James S. Brown's tenement has witnessed a generous slice of local history. It has seen everything from elegant entertaining, with a small oyster farm in the basement, to attempts by an arsonist to burn the building down. Over the years a number of stories have been written about its colorful past with varying degrees of poetic license. Recent findings have not only cleared up some long standing ambiguities, but have unearthed some new mysteries.

The most often repeated "fact" deals with the origin of the knickname, "Brown's Folly." According to all previous accounts, the house was supposedly given the name "because it was considered to be too far out in the country, 'beyond the limits of possible buildings'. At the time it was built, it was at the end of a lane running through the woods." While this paints a romantic picture, it gives a false impression of the neighborhood landscape at that time. True, there were once-thick growths of small bushes interspersed with black, burr, and white oak trees, but that was more than a decade before "Brown's Folly." By the early 1850s Milwaukee's population exceeded 21,000 and the northern city limit was North Avenue.

On a remarkably detailed map of the city published in 1855, the Brown house is shown as the only one in that block, but in the six surrounding blocks twenty houses can be counted. Some of the neighbors, in fact, had been there for more than a decade so it can be seen that the country lane picture is a myth. On the other hand it must not be assumed that Brown built in a highly developed area, because the streets were mud and the neighborhood residents complained about stray pigs and water pools over on Prospect Avenue. When relatives from "out east" came to visit Brown's across-the-street neighbor, John H. Tweedy, they asked both men why they had built in such a "mud hole."

It is the 1855 map which presents the latest unsolved mystery. There, next to Brown's house, is the name R. King, which almost certainly referred to

General Rufus King, the pioneer newspaper editor and school superintendent. What is hard to understand is why, since he never owned the property and never lived there.

The true history of the lot in question begins with the subdivision of the block in 1850 by John B. Vliet. It was then owned by Charles Parker who lived in New York. How James S. Brown came to own it is an unanswered question. We know the lot was his by late 1850 because there is a mortgage recorded between him and Parker in that year. There is no record in the Register of Deeds office to prove that he ever received a deed for the property. A line in an 1853 mortgage proves that the house was already in existence by that time: "said premises containing a first class brick dwelling about 27 feet by 54 feet with outhouses." The dimensions referred to the north half of the doublehouse which Brown sold to Charles E. Wendt in 1855 for $5,000. Brown lived in the nearly identical south half.

James S. Brown was one of the city's greatest pioneer lawyers. Born in Hampton, Maine, in 1824, he left home at the age of sixteen to seek his fortune in the West. After studying law in Cincinnati he was

"Brown's Folly" from the southwest.

"Brown's Folly" sometime between 1900 and 1930. The middle and right (south) porch segments were added decades after the town houses were built. All of the old porches and trees are now gone. Immanuel Presbyterian Church is still a neighbor to the south.

admitted to the bar there. He moved to Milwaukee in 1844 where in a short time he was elected district attorney. He had the honor of being one of the officers in the last self government of the Town of Milwaukee. After his term it was incorporated as a city. According to pioneer historian James Buck, Brown and Jason Downer had greater energy and fight than any of their contemporaries. Brown "passed upward from one public trust to another, the admiration of young men and the wonder of old." He was district attorney at the age of twenty-one, state attorney general at twenty-four, and in 1861 he was elected Milwaukee's eleventh

mayor. After declining a second mayoral term he was elected to congress from the first district.

When Brown came to Milwaukee he practiced alone, but soon formed a partnership with James Holliday and Thomas L. Ogden. After Holliday died (while pleading a case in court) the firm became known as Brown and Ogden. In the early years Brown boarded with the prominent auctioneer, Caleb Wall, while his partner Ogden had a house in the southwest corner of Division (now East Juneau Avenue) and Astor. It is very likely that Ogden was responsible for talking Brown into building right across the street from him on the southeast corner. The neighborhood was known as "Yankee Hill" because of the preponderance of New Englanders and New Yorkers who settled there. The "Hill" part of the epithet is also based in fact: "Brown's Folly" sits on a three-square block plateau which is 670 feet above sea level and represents the highest ground between the Milwaukee River and Lake Michigan. Among his many and varied activities, James Brown and his partner Ogden joined Alexander Mitchell to build a handsome addition to the Albany Hotel on the southwest corner of Michigan and Broadway. It was rebuilt after an 1862 fire and used as the Chamber of Commerce until Mitchell bought out his partners in 1879 and erected the new Chamber of Commerce building which still stands on that corner. It is now called the Mackie Building.

But his first investment building, about five years earlier, was the brick double-house on Astor Street. In 1865 Brown brought his new bride, Elizabeth Shepard, to live in the south half. Only three years later, on August 18, the house narrowly escaped doom. A newspaper story read, "Before the celebration had closed last night, our city was startled by the cry of fire, which was caused by the burning of a barn and wood shed connected with the residence of James S. Brown, corner of Astor and Division Streets." The celebration, called the most universal jubilee in the

history of the world, commemorated the first message sent over the trans-Atlantic cable. Locally there were parades, fireworks, speeches, and an aquatic procession. The fire was glossed over in the shadow of the celebration, but the next day a follow-up story came out with the truth. The damage estimate was tripled and it was stated, "there is good reason to believe, however, that it was the work of an incendiary, as the house had been fired a few days previous."

But the Browns also had pleasant memories of the house: in 1861, four months after he became mayor, several hundred Germans serenaded them on the lawn. A couple of years later Brown sold his half of the still-young house to Theophilus Baker. In the next few years his wife died, he remarried, and after two terms in congress he took an extended trip to Europe for his health. Historian Buck observed "James S. Brown was a living illustration of a precociously active brain embodied in a constitution which was unequal to the task imposed upon it." The strain finally overcame him and at the early age of fifty-four, he died "a victim of complete nervous prostration."

As might be expected, this double-house has seen dozens of owners, including the first coal dealer in the state (Riverius P. Elmore), and a postmaster general of the United States (Henry C. Payne). But the building's most illustrious owner and longest tenant was the

Bird's-eye view of the north side of "Brown's Folly" taken from the roof of the Knickerbocker Hotel. The heavy line indicates the original 1850 building while the light line shows later additions.

family of Charles Schley. The Schleys had come from a plantation near Baltimore and brought with them the refinement and gentility which would become synonymous with the house for fifty-five years. Mrs. Schley, whose great uncle was the first governor of the State of Maryland, once enjoyed the reputation of being the most beautiful woman in Maryland. According to her obituary, "her home was the abode of free-hearted hospitality. Never affecting great entertainments, she kept her parlor and her dining room open to her friends and presided with cordiality, grace and withal, simplicity."

Schley was the first cousin of Admiral Winfield Scott Schley U.S.N., and was the oldest stock and bond broker in Milwaukee. Never forgetting their home state, the Schleys had Maryland hams shipped to the house along with fresh Atlantic oysters which they kept alive in saltwater "flats" in the basement. Of their five children, two daughters, Eleanor and Sibyl, were the last to live in the house.

In 1927 the house was rented for business purposes with the Zita dress shop in the south half and the William Quigley Co., interior decorators, in the north. Today Zita Inc. (a woman's fine apparel shop) occupies that whole building which is owned by the Bradley Family Foundation.

Although the old house has been worked over many times there are still enough original features to gain some impression of its early elegance. Both sides of the central dividing wall are symmetrically identical, but opposite in floor plan. Both entrance doors were side by side in the center and once led to staircases. The one remaining staircase winds up to the roof in straight flights with gracefully curved reverses. Unfortunately the mahogany handrail and its gently tapered ballusters are now painted over. At the top is an oval skylight. The parlor in the southwest corner of the first floor is the most original room remaining with its finely carved gray-and-white marble mantel. The most elegant and unusual feature to be seen is the fine Greek Revival doorway leading to the parlor. Made of wood, the opening is framed by a pair of un-tapered columns on half-octagon bases which support a deep entablature.

With the exception of the entrances and the broad wooden porch which was removed decades ago, the façade is much the same today as when Brown saw it completed. It is fortunate that this historic townhouse has found a dignified tenant who cares about its upkeep. ●

Looking up to third floor skylight through the open stairwell of Brown's (south) half of the double house. Below, the base of the only surviving original staircase. The mahogany handrail, newel post and turned balusters have all been painted over.

Rare, modified, Greek doorway to the southwest
corner room. This would have been James S.
Brown's "front" parlor. Note the non-tapered,
fluted columns set on half-octagon bases.

Standing nearly twenty feet tall, this spectacular cast iron fountain was shipped here from Philadelphia. It may well have been the largest privately-owned fountain ever built in Milwaukee.

Villa Uhrig
1724 North 34th Street

"Villa Uhrig" was once the palatial estate of a St. Louis brewer, Franz Joseph Uhrig. The beautifully proportioned mansion, which once overlooked twenty acres of formal landscaping, is now uncomfortably wedged between bungalows and duplexes. It was built in 1851 as a summer home and occupied by four generations of the family before the changing neighborhood began to nibble away at its gracious acreage.

An interesting twist of fate brought Uhrig to Milwaukee. He was a river raftsman in his native Bavaria, so when he came to Baltimore in 1836, he pursued his occupation on the Susquehanna River. These were the days before the great railroad boom when steamboat traffic on America's inland waterways dominated travel and commerce. Uhrig later found himself operating a packet boat named "Pearl" on the Ohio River between St. Louis and Louisville.

It was during those early years on the river that he loaned $1,500 to a man who later had to give him a brewery instead of the cash re-payment. Uhrig, who had no previous knowledge of brewing, suddenly changed the focus of his life to the corner of 18th and Market streets in St. Louis where he began to produce beer.

Because of his new business, Uhrig began to make frequent trips to Milwaukee to buy barley. After a while, one of his friends, Joseph Schlitz, suggested that he escape the unbearably hot and humid summers in St. Louis by building a second home here.

Afraid that it would be too damp near the lake, he found a piece of property on the west side bounded by the Lisbon Plank toll road (Lisbon Avenue) on the north, Walnut Street on the south, the Milwaukee Road tracks on the east (near 30th Street), and Western Avenue (35th Street) on the west. He bought twenty acres for $100 an acre. It took a man with great foresight to attempt a project like this on what then looked anything but attractive: the land was swampy in one corner and the hilltop was cutover and barren. But Uhrig had visions of the exquisite villas and palaces of German princes and he was determined to civilize this coarse piece of country.

He built his mansion high on the property and then, one-by-one, out-buildings and improvements of all kinds began to spring up. First there was a large stable-barn, a brick gardener's residence, a delicate lattice-work garden pavilion and a very pretty little out-house which came to be called the "eagle house."

Later there came a special building for pheasants, a chicken house and a spectacular three-story-high pump house with a windmill on top. No mean cover for a well-head, this wooden structure had four corner turrets with conical caps, a balcony which circled the building, colored glass windows and an observation platform on the roof.

But architecture was only the beginning of this dream. Franz Joseph decided to pattern his estate after the grounds of a specific villa which he admired in Germany. A neat gravel driveway was cut south from the Lisbon Plank Road and it then split halfway up the hill to form a large circle which swept past the front of the house. A section of the circle — directly in front of the house — was paved with brick. A footpath bisected the circle and went north from the front door, passing between two rows of lilacs, to a fountain surrounded by benches.

Uhrig bought this spectacular cast iron fountain in Philadelphia and had it shipped here in pieces. Standing nearly twenty feet tall, it might well have been the largest privately-owned fountain ever built in Milwaukee. The local trend was to paint such structures black, but Uhrig painted his white, a fact which made its full beauty stand out sharply against the surrounding plantings. A full-size female figure and four large swans made this fountain memorable.

Spreading away from this focal point were two apple orchards, numerous flower beds, gooseberries, currants and two rows of poplar trees which formed an "allee" through which Uhrig would later take his daily walks.

The mansion, which was patterned after the Uhrig home in St. Louis, was of Italianate or "Italian Villa" design. Its hipped roof was surmounted by a shuttered cupola from which Lake Michigan could be seen. Eight wooden Corinthian columns supported the stately front porch.

All trim was made of unusually heavy stock with rich moldings and generous hand carving. The roof overhang was supported by numerous scroll-cut brackets with turned drop finials and the fascia board was paneled between them. The already complex cornice was further embellished with a scalloped cresting.

Inside, a magnificent hallway with a fourteen-foot ceiling divided the house into equal halves and a graceful staircase led to the four bedrooms above. All the windows were "French" and opened to the floor with large china knobs.

In 1865, Uhrig's daughter Josephine married a handsome Civil War veteran, Colonel Otto K. Lademan. Every summer thereafter, the Uhrigs and the Lademans gathered their horses and coachmen and set out for Milwaukee, taking a wagonload of Grandpa's imported wine from the Rhineland with them. Joseph Uhrig Lademan, the colonel's son, remembered tending the horses on the trip east and being sidetracked where he had to wave at the rest of the family as they whizzed by on a passenger train.

When they arrived in Milwaukee they were greeted by their caretaker, "Lisbett," a woman who was the estate's only inhabitant through the winter. The wine was then unloaded and neatly stacked in the two brick-vaulted wine cellars.

By 1871 the two families had outgrown the square mansion, so Uhrig hired the architect of the old Milwaukee courthouse, L. A. Schmidtner, to design an addition. The result was a pleasingly proportioned pair of wings on both sides of the house. Grandpa and Grandma Uhrig lived in the east wing and Col. and Mrs. Lademan lived in the west with their children (eventually eight).

A mansion of that size was bound to provide a variety of possibilities for entertaining curious children. The tall sweeping staircase was just asking to become a sliding board. It was forbidden, but the children could always find a moment to zip down the banister when no one was looking. One of the girls later recalled pushing parental patience to the limit: "I know I put the deepest scratch in it with some cheap pin I was wearing. I was about twelve years old. I never admitted it though."

The dumbwaiter, which lifted food from the ground floor kitchen to the dining room, was another favorite. The children liked to secretly haul themselves up and down on it. "Uncle Oscar" kept a human skull he'd obtained in medical school up in the cupola, and when the children could muster the courage, they would sneak up for a peek.

In the 1890s Uhrig sold the brewery in St. Louis and the two families moved to their villa in Milwaukee to live year round. They brought with them two precious souvenirs, a fine mantel from their home and the wrought iron gates from the entrance to the brewery.

The mantel, in front of which Col. and Mrs. Lademan were married, was installed in the parlor of the Milwaukee home where it remains today. There it became the setting for still another wedding. Joseph U. Lademan Jr. remembers, "As the pillow bearer for my Aunt Walburga's wedding, they decked me out in some

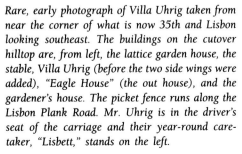

Rare, early photograph of Villa Uhrig taken from near the corner of what is now 35th and Lisbon looking southeast. The buildings on the cutover hilltop are, from left, the lattice garden house, the stable, Villa Uhrig (before the two side wings were added), "Eagle House" (the out house), and the gardener's house. The picket fence runs along the Lisbon Plank Road. Mr. Uhrig is in the driver's seat of the carriage and their year-round caretaker, "Lisbett," stands on the left.

Above, the front of Villa Uhrig from the northeast. Note the shortened one-story eastern wing which had to be lopped off on an angle when 34th Street was cut through. The duplex at the right occupies the spot where the fountain once stood. Right, a view of Uhrig's estate in 1967 taken from the roof of a tall building which now stands at the location of the original entrance to the property on Lisbon Avenue. The two-story white building to the far right of Villa Uhrig is the old gardener's cottage.

This 1880s view shows Villa Uhrig from the northwest after the two one-story wings were added. On this close-up one can see how much of the carved and scroll-out wooden trim is now missing.

kind of Buster Brown suit. I took a razzing later from the guys in the neighborhood who had watched the affair through one of the windows."

The old iron gates were installed at the entrance to the property at the exact point where the sidewalks meet today on the southwest corner of 34th and Lisbon. From there the gravel driveway stretched up the hill to the fountain.

Later, another Lademan married and moved into the house, adding improvements such as hardwood floors and the second floor bathroom. After grandma Lademan's death, her son and Dr. Lademan bought the home from the estate. In the winter they began to close off the eastern part of the house to conserve heat. Meals were served on the ground floor, as it became too much trouble to haul food up on the dumbwaiter to the formal dining room.

Shortly after the turn of the century, the pressures of the expanding city began to cramp the spacious estate and its days of glory were numbered. One by one parcels of the property were sold and buildings began to sprout, cluttering the skyline around the stately mansion.

As the land was sold off certain parcels temporarily became vacant lots and neighbors helped themselves to nursery stock. Gooseberries and currants began to

show up throughout the area. One lady relished the memory of the "homemade current jelly and mouthwatering gooseberry pies" that descended from the Uhrig plants. She also remembered taking home a tiny poplar tree that sprouted beside the lilac row, and then living to see it grow into "an enormous tree."

As time passed the property shrank, the entertaining dwindled and the occupants of the old mansion kept to themselves. No activity was seen on the grounds and neighborhood children spoke of the house as being "haunted." The temptation was too great and a few of the local youth finally, in the words of one of them, "loosened some boards in the fence and stepped into the enchanting and forbidden garden."

In 1913 the worst insult to the mansion's fading elegance happened when 34th Street was cut through to connect Lisbon Avenue with Walnut Street. This intrusion slashed through the fountain circle and necessitated the removal of two-thirds of the house's east wing. The final indignity was a house which then appeared in the front yard where the lilac rows had once been.

By the summer of 1943, after four generations in the same family, the lengthy staircases and maintenance problems forced the Lademan descendants to move. The "Villa" and its now tiny lot were sold for $5,000.

Shortly thereafter the house fell into the hands of a woman who opened it as a spiritualist cult church. Later it was divided into five apartments.

In 1964 it was purchased by a sympathetic couple who lived in the house and rented rooms while working on its restoration. They, however, were forced to abandon the project as the area deteriorated into what in 1986 was called one of the poorest and most depressed neighborhoods in the city.

The fountain was given to Jacob Donges, a friend of the Lademans, but it has since disappeared. The wrought iron gates, which had come all the way from the St. Louis brewery, were donated to the House of the Good Shepherd. They survived there until 1967 when they were sent to the junk yard. Of the once gracious grounds only a small segment of the brick driveway circle remains to be seen in front of the porch today. And the brick gardener's cottage is still in use, with a new pitched roof, at what is now the intersection of two alleys behind the house.

Pieces may be missing, but the majesty of Franz Joseph Uhrig's hilltop mansion is hard to eradicate. Its tall and stately form still dominates the neighborhood. And, when an unsuspecting stranger turns down 34th Street for the first time, the sight of this very special villa must be startling. ●

Main entrance to the estate on the Lisbon Plank Road. The iron fence, posts and gates were shipped here from Uhrig's brewery in St. Louis. Thirty-fourth Street sliced through the property about where the left brick post stands in this June, 1900 photograph. Right, this estate plan was drawn from memory by one of Uhrig's granddaughters who was raised in the house.

Above, the Lion House in 1986 with its small pane windows, one-step stair-side plinths and lions restored. Facing page, the Diederichs' house as it looked between 1895, when the second story was added, and 1985 when the restoration was completed. During this period the house was painted to disguise the less-than-perfect match of building materials and the contrast between new and old.

The "Lion House," at 1241 North Franklin Place, has received more attention in print than almost any other residential landmark in Milwaukee. More than a dozen times its romantic and colorful story has been told with more or less artistic license. Recent discoveries have proven that a number of the oft-repeated legends about the house and its owners have been erroneous, and that the sad life of Edward Diederichs, its builder, was probably more tragic than anyone realizes.

The story begins when Diederichs, who had been living in the "Riga" district of Russia, moved to Milwaukee in 1849. An early writer described him as "one of Milwaukee's early German settlers of the cultivated type." He is said to have arrived with $80,000 cash which he invested in a variety of schemes, particularly real estate. The house, according to most stories, was built in 1851.

Records show that he purchased his lot in three small strips beginning in 1852. It was not until December of 1855, when he received the deed for the final thirty-five foot parcel, that Diederichs actually owned all of the land on which to build his house.

Earlier accounts seem to agree that Diederichs planned his own house and had even made the drawings himself. An 1899 interview with the famous Milwaukee architect Henry C. Koch, sheds new light on the subject. What was thought for years to have been an amateur job can now be connected with three of Milwaukee's most important early architects.

The plans for Diederichs' house were drawn by the firm of Mygatt and Schmidtner. George W. Mygatt, one of the city's first and most accomplished architects, was responsible for Plymouth Church, the old United States Hotel, and numerous early mansions. His partner was Leonhard A. Schmidtner, whose father was said to have been the royal architect of Russia. Schmidtner received the most prominent and largest commission to be awarded in the early days when he designed the Milwaukee County Courthouse. (That $650,000 job, completed in 1873, stood in what is now a square park in front of St. John's Cathedral on Jackson Street.) Diederichs, however, was involved to the extent that he supplied "sketches and pictures" of a house in the old country which he liked and wanted to simulate.

Henry Koch, who had just begun with Mygatt and Schmidtner as a draftsman, went on to become one of the city's greatest architects. Among his surviving works are City Hall, Calvary Church, and the Wells Building. It was young Henry Koch who produced drawings for the original lions which gave the house its nickname. Again, Diederichs supplied "sketches," while Koch enlarged and refined them under his supervision. The lions, which flanked the steps to the front porch, were executed by Richard H. White, an ornamental woodcarver. According to the 1899 interview, "they were made of all-clear white pine taken from an old mast, and that is the reason they have never decayed." However, even the best wood has its limitations in Wisconsin weather, and they did finally decay. In 1944 the lions, which had spent nearly ninety years in front of this house, had to be removed and scrapped. But the name "Lion House" was so deeply entrenched that it persisted in common usage for another thirty years.

Edward Diederichs was supposed to have invested his "fortune" in real estate, a distillery, and a curious scheme of landscaping the bluff along the lake front. The latter project, called the "Lighthouse Pleasure Garden," was created by terracing the bluff between Wisconsin and Mason streets, adding gravel walkways leading to the beach, and building a breakwater. An equivalent to the modern refreshment stand was

provided at the top of the park. But while Diederichs found the lake bluff and bay view desirable, he did not reckon with the public's misconception that damp lake air was dangerous and unhealthy. His was an idea way ahead of its time and he was not successful in making this a popular public resort.

It would seem, by looking at his pretentious mansion and the grandiose projects with which his name was associated, that Diederichs was indeed a wealthy man. In truth, however, his financial condition was so questionable at the time he built the house, one wonders if he ever had possessed the so called "fortune." County records indicate he acquired money from relatives in Switzerland to buy his property and that he was often in arrears on his taxes. It would seem that he was either a naive immigrant whose ideas were costlier than he could afford or that he really had no money and was just an ambitious and reckless promoter.

In either case Diederichs' last straw was a disastrous fire which struck his new mansion in December of 1859. According to the newspaper account, "Saturday evening a fire broke out in the large and handsome mansion of Edward Diederichs on Franklin Street at the junction of Prospect Street, in the first ward, and before the engines arrived on the spot [it] was enveloped in flames, the conflagration

Right, Greek ornamental detail on the southeast corner. The roof cresting was added in the 1895 re-building and is made of hammered sheet zinc. The window lintel is decorated with a carving in white pine.

The best early photograph of the house was taken in 1895, probably as a documentation just before the second story was added. Note the original lions and the shallow portico with only four columns.

The entrance portico was originally shallow and had only the front row of four columns. When the upper story was added the architect pulled the existing structure forward and added two "sleeper" columns behind the corners.

causing an immense lurid reflection in the sky. The firemen, when they arrived on the ground, worked manfully to arrest the progress of destruction. But owing to the strong wind and the combustible nature of the edifice, the most strenuous exertions seemed unavailing to save the building, or indeed the contents, and we were told that the greater part of the furniture was destroyed."

Tradition says that Diederichs' wife, Bertha, could not bear to live in any other house and she implored him to rebuild the ruin "exactly as it was." His investments having largely failed by this time, Diederichs did not have the money for the project. But, to please Bertha, he was forced to secure a $7,000 mortgage loan to finance the job. Shortly thereafter his bank began foreclosure proceedings and by 1863

Diederichs had left town. Years later word came back to his Milwaukee friends that Edward Diederichs had died in a poorhouse in New York.

The newly rebuilt house was sold in 1864 to Henry Mann, the owner of a chair and woodenware factory. Although he left no mark on the house, Mann did purchase an additional fifty feet of land to the north, extending the property to the corner of Knapp Street. Mann loved the carved lions which had come to be a household word in Milwaukee. They had escaped damage in the earlier fire and he was not about to put them at risk again. In 1875, during his occupancy, a minor fire broke out and it was reported that he instructed the firemen to "save the lions, whatever else might burn."

21

The present portico looking south past the two "sleeper" columns added in 1895. The new carved mahogany lions were added in the 1985 restoration.

In 1895 Mann sold the house to John Johnston whose uncle, Alexander Mitchell, was at one time the richest man in the state of Wisconsin. Johnston had come here from his native Scotland to work in Mitchell's Bank. He later became one of the city's most prominent citizens. Johnston made a greater permanent impact on the house than the fire which gutted its interior earlier. Diederichs' original structure was one story tall set on a high well-lit "ground floor" or basement with a large cupola on the roof. Johnston added the second story and re-fitted the old cupola to the new roof.

The alterations were done with such proportional sensitivity that they appear to be a part of the original design. The plans were prepared by architect Howland Russel who, when he first opened his office in 1880, was sneeringly called a "down east school architect." One of his local competitors predicted that he wouldn't be able to earn his rent, but he went on to become a highly respected member of the profession.

His sensitivity can be seen here where he correctly judged that the addition of a large second story mass would overwhelm the original portico. He therefore pulled the pediment forward and added two sleeper columns behind the existing corner pair to give a more appropriate visual support.

On the interior even more drastic changes were made, including the necessary addition of a staircase to service the new upper level. This stairwell, which opens to the ceiling of the second floor, used up one of the original three rooms on the north side of the house. In the beginning a central hall cut through the middle of the house, dividing it into six rooms, three nearly-square ones to a side. Today, almost nothing of the original interior remains, although the style of the remodeling has been carried out with respect for the exterior.

After forty years there, John Johnston's widow put the mansion and its contents up for sale. On October 27, 1936, the Lion House hosted the largest crowd in its history when socialites, serious buyers and curiosity seekers jammed its rooms for a spectacular sale.

From this high point, the venerable landmark started a decline which ended with its becoming a rooming house. In 1943, Eliot Grant Fitch, then-president of the Marine National Exchange Bank, bought the house. It was purchased as an investment, but he later moved in and lived there thirty years. His strong feeling for the historical importance of the house, and his attentive maintenance, pulled the old

structure through the years when nineteenth century architecture was anything but popular.

Now listed on the National Register of Historic Places, this landmark was described by the historic American Buildings Survey as "The finest ante-bellum house in Milwaukee." It presently serves as headquarters for a management company which appreciates its fine qualities and which has invested heavily in its continued good health.

The architecture of the street façade has been variously described as "the classic style of the French Renaissance," "Greek Revival" and "Roman temple style." In fact, its origin cannot even be ascribed to a specific nineteenth century sub-style. The porch columns are clearly derived from the Tuscan order as described by sixteenth century Italians, Palladio and Scamozzi.

An inconsistency arises in the entablature (the horizontal member which is supported by the columns). Here we can identify a different style, the Roman Mutular Doric, a very similar example of which can be seen in the ancient Theater of Marcellus in Rome. Whatever its origin, there can be no doubt that this is a very fine classically-inspired design which has no peers in Wisconsin.

In 1985 the present owner commissioned a feasibility study and the first phase of a major restoration project. Many intriguing questions were answered by the study and a few unexpected surprises turned up. A microscopic analysis of the accumulated paint buildup showed that on certain areas, such as the front door woodwork, there were up to twenty-nine coats. After chemically stripping the building it was discovered that while the sides and back of the mansion were built with "common brick," the east (front) façade was made of the "preferred," or pressed, variety. On this side only the more precise brick was laid with tighter joints and the mortar was dyed a bright orange.

The surprise was that these original orange lines were not visible from a distance, but they served to warm up the slightly greenish-yellow of Milwaukee's famous "cream city" brick. The mansion's masonry was probably not painted before 1895, and then only to disguise the less-than-perfect match of materials and colors that came in the major remodeling that year. The bottom layer of paint removed was used as a guide for the light cream color which has been re-applied to the wood trim.

The large plate glass windows, added in the 1895 project, were removed and replaced with original design double-hung small-pane sash. The wrought iron porch railings had been salvaged from the mansion of Emil Schandein (a vice-president of Pabst Brewing Co.) and put up here later. Their German Renaissance design was very inappropriate so a new Greek honeysuckle design was fabricated to replace them.

But the big decision was to commission the carving of another pair of lions. Great care was taken to achieve the proper proportional relationship with the house. First the plinths, which had been re-built with two steps after the original lions were removed, had to be replaced. A new high one-level plinth, with molded trim, was carefully scaled from old photographs.

Then several lions of different sizes were drawn on cardboard, cut out, and set on the new plinths. By photographing these from different angles and comparing with the old pictures a size was set and a large clay model was produced for approval.

The sculptor chiseled for over a year to carve the almost life-sized lions from huge glued-up blocks of Honduras mahogany. He made them as a symetrically-opposed pair facing slightly outward in opposite directions. Now, after a hiatus of forty-two years, the never-forgotten nickname can be correctly used. The lions have finally returned to the "Lion House."●

The earliest known photograph of the Diederichs house, taken before 1875. Notice the muddy street, wooden sidewalk, and fence which disappeared before 1895.

Above, the White Manor from the south. The closest section encapsulated the old Hull house. Right, a view of today's "White Manor" from the southeast. The high bluff overlooking Lake Michigan is at the far right.

Over the years an intriguing "legend" has been repeated about the origin of the White Manor apartments at 1228-36 East Juneau Avenue. Recent discoveries have shown that story to be false. In the process, the true history has unfolded and it has proven to be stranger and more fascinating than the fiction. Begun in anger, this one-time single dwelling has endured over a century of controversy and change and is now a sprawling maze of wings and additions.

According to the old legend the apartment complex was created by moving three or four houses onto the lot where they were joined together. This was supposed to have taken place around 1926 when Juneau Place (a short street which ran from Juneau Avenue to the south along the lake bluff) was plowed under for the purpose of enlarging Juneau Park. The three or four houses involved were said to have been among those which had to be abandoned for the park expansion. The legend further claimed that these houses were all two-story and that a third floor had been added to each at the time.

It is not difficult to understand why this story has been so popular through the years. When one looks at the White Manor today, it seems quite logical: the fifty-six changes of direction on the exterior wall surfaces create an architectural crazy-quilt which can easily be imagined as three or four old houses. To further convince the non-believer, the materials used in the foundation differ from section to section.

Interesting as it may be, there is not a shred of evidence to support this house-moving theory. In truth all of the angles and sections of the present complex were added at different times, but they all still occupy their original positions on the lot.

The true story begins in 1856 when when David P. Hull purchased the property and started construction of a large house. According to pioneer historian James Buck, "This building was erected with the avowed purpose of preventing the farther extension of a street along the bluff, as talked of at that time . . ." The street, Juneau Place, ran north from Biddle (now East Kilbourn Avenue) to Division Street (now East Juneau Avenue) along the bluff. It terminated on the north by flowing into the eastern extremity of Division Street, a fact which explains the short segment of Juneau Avenue which continues eastward from Prospect Avenue and dead-ends at the bluff.

In a land contract dated November 18, 1856, the property was conveyed from Hans Rees to David Hull with the following provision: "Second party agrees as a further consideration to erect upon the same a good first class brick dwelling house at an expense of at least $8,000. To erect the walls of such house and have the same entirely enclosed within one year from the first of December 1856 and to complete the same ready for occupation at or before the expiration of eighteen months from the day last named." Failure to comply with the above was to have been punishable be a $2,000 fine.

The deadline finally arrived and the house was still far from complete. Hull not only lost the house, and had to pay the penalty, but some of the workmen on the job filed mechanic's liens for unpaid wages.

Hull may have lost financially, but he succeeded in getting up enough of a roadblock to stop Juneau Place. In his biography of Hull, historian Buck observed, "His fault, if he has any, was in going too deep sometimes."

David P. Hull was, however, an honest and respected businessman in Milwaukee and had come here in 1850 from Cincinnati. He opened a banking establishment on Water Street with James Kneeland and later became a dealer in real estate. The Italianate mansion, which he had created as a tactical maneuver, was destined to live for more than a century and to serve an unexpected variety of needs.

Being so close to the bluff, the huge house was for decades the most obvious landmark on the North Shore. It stood in its half-finished condition for several years until it was purchased by Charles L. Rice in 1863. Rice, then master mechanic at the shops of the Milwaukee & Mississippi Railway Co., completed the work on the house but never lived there. He in turn sold it to the Wallace Pratts who turned out to be the only ones to use the structure as a single family residence.

Pratt made improvements which were to have far-reaching effects on the neighborhood. He pioneered

Vignette from an 1872 lithograph. This bird's-eye view shows how effectively the Hull House blocked the northward extension of Juneau Place.

the use of tile draining on the slope and therefore made it possible to plant shade trees where nothing would grow before, "and it was his success with this experiment," wrote Buck, "that gave the key and led to the construction of the present Juneau Park."

In 1869, Pratt left his home and moved to Kansas City where he became a prominent railroad corporation attorney.

The house was sold at auction on April 21, 1869, and the newspaper announced the price: "The bidding was very spirited up to $14,000. The property was finally bid in by Professor Sherman for the Milwaukee Protestant Orphan Asylum at $15,300."

When the nearby homeowners heard that orphans would be moving into their posh residential neighborhood, they were horrified. They banded together and filed a remonstrance against occupation to block the move. But, in spite of the uprising, the Pratt house became an orphan asylum and remained so for twenty years.

The Milwaukee Asylum was founded in 1850 and until this purchase had been quartered in a building on Marshall Street. The news of the purchase not only caused dissention in the neighborhood, but caused a feud among the directors of the institution. Those against moving to the Pratt residence called it a temporary move and not much improvement over their

old building ". . . for the reason, that its ground floor was devoted to an immense parlor, wholly unmerited for the uses of the Asylum." Their opponents claimed that it was a good enough solution ". . . and that the managers should be satisfied with what they had and move in at once before bad boys, not members of an orphan asylum, should break out the windows and otherwise destroy the property."

The neighborhood opposition lost and the asylum moved in. From time to time the house was added to in all directions as the need for space increased. In 1874 a major two-story wing was erected. Two years later, "because it had become a haunt for tramps to sleep in," the original barn was torn down. In 1889, the numerous additions having used up most of the available space, it was decided to move again. This time the directors accepted an offer of 4.75 acres of land which the Milwaukee Common Council had made in 1860. On this plot, at the northeast corner of Prospect and North avenues, they built a huge new building. Although the "new" building is now gone, the institution still occupies that site. (It has since been restructured and renamed the Lakeside Child & Family Center.)

In the meantime Frank B. Van Valkenburgh bought the old mansion, which by that time looked more like a hotel. Immediately he called in an architect

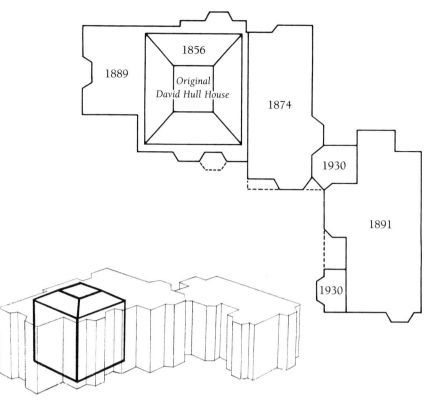

Looking down on the roof of the White Manor, one can still see the very top of David Hull's hipped roof rising slightly above the flat deck. The plan of present day White Manor shows the original Hull House with all of the additions and their dates. Phantom perspective drawing showing the present White Manor complex from the southeast. The heavy line shows the position and size of the original 1856 David P. Hull house.

and spent an additional $14,900 on expansion and repairs. Among these 1889 projects was the construction of plank seats on the slope and level ground.

The Van Valkenburghs moved into the house in 1890, and the next year they sold a piece of their property to the recently widowed Mrs. Cyrus Knight. In Mrs. Knight's deed there can be found a clue which sets the date on the northernmost segment of the present complex. In describing the boundaries of the Knight lot the document reads ". . . and for a part of the way along the northerly line of the brick wall of a dwelling house now in the course of erection upon the premises hereby conveyed." This is further corroborated by Mrs. Knight's first address listing in the 1892 city directory (356 then, 1236 by today's numbering system).

It is now clear that Van Valkenburgh's repairs and additions were not to trim up a single residence, but to create apartments. The owners lived in the front section and the back was divided into units. With Mrs. Knight's separate house there were four apartments in all, a situation which lasted until 1930.

In 1926, Martin Tullfren & Sons Co. began purchase of the complex which was to become the White Manor. By 1930, they had completed the negotiations and had taken out a building permit which outlined a $100,000 remodeling. This, the most extensive of a long line of rebuildings, finally connected all the pieces and rearranged them into fifteen apartments.

Today the White Manor is much the same as when the Tullgrens left, with its coat of white paint to conceal a century of surgical scars. David Hull's house is still there but it is so deeply buried that only an experienced investigator would be able to find evidences of it. The one obvious remnant of the old house, which can still be seen, is its large, square, hipped-roof which rises above the otherwise flat deck. Under it, in a crawl space between the present third floor ceiling and the hip roof, is the only other visible clue. There one can see large segments of an old coved ceiling in lath and plaster.

In spite of its erratic construction, the White Manor, with its sunken courtyard and splendid view of the lake, possesses a charming character unlike any other apartment in the city. It seems to have always had a tenant waiting list and those who have "discovered" it try to keep the secret. But no secret is better concealed than the sturdy pre-Civil War mansion with which one stubborn man permanently blocked a street. ●

Looking north toward Cathedral Square from
Keenan's high front porch. The quality of its pine
millwork and hand-carved ornament exceeds any
other Italianate porch in the region.

*T*he old Matthew Keenan home at 775-781 North Jefferson Street is a rare exception to the rule of survival. This venerable mansion has managed to hold its own against the complicated process of urban growth. It is unusual for a residential structure of this age (over a century and a quarter) to remain so close to the business center of the city.

Typically, a city grows as an expanding circle from its point of origin. Such interrelated factors as changes in zoning, increasing tax base, and rising maintenance costs are responsible for the "decay" and later rebuilding of the core. This renewal then follows the growth in concentric circles. Many areas in downtown Milwaukee are being rebuilt for the fourth time, while the Keenan home still stands, revealing little exterior change.

In 1837, when Matthew Keenan (age twelve) arrived with his parents in Milwaukee, there was "a straggling aggregation of huts and crude houses constituting the village." In later years pioneer Keenan recalled having seen Solomon Juneau's house on the present site of the Mitchell building as well as Spring Street (now West Wisconsin Avenue) when it was only a block and a half long. There were no bridges across the Milwaukee River to connect "Juneautown" (east side) to "Kilbourntown" (west side); only a ferry at Spring Street.

Matthew's first job, in the summer of 1839, was operating this ferry, which was powered by a windlass and rope. In 1841 when Keenan was sixteen, his father died, leaving him the responsibility of supporting himself and two sisters. He quit school and became a clerk in the general merchandise store of William Brown Jr. A few years later H. A. Hayden bought the business and took on the young clerk as a partner, changing the name to Hayden and Keenan.

After a successful eight years in the business, Keenan's ambition to rank as a man of affairs led him into politics. He was elected circuit court clerk in 1852, a position which he held for four consecutive terms (eight years).

Keenan had invested wisely and by 1860 he had sufficient wealth and position to warrant a mansion. This lot on Jefferson Street was one which had been

purchased by his parents in 1844. Keenan employed Edward Townsend Mix, a young architect who had arrived and established his practice in Milwaukee only four years earlier. Mix was later to become one the the city's most popular, successful and respected architects. Among his designs were the Mitchell and Mackie buildings, the National Soldiers Home, St. James and St. Paul's Episcopal Churches, Immanuel Presbyterian Church, and according to a contemporary, "not less than three quarters of the most costly and ornate private residences in Milwaukee."

Mix designed the Keenan house in the Victorian Italianate sub-style. Originally inspired by the rural villas of northern Italy, this style took America by storm in the decade before the Civil War. Because it was not regulated by rules of proportion or geometry, the Italianate was adaptable to all needs. Architects and builders were free to adjust elevations, plans and trim to accommodate any budget or requirement. For this reason it became the most popular of all the nineteenth century sub-styles.

While the most common Italianates are informal single-family homes, the Keenan example is a formal two-family urban town house. As such it is rare in Milwaukee where very few town houses were ever built.

Detail of the front elevation showing the fine carved limestone trim and the high quality cream city brick work.

29

It is rarer still because the refinement of the design and the richness of its ornamentation ranks this town house among the finest Italianates ever built here of any type.

In a day when the newspaper was eight pages and matters of building received a two-line mention in the "Brevities" column on the last page, Keenan's house rated a handsome description on page one.

On May 8, 1860, the exuberant *Milwaukee Sentinel* reporter wrote: "The two splendid brick houses on Jefferson Street just above St. Paul's Church, built by Matthew Keenan, are nearly finished, and their interior presents the most elaborately ornate appearance of any building it has been our good fortune to inspect this year. The parlours are literally covered with stucco and carving, and the eyesight becomes bewildered — we came near saying entangled — amid scrolls and arabesque twists and graceful convolutions of leaves and vines. Such a display of stucco work is rarely to be met with — combining chaste design with so much profusion. It is the work, we believe, of John Cosgrove.

"These buildings are, throughout, models of elegance and comfort. All the modern appliances of household economy that come under the builder's eye are here combined. Mr. Keenan has already rented one of the houses for $900 a year."

"Splendid" was an apt description, but "gracious" and "magnificent" may have been better. The elegant spaces began just inside the massive pair of front doors which were fitted with rich silver-plated knobs and keyhole escutcheons. The thirteen-foot high ceiling of the entrance vestibule was finished with three stepped cornice moldings: classical "egg and dart," "leaf and dart," and acanthus leaf. A semicircular transom window over each doorway featured a delicate leafy design etched in glass.

The main hall was dominated by a graceful staircase which began with an exquisitely carved mahogany newel post. The eight-sided post and cap was much lighter than many of the period and was heavily carved with acanthus leaves. Tapered octagonal balusters and a finely carved open string (the sides of the steps) completed the composition. Unlike many steep staircases — where climbing could be work — this one was designed to rise at a gentle pace (around thirty degrees).

The most impressive feature of the interior was the treatment of door and window openings. Wide pine casings with deep moldings were embellished with carved acanthus leaves and rope twists. These thick frames, with their high-relief ornaments, project nearly three inches from the wall. Four different designs were used on the first floor alone. Window shutters were made to accordion-fold back into hollow recesses in the jambs.

The great first floor rooms (sitting room, parlor, dining room, library) were opened to each other through a series of arches which stretched from the front of the house to the back. To complement the richly crafted woodwork in these rooms, the architect supplied the highest grade of carved Carrara marble fireplace mantels. And the ornamental plaster ceilings, by Cosgrove, were as fine as any in the Midwest. Each ceiling cornice consisted of a lavish series of plaster moldings stacked one-on-the-other for a total depth of over a foot. One of these segments was set away from the main body of the plaster to create a delicate undercut lace-like effect.

The second floor was devoted to bedrooms while the kitchen and maids' quarters were located in the high English-styled basement.

The house's exterior is enhanced with limestone quoins (corner blocks) and window lintels. A winding double stairway with an ornate cast-iron balustrade leads to the graceful front porch. Handsomely carved wooden brackets support both the porch canopy and the roof's dramatic overhang.

Matthew Keenan lived in the southern half of this town house and rented the identical northern half until 1870 when he decided to sell it off to John Eldred for $15,000. By that time he had been clerk of the circuit court, city assessor, tax commissioner, member of the common council and vice president of the Chamber of Commerce.

That year historian John Gregory wrote, "Matthew Keenan is not an ordinary man. His success through life and the high estimation in which he is held by all who know him are the best proofs that honesty is the best policy . . . His kindly disposition, inostentatious manner, good talent, and above all, his general character will in time, place him in a position which he does not at present, perhaps contemplate. The City or County should never dispense with his services, as a public officer."

In the following years he was elected to the state assembly, became supervisor of the Milwaukee Waterworks and held a number of additional civic and executive positions. In 1876, he was elected vice president of Northwestern Mutual Life Insurance Company.

This bird's-eye view of the neighborhood was taken between 1860 and 1862 when Matthew Keenan's townhouse was new. The triple row house to the left survives in a greatly-altered state; the two square houses to the right have also survived. Everything else in the photograph is now gone.

Left, one of the many beautiful door casings with heavy moldings and exquisitely carved pine ornaments in high relief. Some of these were salvaged and reinstalled in the new interior. The ceiling chandelier rose in the southeast parlor. This unusually deep and handsome piece of ornamental plasterwork was executed by John Cosgrove. Looking through the southeast parlor arch from the stair hall. Below, the east (front) façade of Matthew Keenan's double town house showing the house shortly after twenty-two coats of paint were removed in November of 1972.

After Keenan's death in 1898, his widow lived in the house for eight years. Shortly before 1910 the gracious home ceased to be a two family dwelling. The Milwaukee County House of Detention moved into the north half of the building. The Walrus Club, the Wisconsin Players Drama Club, and a school of music shared tenancy until 1925. After a two year vacancy, the old home was again occupied by shops and offices.

In the early 1970s, after many decades of piling on paint, the decision was made to strip the aging townhouse. In one of Milwaukee's first major chemical restorations twenty-two coats of paint were removed from the exterior. This included one layer which had been mixed with ox blood and which was exceptionally difficult to dissolve. The resulting light-yellow "cream city" brick was, with its painted carving and ornament, as pretty as a wedding cake.

But the good news was to last only a decade. On February 23, 1984, the building was all but gutted in a two-alarm fire. After evaluating the damage, the owner decided to save what he could and a year later wrecking cranes began to nibble away at the building. The front and two side walls were stabilized while the rear, the roof and the entire interior of the house were carefully removed.

Inside the remaining walls a new steel-framed office building was erected and there are plans to re-use some of the salvaged fireplaces and wooden trim.

In spite of countless abuses and the final indignity of a major fire, Matthew Keenan's splendid façade will end up delighting the eyes of passersby for many more years to come. ●

Left, looking down into the gutted shell of Keenan's house, January 1986. Note the back wall has been removed and a new steel skeleton is being erected inside. Above, the townhouse burning on February 23, 1984.

34

This handsome window is centered in the front of the second floor. Its richly ornamented lintel is made of salmon-colored terra cotta; the sill is cut from local limestone.

*T*ucked away on a little-known side street is one of the Midwest's finest architectural gems. This superb Italianate residence, at 1105 Waverly Place, was built over a century ago by James S. Peck. Its handsome proportions and true beauty have been partly disguised by a well-designed, but inappropriate, porch addition. In spite of this and a few other minor intrusions, the 116-year-old house has managed to survive largely intact and in very fine condition.

The Peck home is the last of eight single-family residences to grace this once fashionable block-long street. While the origin of Waverly Place is still unclear, we know that the first house appeared there a couple of years after the Civil War. In 1875 the street had already developed an enviable reputation and was described by *Milwaukee Monthly* magazine as, "the most delightful locality in the city." The 1875 article continued: "Not only is Waverly Place pleasantly located, but it has the advantage of a charming social atmosphere, for in every house resides a family of culture, wealth and refinement." Two years later the street was further praised as "a favorite residence portion (of the city)." An 1877 Milwaukee souvenir book noted, "here on Waverly Place was first put into practice the pretty idea of removing all fences, thus throwing the beautiful grounds into one immense and beautiful park."

What the author meant by "first put into practice" is unknown, but history shows that in the last half of the nineteenth century, the idea of Fences-Versus-No-Fences grew into a major social issue. Just how big an issue it was can be seen by its inclusion in such an unlikely publication as Thomas Hill's *Manual of Social and Business Forms.* In this 1881 guide to penmanship and spelling there is a chapter on "Etiquette among Neighbors." A residential street is pictured with fences everywhere and the author explains that "the neighbors suspect each other, and they destroy the beauty of their grounds in the attempt to shut each other out . . . . inharmony, disorder, and ill-feeling among the people are characteristics of the neighborhood."

In a corresponding engraving Hill shows the same view without fences and pictures the neighbors strolling over open landscape and congregating under the trees. "Enjoying peace and beauty," he wrote, "they evidently desire that the neighbor shall share the same. This cooperation, kindness and regard for all, gives the beauty, the harmony, the peace, and the evident contentment which are here presented."

One would like to think that Waverly Place was indeed the spot where this idea was born, but the old guidebook probably meant that this was where the concept was first practiced in Milwaukee. In either case these neighbors displayed the proper spirit by holding many "summernight's entertainments" and illuminated lawn parties. One recorded party was a benefit to raise money for the Wisconsin Industrial School for Girls.

Who then were these families of "culture, wealth

FIG. 22. PEOPLE WHO ARE TROUBLED BY THEIR NEIGHBORS.

FIG. 23. THE NEIGHBORHOOD WHERE PEOPLE LIVE IN HARMONY.

Peck house from the southeast showing the Waverly Place front and the south (side) elevation.

and refinement"? The first to appear on the block was James G. Baldwin, a tea dealer, who erected his house in 1867. The next year Edward Townsend Mix built on the southwest corner of Waverly and Division (now Juneau). Mix, who was on his way to becoming the city's most celebrated nineteenth century architect, would later design Immanuel Presbyterian Church in the same block. Then followed the houses of banker, William G. Fitch, iron merchant; Charles L. Pierce, drug wholesaler; Dr. Henry Harrison Button, and James Peck.

In the beginning, city directories listed the residents of Waverly Place in the predictable 500 block of the Milwaukee numbering grid. First resident, Baldwin, for example, was assigned the number 585. But this was too prosaic for a unique, short street with such influential inhabitants. In a few years Waverly Place broke with tradition and took on its own, unique, single-digit numbering system. Mix was #1, Peck was #5, and #9 turned out to be the highest address on the block.

A 1875 wood engraving of Waverly Place looking north. From the left are the residences of G.W. Fitch, O.M. Norris, James S. Peck, Charles L. Pierce (barely showing) and - on the corner - Edward Townsend Mix. Immanuel Presbyterian Church looms in the background.

Waverly Place

The main staircase begins at a walnut newel post that is capped with a finely carved acanthus flower. Its massive five-inch-wide handrail follows a sinuous curve to the second floor. Below, detail of the main staircase open stringer showing applied moldings and ornate scroll-cut ornament.

Waverly Place neighborhood in 1898.

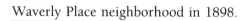 -James S. Peck residence
A -Immanuel Presbyterian Church
B -Edward Townsend Mix residence
C -Dr. H.H. Button residence
    (still standing at 1024 E. State St.)
D -Charles L. Pierce
E -O.M. Norris
F -William G. Fitch

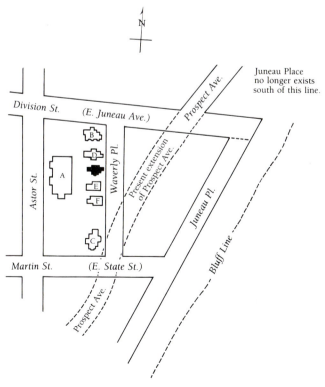

Juneau Place
no longer exists
south of this line.

"Unique" seems to have been the watchword for Waverly Place since its very inception. The original owner of the entire neighborhood was an out-of-state speculator by the name of Parker C. Cole. A New Yorker, Cole was well known here for his substantial purchases at the Green Bay land sale in 1835. He had a special love for the lake bluff and, at one time intended to improve it with landscaping. According to Matthew Keenan, who knew Cole, ". . . he fenced in a strip three blocks wide with a view to its utilization as a park and in the hope that other owners to the north would join him, but at that time the project fell through."

It is difficult to visualize, with today's property values, but in Milwaukee's earliest decades the lakefront was avoided like a dump. No money was allocated for improvement and in those days the lake breezes were considered to be unhealthy. Parker Cole, then, finally gave up his dream of making the bluff into one which "would surpass in loveliness the famous Bay of Naples."

In 1850, he hired John Vliet to survey his block no. 105 and subdivide it into lots. Peck's lot (no. 3) was first sold to a commission merchant, Charles P. Jones, for $5,250 — an astronomical sum in 1867. Jones did nothing to improve the lot and, three years later, sold it to Peck for a $1,250 profit.

For all of his apparent wealth and connections here, James Sidney Peck left little more than the residence as evidence of his forty-years in Milwaukee. Very little was written about him in standard histories or newspapers and only in his obituaries do we find a few clues to his life and pursuits. He was once a supervisor of the 7th ward and was more than once elected a director of the Chamber of Commerce.

Most of his business activities were centered around Angus Smith & Co., at one time the world's largest handler of grain. After the death of his first wife, Angus Smith married James Peck's sister and, thereafter, the two families remained close both in business and socially. Peck worked as one of the three highest paid men in his brother-in-law's company. On the side he invested in real estate and speculated in iron mining.

James Peck's principal accomplishment seems to have been the Converse Cattle Company which had offices here and in Cheyenne, Wyoming. As president of the company he spent a lot of time out west, which explains his low profile in this city. When he was in town, Peck ran the company from a desk in Angus Smith's office.

In July of 1870, James Peck married Nellie M.

Hayes in Palmyra. Four months later he purchased the property on Waverly Place and, within a year, built the house for his new bride. It is said that the first three houses south of Juneau (on the west side of Waverly) were designed by Edward Townsend Mix. There can be no question that the prominent architect drew the plans for his own house on the corner (#1). But there are no known photographs of the next one south which was built by Baldwin and later occupied by Charles L. Pierce.

The Peck house, though, can easily be compared to other Mix designs. Perhaps the best parallels can be seen in an old photograph of the Mix house which was built only a couple of years earlier. Similarities include window details, roof pitch, floor plan and the same unusually wide overhang of the eaves.

Generically, the Peck house is a mid-Victorian period design in the Italianate substyle. There are still hundreds of this type remaining in Milwaukee but this one is special because it has elegant proportions, superbly designed details and the finest craftsmanship. It is an architectural jewel which, unlike many of its builder-designed contemporaries, shows the sensitive touch of a master architect.

The house is built of pressed cream city brick, set on a rock-faced stone foundation. The limestone water table is finished in the best fashion with chiseled margins and bush hammered texture. Window sills share the same quality finish and each is supported by a pair of stone corbels. The eaves overhang forty inches and are decorated by a large carved wood rope molding. This generous overhang casts heavy shadows and is responsible for much of the design's character.

Six different window shapes give interest and variety to the walls. But the trim and detail on these beautiful windows are the true glory of the house. Each is set in a deeply molded wood frame, some of which contain carved ropes. A few lintels are made of salmon colored terra cotta and are decorated with ivy and clover. The single greatest piece of design and craftsmanship, however, is the spectacular round attic window above the front porch. Surrounding this humble circle of brick is a deeply carved riot of acanthus whorls, fruit, flowers and rope. This is certainly one of the finest pieces of exterior wood carving in the Midwest. In a similar manner the front door is framed with handsomely carved pine.

On the south wall is an all-wood five-sided bay window supported on an unusual corbel which is shaped like an octagonal trumpet bell. Two of the oval

39

The upper half of the Waverly Place façade after the brick was stripped of paint and cleaned. Here one can appreciate the fine proportions and elegant detailing which set this house apart from the more common Italianate houses in the area. The little round attic window is highlighted with an exquisite pine carving in deep relief. Its acanthus whorls, fruit and flowers rank among the finest exterior carvings in the Midwest. Right, detail of the roof corner showing its handsome moldings and the unusually deep (40") overhanging eaves.

windows have sandblasted plate glass centers into one of which *V*-cut grooves have been ground in a diamond grid. Both have surrounding borders of ruby flashed glass. Leaves and flowers have been cut through their rich, red layers creating a superb, delicate, white wreath.

Inside, the quality continues in parquet floors, deep plaster ceiling cornices, carved fireplaces in marble and unusually rich wooden moldings. The mop boards, for instance, are so heavy that they had to be built up from four pieces. Where these abut the even bolder door casings, the architect provided an unusual corner trim board with a twelve-inch radius.

The spectacular staircase follows the same example with its walnut newel post capped by an exquisitely carved classical acanthus flower. A massive five-inch-wide handrail follows a very complex undulating curve as it winds up to the second floor. Upstairs, in the master bedroom, is a carrara marble fireplace with realistically carved grapevines.

In the same bedroom is a one-of-a-kind surprise. Set in the wall, like a statuary niche, is a half-octagon

The main parlor fireplace is carved in pure white statuary grade carrara marble from Italy. Its gadrooned arch is broken at the peak by a deep relief keystone in the shape of a cartouche.

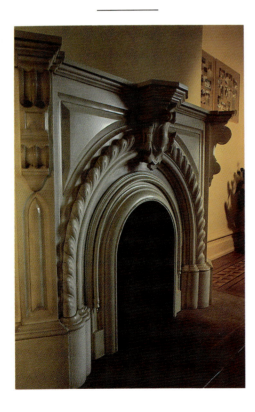

drum with a built in marble wash basin. This is framed by a pair of small plaster female heads supporting an arch.

The Pecks enjoyed their splendid house and entertained frequently. After Peck's death in 1897, his widow did a lot of traveling, but continued to occupy their original residence until she died in 1909. Unlike her husband, Mrs. Peck made a conspicuous dent in Milwaukee history. She was active in many charities, and was a charter member of the Woman's Club of Wisconsin, the Atheneum Association, the College Endowment Association, and the Wisconsin Chapter of the Society of Colonial Dames. She organized the Milwaukee Branch of the Consumers' League and assisted in the organization of the Milwaukee D.A.R. and the Society of Mayflower Descendants. Mrs. Peck even wrote a chapter in Conard's *History of Milwaukee.*

The Pecks' only daughter, Katherine Hubbard, inherited the house and promptly sold it to William H. Dodsworth, who was general agent for the American Express Company office here. It was Dodsworth who added the large wrap-around porch in 1912. His architect, the distinguished firm of H.C. Koch & Sons, designed such a fine porch that it has been taken as original for many decades. It is, in fact, clearly from a different period and it overpowers the delicacy of house. The original porch was a much smaller, rectangular design that extended a short distance out from the front door.

Dodsworth never occupied the house, but he let his daughter (Mrs. Samuel J. Pierce) and son-in-law live there. In May of 1930 he leased the premises to Mrs. C.R. Gilman, an interior decorator from Elm Grove. Marjorie Fielder, who worked for Mrs. Gilman and later succeeded her in business, purchased the house in 1948 and used it as her office and dwelling until she sold it in 1981. The present owner uses the house as offices for a real estate management company.

Finally, after a confrontation that lasted for decades, the Milwaukee building inspector has granted a special use exception for this very special house. Claiming a zoning violation, that office never stopped complaining to first Dodsworth, then Gilman and then Fiedler about their using this residence as an interior decorator's studio and antique shop. But it was probably that ongoing violation, by two very sympathetic ladies, which has been responsible for preserving this architectural gem.

The finest house ever built on Waverly Place is the only one to survive. ●

One of two beautiful oval windows on the north façade. The four-piece ornamental border is made of ruby flashed glass. A delicate wreath of leaves and flowers has been hand ground through the thin layer of deep crimson glass to the clear base layer. This photograph was taken before the light yellow brick was cleaned.

Above, the best early view (ca. 1880) showing both of the stick-style porches which are now gone. Right, in this print from a glass-plate negative, the stable barn, built by Dr. Day himself, can be seen in its relationship to the mansion. The barn is long gone but a substantial segment of its stone foundation remains.

Dr. Fisk Holbrook Day, who was once called Wauwatosa's most prominent citizen, built three houses here and named them "The Bird's Nest," "Evergreen Hall," and "Sunnyhill Home." The Bird's Nest disappeared so long ago that no one living remembers it. Evergreen Hall, a romantic Gothic Revival cottage of National Landmark importance, was destroyed in 1967 for a parking lot. Only Sunnyhill Home, at 8000 West Milwaukee Avenue, remains as a monument to that cultured and highly intelligent pioneer. Built around 1874, it was Dr. Day's third and largest residence and it is now listed on the National Register of Historic Places.

The old mansion is beautifully sited on a spectacular wooded lot — the largest residential lot in the City of Wauwatosa — and it is architecturally significant for many reasons. But even more interesting than the landmark is the story of the amazing Dr. Day. An intense and dedicated man with an insatiable thirst for knowledge, he came as close as anyone in Wauwatosa history to being a true "Universal Man of the Renaissance."

It is well known that Day was an appointed physician for the County Hospital, the Poor Farm, and the Insane Asylum and that he also conducted an extensive private practice in the area, but few know of his distinguished accomplishments in other fields. He was interested in architecture and astronomy and was a serious lifetime student of botany and archaeology. All of these paled, however, when compared to his consuming passion for geology and paleontology.

He was one of the first men to study the geology of the Milwaukee area and his fossil collections brought him national recognition. He personally knew, and often supplied specimens to, many of the country's most prominent scientists. As a member of numerous medical and scientific societies he gave lectures, wrote for publications, and entertained countless professionals in his home. Today his fossils and geological specimens can be found in collections of the Smithsonian Institution and Harvard University.

Fisk was born in Richmond, New York, in 1826. His father, Rev. Warren Day, was a long-time Presbyterian and later Congregational minister and an intimate friend of Daniel Webster. His mother, Lydia Holbrook Day, was a schoolmate and close friend of William Cullen Bryant. After preliminary studies at the academies of Ithaca and Geneva, Fisk decided to attend the Jefferson Medical College in Philadelphia. Although his parents had supplied him with ample cultural stimulation, they were unable to pay his way through college. In fact, their financial means were so slim that when he was leaving for Philadelphia, Fisk's father gave him his blessing along with fifty cents in cash (which was all he then could spare). According to a daughter he had to work his way through college and his "meals were frugal — often cooked (in) or eaten out of a tin can."

Dr. Fisk Holbrook Day.

After graduation in 1849, Fisk practiced a few years in Rushville and Warsaw, New York. Then, for some now-forgotten reason, he decided to move to Wauwatosa in 1854. His father, sixty-five, had just retired from his pastorate and both parents joined their son on the trip west. Soon after the Days arrived here, Fisk built a charming little frame cottage on lower Church Street. (This section of the street, which angled southeastward into the village center, has now become a part of Menomonee River Parkway.) This first house, dubbed The Bird's Nest, was built as a residence for his parents, although it is possible that Fisk lived there for a short time until the brick house was completed.

43

*View of the Day house looking northwest in Sep-
tember of 1979. Compare this to the earliest
known view taken over 100 years before and from
nearly the same vantage point. Right, this detail
of the upper half of the front (south) elevation
shows the white-painted brick and the remarkably
fine condition of the scroll-cut stick-work under
the eaves.*

The origin of the second house is somewhat nebulous, but it might be explained by a romantic narrative which appeared in *The Milwaukee Monthly Magazine* in 1872. The author, prominent Milwaukee architect James Douglas, admitted that his story was based on real people still living in Wauwatosa. The hero of his romance, Dr. Fred Dayton, is a thinly disguised carbon copy of Dr. Day. Almost every fact in the story, from the Doctor's hobbies to the number of and interests of his children, accurately parallels the truth.

According to the story — entitled "Marion Hunter's Mistake" — the Doctor fell in love with Marion and built a house for her. "He sketched the design himself, and sent it to be completed by one of Milwaukee's most talented architects" [probably the author]. "She [Marion] could watch from the window of her room across the river, the erection of each arch, balcony, gable, verandah and porch . . . as the pretty Gothic Villa ran into fine proportions among the trees, in charming harmony with the surrounding scenery." That passage was a perfect description of the real house at 1533 Church Street which Dr. Day affectionately named Evergreen Hall. It was a textbook-perfect example of Gothic Revival design, executed in cream city brick with scroll-cut gingerbread and carved gothic trim.

The description continued: "The ceiling and walls [of Marion's room] were frescoed in violet and fawn colors, intermingled with ashes of roses and the more delicate hues of lilac. Over the arch of the south window was frescoed in old English characters, 'Marion's Room' and in the garden in front was planted a bed of flowers, so as to blossom out into the name of Marion. Everything was at last completed and Fred had arranged with a prominent Milwaukee firm for the furnishing; about all of which Marion's tastes were consulted. Her monogram was on each chair, sofa and mirror. Her beautiful chamber set and dressing case, all of her table linen and silver, were marked with her name. The home was ready, and Fred had expended upon it all he had earned."

At this juncture Marion fell in love with another man and left the doctor. "His beautiful home stood vacant for a long time. He was never known to enter the grounds after his separation from Marion . . . the beautiful grounds grew up to weeds, the long grass obscured the walks with the weeds loped over and decayed upon the porch and verandas."

The doctor was then called to visit a patient in a "distant town" where he found a young lady in attendance whom he had known from Rhode Island as a teenager. It was love at first sight and the Gothic Villa project was reopened to accommodate his new love. The "distant town" was Waukesha, and the lady was Frances A. Williams. The real wedding took place in 1858.

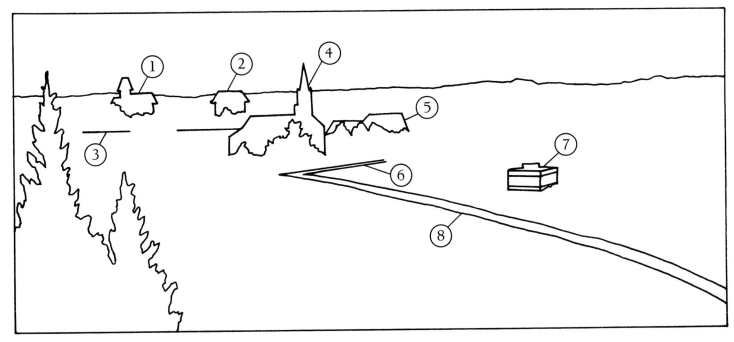

Rare panoramic photograph taken in the late 1870s showing all 3 of Dr. Day's houses. The photographer stood on the hill where the Milwaukee Sanitarium now stands and looked to the northwest. 1) "Sunnyhill Home" 2) stable/barn at "Sunnyhill" (present garage is built inside the foundation of the old structure) 3) Milwaukee and Wauwatosa Plank Road (now W. Milwaukee Ave.) 4) First Congregational Church (the original building — Fisk's father, Rev. Warren Day, often preached here as a guest minister) 5) "Evergreen Hall," Day's Gothic revival house 6) Upper Church Street 7) "The Bird's Nest" First built by Fisk Day around 1854 as a residence for his parents (Rev. & Mrs. Warren Day). This is the only known view of that house. 8) Lower Church Street (now a part of Menomonee River Parkway).

Since ninety percent of the romance is factual it is tempting to assume that the reason for the house, and its subsequent abandonment, is also the truth. Whatever the case, Evergreen Hall appeared in the mid 1850s and remained the residence of Dr. and Mrs. Day until Sunnyhill was built.

In 1864 Dr. Day purchased the hillside land for his next home. That historic 8.5 acre tract, known as the "Brown & Mower" lot, cost $425. By that time Day was already a well established country doctor who made his house calls on horseback while carrying the medicine in his saddlebags. He had already accepted the appointment as Milwaukee County Physician and was making daily trips to the Hospital, the Alms House and the Poor Farm.

It was not an easy life, as we can see by reading a few entries in his handwritten journal of 1862. He was often called out in the middle of the night to keep an around-the-clock vigil over a patient at the hospital. Even on Christmas Day he wrote about making his rounds "as usual."

And the County Board of Supervisors didn't make it any easier. Day found a lot to complain about and was constantly fighting with the board. Typically his complaints made big news and ran one and one-half columns in the newspapers. In 1865 this attack was printed: "I have on several instances seen a whole and new garment torn into shreds by a maniac (even when manacled) in his frenzy, and as most of the insane are brought here to the County Farm Poor House from the station house, or jail, they are generally ragged, filthy and covered with vermin and not withstanding the ablutions and change of garments they undergo upon their arrival at the poor house, and although their cells are daily cleaned, still ventilation is so imperfect that it would be just as reasonable to suppose a horse stable well cleaned would emit no foul smell as that a cell once occupied by one of these 'most miserable of all creatures' could ever be in an endurable condition."

Day called the board "worthless material" and accused them of "gross mismanagement." They called him an impertinent meddler and once they countered by cutting his salary. He was criticized for "throwing dirt at his own house" and the Board claimed that he should have mentioned his complaints privately instead of going to the press. An investigation was ordered after one of Day's attacks and he was vindicated when it was discovered that the hospital was indeed a piece of "botch-work" thrown up carelessly by the administration's building committee.

In spite of these pressures and complications Day found the time to build a barn behind his house, work

47

"Evergreen Hall" as it looked in 1967, the year it was razed by the First Congregational Church to make a parking lot. Built around 1854, its final address was 1533 Church Street.

Rare view of Dr. Day seated in his study at "Evergreen Hall" before 1874. He is surrounded by many of the things he loved most. His geological specimen display cases dominated at least one room in the days before Sunnyhill.

in his garden almost daily, and go into the city frequently to attend auctions. He went to the Cold Spring Race Track with "Frank" (his nickname for Mrs. Day) and he took time to give his daughters almost daily sleigh rides in the winter.

This might have been a full life for most people but for Fisk Day it was only the beginning. He belonged to the Lapham Archeological Society and found time to excavate Indian mounds and deliver lectures.

He was a member of the Lyceum of Natural History of New York, the American Association for the Advancement of Science, the Chicago and Wisconsin Academies of Science, and he was once president of the State Medical Society of Wisconsin.

Before all of these interests, and perhaps even before medicine, came his great love for geology. Fisk knew every rock outcropping and hole in the ground for miles in all directions. He knew all of the quarries and the men who worked in them. The workers kept an eye out for fossils and after heavy blasts they would pick out specimens and set them aside for Day. He even had his patients on the look-out for specimens and sites. It was common to hear the sound of a

geologist's pick around the house, as Day spent a great deal of time hammering fossils out of their rocks.

When he built Sunnyhill Home, around 1874, it came as no surprise that one room was to be known as the "Cabinet Room." Actually more like a small natural history museum, this was the place where Day kept his tall wood and glass display cases. His fossil collection was so impressive and large that many scientific societies came to the house to take a tour.

Day's specimens were considered the finest collection of Milwaukee area Silurian fossils in existence. In recognition of his scholarly dedication in this field two fossils have been named after him. One of these, *Bumastus Dayi,* was so spectacular that he was once offered $100 for it, an astronomical sum for a fossil in the nineteenth century. The word of this man and his collection spread across the country and Day got to know and correspond with most of the prominent paleontologists in North America.

Among the famous visitors to Sunnyhill was professor Alexander Agassiz, son of the great American naturalist Louis Agassiz. After Louis' death Alexander continued his father's work in the Museum of

Comparative Zoology at Harvard. In later years Florence Day remembered sitting on the professor's lap when he came here to evaluate her father's collection in 1880.

Agassiz purchased a large part of the collection and it was shipped to Harvard University. Local newspapers described the packing as "the most important event at Wauwatosa" that week. Although it was only a part of his collection, the net weight of fossils to be packed was an impressive 8,265 pounds. The shipment consisted of sixty-three large boxes, six barrels and three large slabs with glacial markings. A few years later Day sold another sizeable collection to Thomas A. Greene. This is still housed in the Greene Museum at the University of Wisconsin-Milwaukee.

An 1883 newspaper story about Dr. Day claimed that even after his big sale "his cabinet now contains 5000 specimens." It further noted that "there are 1000 Indian relics that the doctor has taken from mounds within a radius of 10 miles from the village . . . it would take pages to describe all of these curiosities. There is a sermon, printed in 1611, by the Lord Bishop of Canterbury, corals from the Philippine Islands, cedar from Lebanon, costly bric-a-brac from China and Japan, rubies, emeralds, and amethysts in their natural state, and gold, silver, copper and salt from the mines of Nebraska. Many valuable pictures adorn the walls."

In light of the foregoing it seems logical to assume that one reason why the Days left a perfectly beautiful Gothic Villa and moved just around the corner, was for the need of more museum space. While no records have survived to indicate the architect of Sunnyhill Home or its date of construction, there is a strong case of circumstantial evidence for James Douglas and 1874. One old time Wauwatosan remembers hearing that the two houses were designed by the same architect. Considering Douglas' intimate knowledge of Day's family and life and his preoccupation with the house in his romantic narrative, it is likely that they were good friends and that Douglas was the family architect. Also, in Douglas' 1874 ledger the words "Dr. Day barn" appear on the endpapers. Another undated 1870s entry mentions "Dr. Day's house" with painting costs. This, plus the strong similarity between Sunnyhill and the other known Douglas-designed houses makes a strong case in his favor.

A rare old stereopticon view, dated November 21, 1876, is the earliest known photograph of Sunnyhill Home. It shows the new mansion set atop an almost treeless hill. In the foreground is the Milwaukee and Wauwatosa Plank Road (now West Milwaukee Avenue)

and a whitewashed picket fence. Barely visible at the entrance to the driveway, is Fisk's "shingle" which simply reads "DOCTOR DAY." It was, perhaps, that very shingle which brought another famous visitor to the house: Ella Wheeler Wilcox was passing through the village on her way to Milwaukee when she got a cinder in her eye. The renowned poet came to Sunnyhill and had it removed by Dr. Day.

Dr. Day's mansion was certainly the most spectacular residence in all of Wauwatosa. Set on 8.5 acres with a stable/barn, two grass tennis courts, vegetable and flower gardens, it must have amazed all passersby. We know it amazed young Florence Day, because she later recalled that when she came home from school she would pause at the gate if there was a carriage approaching. That would allow the traffic to see that the "little girl lived in that beautiful house upon the hill."

Not only is the house set high on the landscape, but its tower is a full five stories higher. When standing on top, one is on a level with the peak of the Congregational Church steeple. The tower was much more than an ornament on the house: Day owned two large telescopes and he used the tower for an observatory. Fisk was a good friend of Dr. Robert J. Faries, who lived on the other side of the river. Faries, a pioneer engraver and dentist, had the distinction of building the first telescope in Wisconsin. He was no doubt influential in Day's astronomical activities.

Two pencil sketches of fossils drawn by Dr. Day.

The tower was also used to receive messages from the County Hospital across the valley. The Doctor had an arrangement where, if he was needed in an emergency, they would set out a signal, such as a white flag. The family made periodic trips up the tower to watch for it. This was not the only creative "extra" that Day contributed to his job. The county grounds got a fine artesian well thanks to their physician's expert knowledge of geology.

A man of Dr. Day's interests might have been expected to let his family life suffer, but he seems to have found ample time for them as well. Fisk would often take a daughter with him as he made his rounds. He was never in such a hurry that he couldn't stop and let her pick wildflowers by the roadside. This would often lead to a botanical lesson and the collection of specimens to transplant at home.

The Days had two sons, who died in infancy, and four daughters (Sarah, Margaret, Minnie, and Florence). They all benefited from their exposure to so much culture and intellectual activity and became accomplished in writing, art, and music. When Minnie married John Busch, a banker from Lansing, Michigan, the wedding took place at Sunnyhill. It was billed in the newspaper as "one of the most brilliant weddings the Village of Wauwatosa has had for years." Guests came from all over the country and according to the reporter, "The house had been handsomely decorated and was darkened by closing the blinds, a beautiful

effect being obtained by the suspension of Chinese lanterns about the parlors." Suddenly Minnie was "taken with a fainting fit" and remained unconscious for nearly three hours. "It was thought advisable . . . to proceed with the wedding program without the ceremony and elegant refreshments were served while the guests tried to be as merry as possible under the circumstances." Later Dr. Day announced that Minnie would recover for a ceremony in the afternoon but, due to her condition, it would have to be private. The guests then left.

In 1886, just before his second daughter left home, Day had a surveyor subdivide his property into six lots. The house was centered on the largest (lot 3) with 400 feet of frontage on the road. In three years Mrs. Day died and Fisk began to change his priorities. By 1892 he had decided to leave Wauwatosa and to go to live in Lansing near Minnie and her husband. In 1895 he sold the mansion, and lot 3 to Abe S. Austin for $5,500. Florence remembered, when it came time to pack for moving, that her father blissfully ignored the vases, statuary and other household treasures and immersed himself in wrapping his beloved fossils for the trip.

After twenty years as County Physician and forty years of general practice, Dr. Day was gone. On the way to Michigan he took his two single daughters to the World Columbian Exposition in Chicago. The doctor settled on Sycamore Street, in Lansing, and

Map showing the original size of the 8.67 acre Day lot. In 1886 it was subdivided into 6 smaller lots with the house centered on the largest (lot 3). The 19 buildings which now occupy the original property are shown with their current addresses. Note the western 150 feet of lot 3 which was sold by Austin in 1897.

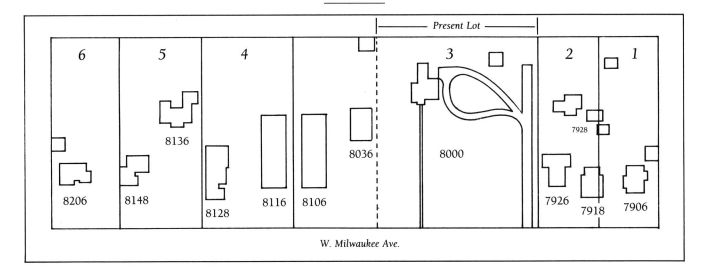

lived there until 1903 when he died of Bright's disease at the age of seventy-seven. By then all of this daughters were married and scattered across the country. Dr. Day's body was returned to Wauwatosa and, after a funeral service at the Irvington Hotel, was buried in the family plot at Wauwatosa cemetery.

What remained of his lifetime preoccupation, 8,000 to 9,000 fossils, was offered for sale. The Day girls rejected numerous offers from interested institutions, including Harvard, because they wanted the collection sold intact. It finally went to the University of Michigan.

Back at the old homestead, Mr. Austin quickly sold off the west 150 feet of lot 3 and created the off-center house relationship that survives today. This reduced what was once a 1,060-front-foot lot to the present 250 feet. Austin turned the house into a multi-family residence and office. Equipment from his coal company and later grading machinery from a family construction company was stored on the property.

In the early 1930s the house was abandoned and partially boarded-up. For nearly ten years it sat vacant while vandals threw rocks at the windows, destroyed two original porches, smashed marble fireplaces and generally enjoyed playing in what had come to be known as "the haunted house." A bed, thrown down from upstairs, splintered out a few balusters and blocked the once graceful sweep of a black walnut circular staircase.

Around 1945 Abe Austin Jr. moved back into his family home, made some necessary repairs, and remained there until his death in 1979.

Just before Austin's death, pianist-entertainer Liberace made an unsuccessful bid to purchase the mansion and convert it into a museum to house his personal memorabilia.

Sunnyhill has since changed hands a few times but it has yet to receive the meaningful restoration it deserves. The city has waited decades for a happy ending to come to the home whose builder was once called, "Wauwatosa's most prominent citizen."●

"Sunnyhill Home" from the southwest around 1880. Note the ornamental roof geometry created by color-dyed sawn cedar shingles. In addition to the two porches, the third floor tower balcony is now missing.

Front elevation of Francis Hinton's double townhouse.

*E*benezer Arnold's townhouse started a Prospect Avenue feud. Or at least that's the accepted legend about the Victorian double-dwelling at 1229-31 North Prospect. Recent findings, however, indicate that Mr. Arnold not only did *not* build the house, but he never lived there.

The feud, on the other hand, is probably based on the truth. According to the popular story, Judge Jason M. Downer built his Victorian Gothic mansion on the northwest corner of Prospect and Juneau in 1874. (It is still standing at 1201 North Prospect Avenue and is now used for offices.) One of Downer's considerations in the selection of this choice lot was the quality of his view. He could look to the south from his eastern bay window and enjoy the lake. From the same vantage he was able to watch a fountain splashing in the little square opposite the old Van Dyke house. The fountain is now gone, but the irregular four-sided park, which was donated to the city by pioneer land speculator James H. Rogers, is still there bounded on three of its sides by North Prospect Avenue, North Franklin Place, and East Knapp Street.

Shortly thereafter, between 1875 and 1879, the townhouse in question was erected. Since it was three stories tall, and was built right up to the sidewalk, it permanently blocked Downer's view of the fountain. Incensed by this intrusion upon the neighborhood's aesthetics, the judge promptly planned his revenge.

He is said to have built the three-story brick dwelling at 1223 North Prospect for the express purpose of blocking the lakeview from the townhouse. This was about a decade before building permits were issued, and Downer had no trouble in pressing his "reply" dwelling right up to the lot line. Since the townhouse was also built on the line, the two structures are so close that it would be difficult to squeeze a butter-knife between them today.

Ebnezer Arnold has, for years, taken the blame for starting this "feud." The confusion is no doubt due to the fact that he did live at this address, but in an earlier structure on the same lot. Considering the unpleasant circumstances that caused him to leave town, it seems only proper that he should be cleared of this additional, and undeserved accusation.

Arnold was one of the city's pioneer booksellers, appearing for the first time in the 1851 city directory. He and his partner, Archibald Wilson, sold and repaired books and were purveyors of paper hangings and stationery.

In 1857 he was elected librarian of the Young Men's Association, a position for which he was perfectly suited. A lifetime familiarity with books and booksellers gave him the background to purchase volumes for the association and to organize and catalog their collection. He brought more new members to the association, acquired more books, and held that position longer than any other librarian in the history of the Y.M.A. In 1878 the Y.M.A. library, consisting of nearly 10,000 volumes, was given to the city and became the nucleus of the Milwaukee Public Library.

Suddenly, in 1871 and to the surprise of everyone, the board of directors voted Ebenezer Arnold out and Mr. Peacock, his assistant of eleven years, in as librarian. The board explained the abolishment of the position as an "economy measure." In an earlier front page story, the newspaper had praised the honorable, hard working, well-loved, librarian and criticized those who complained about his $600 per annum salary. The editors enumerated the great variety of tasks he performed, adding, "we beg leave to say that no man in Milwaukee is more adapted in all respects to this position than Mr. Arnold and that no man will do the work performed by him, for as little money."

Although no one seemed to believe that his dismissal was for purely financial reasons, no record survives to clarify the action of the board. It was an embarrassing and humiliating blow to Arnold and within three months he moved to New York City and took a position with the Catholic Publishing House.

In 1874, Arnold sold his house to Francis Hinton. It was a two-story frame structure with a hipped roof and a central wing on the rear. There was a long veranda across the front of the house and its address was 639 North Franklin. Since this lot is situated at the exact point where Prospect and Franklin come together, it has alternately been assigned addresses on both streets through the years.

Francis Hinton was a traveling salesman for the

53

Bird's-eye view of the west side of North Franklin Place looking north from Prospect Avenue. From the left: Judge Jason Downer's "reply house" built to block the view of Lake Michigan from Hinton's townhouse; Francis Hinton's townhouse; The Diederich's "lion house" and the Bloodgood-Hawley double house.

54

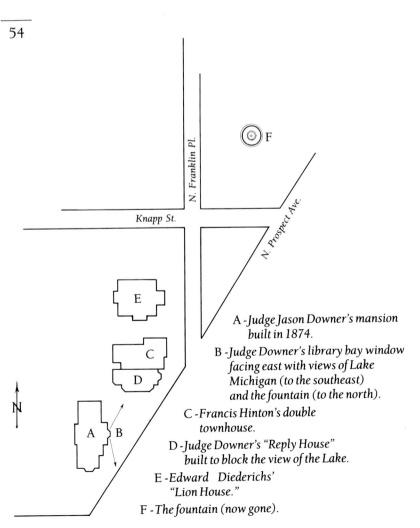

A - *Judge Jason Downer's mansion built in 1874.*

B - *Judge Downer's library bay window facing east with views of Lake Michigan (to the southeast) and the fountain (to the north).*

C - *Francis Hinton's double townhouse.*

D - *Judge Downer's "Reply House" built to block the view of the Lake.*

E - *Edward Diederichs' "Lion House."*

F - *The fountain (now gone).*

Above, detail of an original etched plate glass panel in one of the front doors of the south half.

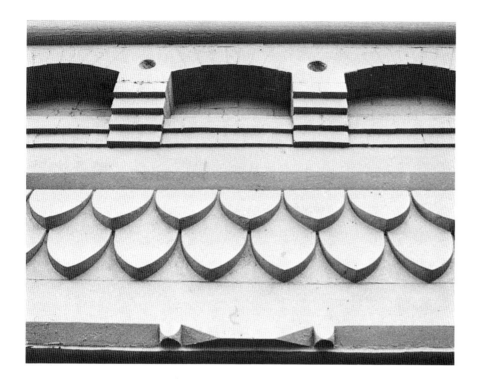

Masonry detail near the roof line. Note the neatly-laid brick corbel course and the cut stone trim which imitates shaped shingles. Compare the chamfered edge at the bottom of the lintel with the similar treatment of interior door casings above.

Milwaukee Iron Company of Bay View and he lived with his parents on Cass Street. After he purchased the property, sometime between 1875 and 1879, he razed the Arnold house and erected the double dwelling which stands there today. He never lived in any of the houses on that lot and it may only be assumed that he built the townhouse as an investment.

Hinton owned the Prospect Avenue property until his tragic death in 1895. At that time he was a wealthy man, manager of the Illinois Steel Company in Bay View, and in his prime at the age of forty-two. He shot himself in the head on a street corner in Paris. The newspapers reported that he was there preparing for his forthcoming marriage to an American woman, and that he had been shopping for presents. Hinton's parents denied any knowledge of the engagement, and the question, "why?" was never answered.

The first known tenants of the townhouse were Mr. and Mrs. William Bigelow, who lived in the north half until 1894. Through the early decades the list of renters included such names as the Herbert Underwoods, the Willet M. Spooners, Mr. and Mrs. George Arthur Harlow, and the prominent Milwaukee architect, George B. Ferry and his wife.

The building was nearly half a century old before one of its owners became a tenant. Elizabeth Shumway, who purchased the house in 1923, also used it as an interior decorating studio and antique shop. The present owners acquired the house in 1956 and occupy one of the six apartments.

In Chicago there are literally thousands of Victorian townhouses — stretching in some neighborhoods, as far as the eye can see. But, in Milwaukee, where there were never never many even in the nineteenth century, only a handful have survived. Among the few remaining here, Hinton's creation is certainly the most elegant.

Like most townhouses, this one was built on a small lot and it uses every inch of the forty-foot frontage. As a result there are two passageways, one under each half of the building, to give access from the sidewalk to the back yard without trespassing on the neighbors property.

The basic structural material is cream city brick trimmed with carved limestone lintels, sills, and gable details. The steep Mansard roof is broken by a Corbie-stepped gable and three dormers.

It is broken into nineteen different planes and is covered by the original slate shingles (four courses rectangular on two courses hexagonal). Additional interest is created in the ornamental brick string courses which form horizontal bands across the façade. The entire composition has a faintly Victorian Gothic flavor.

Considerable remodelings have all but erased the original interior. In the south half the old door casings and the staircase are still intact and the handsome etched glass of the inside front doors is original.

We may never know whether Francis Hinton was aware of the impression his house was making on Judge Downer, or if he just created his investment without a second thought. Whatever the origin, it has become one of the most desirable places to live within walking distance of downtown. ●

East (front) façade of Harrison Ludington's gentleman's farmhouse. Note the two-story front porch added after the Ludington family sold the house. Right, rare early photograph of Harrison Ludington. Sitting beside him is a fellow Wisconsin pioneer, Talbot C. Dousman.

When Harrison Ludington built his "gentleman's farmhouse" in 1881, he had no intention of living there. He had already served three terms as mayor of Milwaukee and had only recently retired from his post as Wisconsin's governor during the American centennial. His property, much of which is now the Ravenswood subdivision of Wauwatosa (a Milwaukee suburb), had been operating as a stock farm since 1870. The Ludingtons, however, were quite comfortable in their handsome Italianate residence in downtown Milwaukee.

Why then the far-above-average "farmhouse"? According to the last family member to occupy that house, Harrison installed his son Frederick there because he "thought he would be better off on this farm." He wanted to teach him the agricultural life instead of leading him into politics. And there was another, unspoken, advantage: Mrs. Frederick Ludington was an excellent cook and the former governor made it a point to show up there for dinner twice a month.

This mansion of a farmhouse, at 343 Glenview Avenue, is in a highly visible location just off the expressway, and is seen by thousands daily. Few passersby, however, realize the importance of the Ludington family, one of the most distinguished ever associated with Wauwatosa.

Harrison was not only a notable public servant, and a very wealthy businessman, but he figured prominently in Milwaukee history as one of its earliest pioneers. His uncle, Lewis Ludington, was the founder of Columbus, Wisconsin; his cousin James founded Ludington, Michigan. A different cousin founded Fort Riley, Kansas. Other cities named after this illustrious family include Ludingtonville, in Putnam County, New York, and the village of Ludington in Eau Claire County, Wisconsin.

Although Harrison was a major Wauwatosa landowner, that city's Ludington Avenue was named after his cousin James, according to the family. The Ludington mine at Iron Mountain, Michigan, however, was named after Harrison. And in Wauwatosa, until just recently, there was a Ludington School.

Harrison Ludington was born in 1812 in Kent, New York. (That Putnam County town would later be renamed after his family.) His parents selected his first name to honor William Henry Harrison, the army general who later became 9th president of the United States. Young Harrison received only a common school education and worked for a while as a clerk in the family store there.

In 1838 he joined his uncle, Lewis Ludington, and Harvey Birchard on a trip to the then-relatively unsettled West. When they arrived in the little village of Milwaukee there were only muddy streets, humble frame dwellings and lots of tamarack swamp. That winter the brave trio ventured out on long trips by horseback through the wild Wisconsin interior. The purpose of these expeditions was to search for rich government timberland. They purchased vast tracts at what would naturally be the lowest prices in history. It was these early and wise investments which formed the cornerstone of Harrison's and his family's later fortunes.

At about the same time, Milwaukee's founder, Solomon Juneau, ran this advertisement in the *Milwaukee Sentinel*: "to rent . . . A large two story store, with a basement, well situated upon the corner of Wisconsin and Water Streets, lately occupied by Solomon Juneau." That corner (northwest) was the location of Juneau's log cabin and is the city's most historic square of real estate. Later the site of the spectacular Pabst building, this prime corner is now a vacant lot awaiting development.

When the pioneer timber speculators returned from their explorations, they recognized the potential of the city's first store building and made this newspaper announcement on June 4, 1839: "New and cheap store — The subscribers have formed a concession in business under the firm of Ludington, Birchard & Co. and are now opening at the old stand of Solomon Juneau, corner of Wisconsin and East Water streets. A large and well selected assortment of seasonable goods."

In a short time their general merchandise store became the largest in the village. Harrison, who actively promoted the development of Milwaukee, was reported to have "brought the first seed wheat from the east to Milwaukee, and bought the first load of grain

57

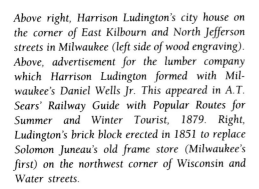

Above right, Harrison Ludington's city house on the corner of East Kilbourn and North Jefferson streets in Milwaukee (left side of wood engraving). Above, advertisement for the lumber company which Harrison Ludington formed with Milwaukee's Daniel Wells Jr. This appeared in A.T. Sears' Railway Guide with Popular Routes for Summer and Winter Tourist, 1879. Right, Ludington's brick block erected in 1851 to replace Solomon Juneau's old frame store (Milwaukee's first) on the northwest corner of Wisconsin and Water streets.

brought to this market." Within a year Harrison's younger brother, Nelson Ludington, came to town and was employed in the family business as a clerk for $150 per year including board.

In 1841 Birchard retired and Nelson was taken into the firm as his replacement. Under the new name of Ludington & Co. they announced a large shipment of goods from New York "as cheap as any store in the western country for ready pay."

Seven years later, in 1848, Nelson broke away from the company to become the first family member in the lumber business. The new firm, N. Ludington & Co., set up a lumber yard at the foot of East Water Street and Nelson's interest in the old store was sold to a cousin, James Ludington.

At about the same time Harrison purchased the property on which the "old store" was built. When that ancient building — once known as "Juneau's warehouse" — outlived its usefulness, it was moved north to a spot now occupied by the Performing Arts Center. In its last days the historic structure is believed to have been a bordello. It burned down in 1882.

In 1851 a fine new brick building called the Ludington Block rose on the original Water and Wisconsin Street corner. When that was removed to make way for Milwaukee's first skyscraper, Harrison leased the lot to Captain Pabst for 99 years for a rental fee of $10,000 per year.

Harrison "drifted" into the lumber trade when, as he said, "I didn't know cull from clear board." After withdrawing from the family store in 1851 he worked with his brother's firm. But Nelson opened a branch in Chicago and then decided to move the business there, closing the Milwaukee operation.

Harrison formed his own company with Daniel Wells Jr., Anthony G. Van Schaick, and Robert and Isaac Stephenson. Later incorporated as the Ludington, Wells & Van Schaick Company, the firm became one of the largest producers of lumber in the world. They owned vast tracts of pine in Wisconsin, Michigan, Louisiana, and Texas and maintained numerous camps and large sawmills in Wisconsin and northern Michigan.

By 1867 Mr. Ludington's wealth and position had grown to the point where a new residence was in order. That year he erected a handsome brick Italianate mansion on a large double lot at 519 Jefferson Street (on the northwest corner of what is now East Kilbourn). Three years later the same wealth enabled him to spend $12,000 on something that was for his pleasure only: From Leander L. Gridley he purchased 100 acres of land in Wauwatosa and started to build his beloved stock farm.

Harrison's interest in agricultural pursuits had been growing alongside his fortune for many years. In 1852 he was elected to the Wisconsin Horticultural Society and in 1861 he became treasurer of the State Agricultural Association — a position he would hold for many years. The 1870 purchase of a farm near the city finally gave him tangible proving grounds with which to work.

His big city life, however, could not be interrupted. Only a year after the land was acquired, he was elected to the first of three terms he would serve as mayor of Milwaukee. It was during his first term, in 1871, that Chicago was devastated by the tragic fire. The mayor responded to his southern neighbors by extending relief to the suffering and homeless and he earned special acknowledgment from Chicago authorities.

But even while serving the public and his various businesses, Ludington found the time to devote to his farm. In 1873 he went to Paris, Kentucky, and spent $2,100 (astronomical at that time) for a cow and two heifers. The local press called them "as handsome specimens of blooded stock as we have ever seen." He created quite a sensation by parading these choice animals west on Spring Street (now West Wisconsin Avenue) and all the way out to Wauwatosa.

The local newspapers regularly announced his purchases and improvements. When two imported Berkshire boars were added, it was reported, "the worthy Mayor is greatly interested in the improvement of the stock of Wisconsin and his farm is already a point of interest to all stock raisers in this and the adjoining states." The *Western Farmer* published this description of his growing farm: "It is well planned, well-built, neatly-painted barns have been erected, costing more than most farmers can afford to expend, but no more, probably, than those of the many well-to-do farmers. The stables and yards are well arranged, and considerable good fence has been built."

Pioneer historian James Buck wrote that "he is also very fond of blooded stock, in the raising of which he has been very successful upon his splendid Wauwatosa farm, in the cultivation and adornment of which . . . he gives his personal attention . . . [he] spares neither time nor money to make it the banner farm in the country." Ludington exhibited his animals in Chicago and at the Wisconsin State Fair where his stock regularly took blue ribbons.

The year 1873 brought personal tragedy when Harrison's wife of thirty-five years died. He was mayor, then, and the council ordered city offices closed on the day of her funeral. Two years later he married Emeline Tobey, a widow from Poughkeepsie. It must have been true love, since the newspapers noted that to marry Ludington, she had forfeited her right to the $80,000 estate of her former husband.

In January of 1876, Harrison Ludington resigned from the office of mayor to become governor of Wisconsin. This was to be his last political office and he declined to be re-nominated at the end of his term. Thereafter Ludington's political and business involvement tapered off as he spent more and more time with his model farm.

A few years later the *Milwaukee Sentinel,* in describing the farm, reported, ". . . . his premises are frequented by those who claim to be experts in this specialty, with profit, too, if their declarations may be taken into account. A statement of two transactions by the ex-Governor . . . indicate that he is as successful in this field as in every other upon which he has ventured. He accepted an offer of $200 for a bull calf of the short horn Durham breed-10 months old — and sold a three-year-old Clyde mare for $400. The ex-governor, so elated over his achievements as an amateur stock raiser, has quite recently declared that if some unconscionable wretch had not deprived him of the means of realizing his wish, by robbing him of that gold-headed cane, he would favor Milwaukeeans with an exhibition of his pets by driving them through the streets as he did several years ago."

While the farm was trim, well-manicured, and equipped with numerous handsome buildings, it was not until 1881 that Harrison Ludington had plans drawn for the huge Queen Anne-styled dwelling which was to be erected there. No ordinary farmhouse, his oversized structure was finished in the style and quality of workmanship that might have been expected on one of Yankee Hill's fine mansions. Elegant hardwood

Living room fireplace made of white carrara marble with grey marble columns. The ornamental, incized carving is delicate and unusually fine for a house in the country.

Top left, view through the entry hall arch into dining room. Note the unusually thick wooden casings and the different parquet floor borders. Bottom left, former boiler house which provided heat for the large greenhouses which are now gone. This is one of only two outbuildings surviving the 100-acre stock farm. Above, newel post at base of the main staircase. This hefty Queen Anne/Eastlake-styled post is typical of the above-average quality of woodwork throughout the house. Note the exposed ornamental parquet floor borders. The post probably sported a lamp standard at one time - the present finial was a later addition.

62

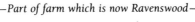

Above, Ludington's farmhouse before the present two-story porch was added. This was taken about 1950 after the last Ludington descendant moved out. Note the original door and window canopies. Right, Harrison Ludington farm today. The heavy black border outlines the original 100 acres purchased from Leander L. Gridley in 1870. Ludington's farm house is indicated as a black square. West of 84th Street/Glenview Avenue is Ravenswood subdivision. The oddly-shaped block bounded by North 84th, West Bluemound Road, Hill Street and Ravenswood circle remained in the hands of Ludington descendants and was not sold for subdivision until later.

Part of farm which is now Ravenswood

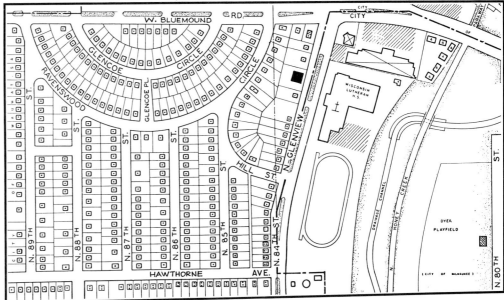

floors with multicolored parquet borders graced the first level and all of the door and window casings were made from expensive heavier-than-average stock. And there were carved and polished marble fireplace mantels the likes of which were found only in the big city houses.

Mr. and Mrs. Ludington elected to stay in their east side mansion, so they installed their son Frederick and his wife in the "farmhouse." This provided not only a place to stay while visiting the farm, but added to the pleasures of each visit. After Harrison's death in 1891, his widow moved to Chicago. Frederick and Elizabeth both lived in the big house for the rest of their lives. In later years, their children ran a business called Ludington Farms Greenhouses, specializing in calla lillies. The two dwellings flanking the big house were wedding presents for Sylvester Ludington (south at 325 Glenview) and Frederick Ludington (north at 407 Glenview).

Today, the boundaries of Harrison Ludington's original 100-acre parcel would be Bluemound Road on the north, Fairview Avenue on the south and from 80th Street to near 89th. The acreage east of Glenview is now mostly occupied as county parkland (Honey Creek Parkway) and by Wisconsin Lutheran High School. Most of the western acreage (62 acres) was purchased by Milwaukee Investment Corporation and developed into the Ravenswood subdivision in 1926.

For years, suburban developments had been springing up all around Wauwatosa; one of the earliest was the Washington Highlands which grew out of the old Pabst hop farm after 1908. The Rockway subdivision, adjacent to Ravenswood, was developed just before this one. "In the country, near the city" was the slogan coined for Ravenswood by developer, realtor and partner in the project, Henry W. Marx. In Marx's attractive sales brochure it was claimed that the new T.M.E.R. & L. Co. elevated rapid transit line would whisk residents to third street, downtown, in fifteen minutes. The transit line, which bordered Ravenswood

on the south, made stops at both 88th Street and Glenview Avenue.

Ravenswood was described as "an exclusive high-class development" that would be "distinctly an area of homes built by cultured people." Average lots were 50'x120' and each came with this restriction: "No residence costing less than $7,500 will be permitted to be erected." During the depression, however, one of these high class lots sold for the sacrifice price of $500. In 1930 the subdivision paid the extra cost to install a better-than-city-standard ornamental street lighting system.

The sales brochure noted that "at the edge of Ravenswood are situated the beautiful homes of Sylvester Ludington and Mrs. Frederick Ludington." The odd-shaped parcel bounded by Glenview, Hill Street and Ravenswood Circle was reserved by the descendants for their own use. It appears as a large wooded block, on the subdivision plat, and bears the title, "ex-Governor Ludington estate." Later Henry Marx was called in to subdivide that last, large, piece into thirty-four saleable lots.

The last Ludington moved out of the big house in 1950 and sold it to a man who kept it only a few months. Mr. and Mrs. Paul E. Tomich, who then bought the house and six of the thirty-four lots, are only the second owners to live in this century-old house.

Little remains of Harrison Ludington's pride-and-joy farm but a sharp eye can still find a clue here and there. In addition to the big house there is still a deep well pump house and a little to the southwest, the tall-chimney boiler house that once supplied the long-gone greenhouses. Occasionally a neighbor, while doing yard work will turn up the remains of an old barn foundation. But the big wooden house is still our best reminder of the pioneer who took over Solomon Juneau's store in 1839, and grew to become one of the czars of the lumber industry. ●

The Sanford Kane house in 1967 when it was still a nursing home. This flat-on view best displays the variety of squares, triangles, rectangles, and carved ornaments typical of Queen Anne design.

Milwaukee's finest remaining example of the Queen Anne style of architecture stands at 1841 North Prospect Avenue. It is such a pure and unspoiled specimen that, even today, it appears to have been lifted from the pages of the architectural pattern books popular during that period. Built in 1883 by Sanford Kane, the house also serves to remind us of an almost forgotten family which once owned the whole neighborhood and after which nearby Kane Place was named.

In 1846, the year Milwaukee became a city, Philander Kane and his five sons, (Alonzo, Charles, George, Sanford and William) arrived here from Waterloo, New York. Their name was soon to become a household word around town and at least two of them were destined for great wealth. The first wise investment was made by their father who bought the American House Hotel on the lot now occupied by the Plankinton Building (West Wisconsin Avenue and North Plankinton Avenue). This pioneer hotel, built in 1843 by Jacob L. Bean, was among the first establishments of its kind in the territory. In 1855 the new owners ("P. Kane & Sons") added two stories, making it the largest hotel in the city. It belonged to the Kanes until it was destroyed by fire in 1861.

Meanwhile, Charles Kane had been acquiring sizeable parcels of real estate. In 1855 he sold 40.5 acres, which included this Prospect Avenue neighborhood, to his brother Alonzo. Then, for reasons unknown, he and his wife left for New York and were not to return until 1895. In fact, by the time their hotel burned down, the whole family had contracted wanderlust. George, William, and Alonzo moved to Chicago and the whereabouts of Sanford remains a mystery.

Not many years later, however, an amazing discovery on part of his Milwaukee land brought Alonzo and his brother back here to stay. An 1872 *Milwaukee Sentinel* headline announced ". . . strange but true-mineral spring discovered in Milwaukee." The enthusiasm continued: "after a very strict and thorough investigation of about four months, it has now become a fixed fact that we have in our own city a mineral spring fully equal, if not preferable, in the cure of all disease of the kidneys, to the Waukesha Bethesda Spring." The spring was actually no new discovery, but its water had just been analyzed in two laboratories and was found to contain the same favorable balance of minerals as the famous Waukesha Spring. "Proof" of its curative powers was furnished by people who claimed complete recovery from diabetes and kidney difficulties.

The exact location seems lost in history, but it was described at the time as being in a deep ravine midway between Prospect Avenue and the Milwaukee River just south of the railroad tracks which cross North Avenue at Oakland. By 1873 Alonzo and Sanford were again listed in the Milwaukee city directories and were to remain here for the rest of their lives. Their occupations were listed as proprietor and secretary of the Siloam Mineral Spring, no doubt named after the Siloam Pool of healing water in biblical Jerusalem.

Detail of the front porch and the principal bay. Here the trim complexity and asymmetrical massing of elements is apparent.

In the first announcement the newspaper stated, "The water is free to all . . . it only costs the dipping. To the afflicted it proves a very cheap medicine." But not for long. Pioneer historian James Buck described Alonzo Kane as "sharp and keen, and usually gets the best end of a bargain." The Kane brothers turned the spring into a commercial venture and made money bottling the water.

With visions of turning Milwaukee into one of those great eastern resort/spas, a group was formed including Kane, Guido Pfister, John Johnston, and Sherbourne Bryant. Architect E. T. Mix prepared sketches for a $120,000 brick and stone resort hotel to be built near the lake bluff. Surrounded by a spacious veranda, it was to be 212 feet long, four stories high and equipped with three towers. The grandiose project never blossomed, but Alonzo Kane soon capitalized on the spring by purchasing the old John Lockwood mansion and converting it into a posh hotel. Today the old Lockwood grounds are a park bounded on the north by Back Bay Road, the west by the foot of Terrace Avenue and the south and east by bluffs.

Sanford worked with his brother Alonzo on the spring and in real estate, from which they both acquired great wealth. For years they lived side-by-side on Farwell Avenue just south of Kane Place. Then, in 1876, a confusing series of events began to unfold. The newspaper announced the Alonzo Kane was building a new residence on Prospect Avenue to be designed by the prominent architect James Douglas.

Alonzo and Sanford Kanes' residences, looking south on North Prospect Avenue in the 1890s. Sanford first lived in Alonzo's House (on the left) which is now gone.

The next year this item appeared: "The elegant residence of Sanford Kane, on Prospect Avenue, was opened on Wednesday evening by one of those old fashioned events known as a house warming. A large company attended the felicitious occasion." But it was his brother's house that Sanford "opened" that evening in 1877, a mansion that Alonzo built but never occupied. It was designed in Douglas' unique termesmordax or "ant-hill" style with a characteristically complex roof and tall tower. About the time he was building this first house, which has since been replaced by the Prospect Health Center (1825 North Prospect Avenue), Alonzo sold the four adjoining north lots to Eli Hoyt. Within a year those lots were purchased by Sanford Kane.

After only six years in the new house, Sanford decided to erect still another large dwelling on his own property next door. In 1884 the Kanes moved one house north and remained there for the rest of their lives. Why the short stay in the house with the tower? It might have been built on speculation by Alonzo and "loaned" to his brother during the planning of the second house or it may have been "tried-out" by the Sanford Kanes and found to be unsatisfactory. Whatever the case, it was then sold to L. J. Petit and finally E. J. Lindsay. During the Second World War it was converted into a resident center for National Youth Administration girls learning war factory skills.

The Sanford Kanes' new house was not as pretentious as the one they left, but it was certainly a modern dwelling in the style which was then the rage country-wide. The Queen Anne style was being heralded as a new national or American vernacular style. It originated in England in the early 1870s in the work and teachings of Richard Norman Shaw and J. J. Stevenson who criticized the earlier Gothic style as being an "artistic expression of an obsolete mode of construction." The new Queen Anne style on the other hand, was an amalgamation of a number of English styles including Elizabethan and Jacobean, along with later Renaissance forms.

Among the style's characteristics were irregular projections and bays, numerous gables and dormers, and a very informal massing of elements overall. A liberal use of wood framing with coarsely carved detail, shingles for siding, and tall prominently sculptured chimneys also distinguished this from previous designs. The Sanford Kane house is not only a remarkably well preserved example of its style, but it is so typical in every respect that it almost becomes a dictionary of

Taken with a telephoto lens, this upper front detail has almost no perspective and shows the design as it would have appeared on the architect's drawing. Here the asymmetrical balances and complex composition can best be appreciated.

This second floor-front window complex is the visual focal point of the exterior. Note the applied moldings, incised chip carving and full-round naturalistic carving. The stylized potted daisy was a favorite Queen Anne theme in the 1880s. At right, detail of the front porch.

The main staircase is the finest and most typically Queen Anne feature of the interior. Above, looking down to the landing of the main staircase from the second floor. Note the unusual quarter circle arc of the balustrade.

Queen Anne characteristics.

Inside, the illusion is destroyed. Not only has it been somewhat altered, but the quality of proportion and workmanship falls short of the exterior and the overall impression is one of disappointment. A single exception — the staircase — makes an exciting contrast on the first and second floors. Rising in three flights, with two landings, it terminates in a second floor balustrade which describes a quarter circle arc around a pie-shaped opening in the stairwell.

Sanford Kane died in the house in 1894 and his widow sold it to another widow, Jane Follansbee. In 1901 it became the home of George Stanley Mitchell, described in an early account as a "lumber king." A native of Plover, Wisconsin, Mitchell was vice president of a Waupun bank and an officer of the William Becker Leather Company here. After his death in 1910, the house remained in his family for thirty years during which time it became a rooming house. In 1957 the Mary Clare Nursing Home converted the aging mansion to serve its purposes. It continued in this capacity until 1984 when it was again given a new lease on life as the Lakeshore Montessori School.

With the Siloam Spring dried up and the old resort hotel gone for so long that nobody remembers it, the Lakeshore school has become our last reminder of the illustrious Kanes of Kane Place. ●

Interior woodwork detail showing a typical paneled door, its casing, and wainscot paneling. Note how the popular sunflower theme appears in the carved oak and the doorknob.

Above, the upper exterior from the southeast. Note the copper-clad dormer. Almost nothing on the exterior has changed since 1887. The many stained glass transom windows were covered on the inside during the Tiffany remodeling and can no longer be appreciated from within. Right, miniature portrait of T.A. Chapman in the parlor. This beautifully painted image was executed on a tile by F.H. Thallmaier of Munich. Far right, the front porch balustrade consisting of fluted sandstone posts and railing with decorative iron panels. These panels are unusually delicate for the period and are made of both hand wrought and cast iron pieces.

When T. A. Chapman decided to give his daughter a mansion for a wedding present, he was not about to take no for an answer. The fact that Laura showed little interest in the planning did not deter him. Chapman hired the architect, developed a plan, and spent a lot of time supervising construction. When his future son-in-law, George P. Miller, said, "I can't afford to live in a house like this . . . I'm only a lawyer," Chapman replied, according to the family, "Then I'll endow it." In fact, Chapman's determination was so strong that, while the newlyweds were away on their honeymoon, he finished the building, hired a complete staff of servants and had dinner on the table when they returned.

But today this is more than just a world-class wedding gift. It is a rare time capsule preserving the tastes and expensive life style of three generations of a prominent Milwaukee family. Like Tutankhamun's tomb, it has not been violated or plundered. Almost all of the original furniture, paintings, oriental rugs and objets d'art are still there — in the same spot where they have resided for 100 years. There is still wine in the wine cellar, family portraits on the walls, and the library is still filled with books accumulated over three generations.

Chapman's granddaughter, Isabelle Miller, was the last family member to live in the house. She was born in a second floor bedroom, shortly after the mansion was completed, and died in the same room in 1980. After living 91 years in the same house Isabelle can be forgiven for her seeming indifference toward it in the later years. Her casual attitude is best remembered when I came to photograph the interior in 1968. Miss Miller seemed puzzled and said, "Mr. Zimmermann, I really cannot understand why you are so interested. It's not original, it's been remodeled." The delicious irony here is that the remodeling was done by the world-famous Louis C. Tiffany of New York. This is a rare case where, instead of detracting from the original, the alterations have given the mansion greater artistic quality and greater historical importance.

The man who was completely responsible for this landmark was somewhat of a landmark himself. Timothy Appleton Chapman, once called the "Merchant Prince" of Milwaukee, built a company which was recognized as being "at the head of the retail dry goods trade in the city and state." His "old store" on the corner of East Wisconsin Avenue and Milwaukee Street, was more like one would expect to see in Philadelphia or New York than on the muddy streets of a small Midwestern town.

In 1895 a local historian wrote, "not content with building for utility only, Mr. Chapman called decorative art to his aid, creating an establishment which fitly came to be spoken of as the 'palace store' and was the pride of the whole northwest." When this spectacular establishment was destroyed by a fire on the night of October 23, 1884 , T.A. Chapman was sixty years old and still full of energy. While the ashes were still smoking he began to plan a new — and even more elaborate — store for the same lot.

With this determination, and Chapman's obvious love for architectural beauty, it probably surprised no one when he announced another building project only two years later. On August 20, 1886, the local press noted, "The stone residence to be erected by T. A. Chapman at Juneau and Prospect Avenues at a cost of $16,000 will be occupied by his youngest daughter. It will be 40 x 80 feet in extent and two stories high."

A year later, during what must have been the final stages of construction, Laura Chapman married George Peckham Miller. A newspaper story claimed that "The social history of Milwaukee has not chronicled a more notable wedding." The streets of Yankee Hill were jammed with fashionable carriages as 1,200 invited guests converged on T. A. Chapman's Cass Street residence for the reception.

Laura's sister Alice composed a wedding march for the occasion and a special wallpapered pavilion was erected on the grounds in which to serve dinner. The pavilion was connected to the parlors and kitchen of the house and was decorated with hanging fruits and flowers. Large pyramids of "tropical and native plants" filled the corners of this remarkable temporary room.

With Laura married and away on her honeymoon, Chapman resumed his daily visits to the mansion project, which he thoroughly enjoyed. The fatherly love for his daughter, the substantial expenditure by a

71

wealthy man, and the consuming interest in a pet building project all seem logical and reasonable. But Chapman's choice of an architect is still an unsolved mystery. He employed local talent for his own house and for the two stores he built here but went to Chicago and sought out a German architect, August Fiedler, for his daughter's house.

Fiedler was the man who created the gemuetlichkeit atmosphere of Chicago's famous Henrici's restaurant. And he designed the handsome club house of the Germania Manerchor about which an 1891 guidebook said, "Germania Hall . . . is from an architectural point of view, one of the most impressive buildings in Chicago, and one of the finest club houses in the whole country." Fiedler was known for at least one other Milwaukee commission, the Samuel Field house which once stood in what is now Juneau Park and was later moved, stone-by-stone, to North Lake Drive.

From the beginning the Chapman/Miller house attracted more than ordinary attention. It was pictured in Milwaukee souvenir books, a local newspaper ran a

pen sketch of it, and it was used as a decorative illustration in the 1891-92 Milwaukee Elite Directory (a society "blue book"). But Fiedler was probably most pleased by the attention shown to his design in his native land. A photograph and three drawings of the house appeared in *Architektonische Rundschau,* a German periodical. Roughly translated that article noted, ". . . Architect's assignment was to create rich color but not to the point of being loud or garrish. He [Fiedler] paid more attention to the interior and therefore the outside was rather simple." Simple perhaps when compared to similar projects in nineteenth century Germany, but by Milwaukee standards, this could only be described as an elegant mansion. Even if one ignores the ornament, the house is rich in the variety and quality of its materials. The walls consist of carved pink Minnesota sandstone, Milwaukee pressed cream city brick and molded buff terra cotta. These materials are complemented by black hand-wrought iron, green sheet copper, leaded cathedral glass and gray slate roofing. Fiedler's design does not fit into any of the usual stylistic categories. It borrows from such a

Opposite, the massive Romanesque arches of the porch looking west. Note the heavily weathered goats' heads on the column supports carved in soft pink Minnesota sandstone. Detail of the complex and highly unusual frieze under the eaves. From the top are naturalistic leaves hammered from copper, buff terra cotta tiles and a band of carved and rusticated sandstone. The carved head, representing Laura Chapman Miller, was dismissed by her as "German sentimentality" and not a faithful representation. Left, a highly unusual decorative grille on one of the front doors. The very stylistic leaves and flowers are hammered from flat sheets and filed to shape.

73

wide range of influences that it might best be described as eclectic Victorian. In fact it may be Milwaukee's finest remaining example of purely Victorian work. When Frank Lloyd Wright's son toured the house some years ago, he called it a good example of bad architecture, but he nonetheless conceded that it should be preserved. Richard Perrin, former director of city development, put it more strongly: "It is one of the city's principal residential landmarks which should be preserved under all circumstances."

The mansion qualifies as a landmark in all of the usual categories, but it has one additional attribute which is rarer and more valuable than the rest. This is still a one-family house which was kept in mint condition by a staff of servants until 1980. The Pabst Mansion, by comparison, was in unusually fine condition when it became a museum, but its conservatory had been converted into a chapel by the Milwaukee Archdiocese and a vast quantity of original furniture, paintings, lighting fixtures and objets d'art had slipped away. Although some pieces have been found there are still countless furnishings which can

never be recovered.

One other rarity came close to surviving — the Joseph Uihlein mansion at 3318 North Lake Drive. Until Mrs. Uihlein died in 1983 it too was filled with original furnishings, occupied by the lady who conceived it and kept brightly polished by servants. Unfortunately its contents have now been dissipated and the interior has been converted into a number of condominiums. The Miller house, therefore, is even more precious as time passes.

The mansion's exterior has both a rich complement of materials and an extraordinary amount of finely-crafted ornament. The third floor dormer is almost completely sheathed in sheet copper fashioned to look like carved and rusticated stone. Just below the eaves is a feature not found anywhere else in Milwaukee: a large-scale metal frieze decorated with realistic leaves hammered out of copper. This sits on another rarity — a wide band of buff terra-cotta tiles in an ornamental pattern. Below is still another band with leaf-work hand carved in pink sandstone.

Over two of the second floor windows are carved heads representing Mr. and Mrs. Miller. Isabelle Miller remembered her mother describing this exterior feature with disdain. Laura Miller said that they were not faithful representations and dismissed them as "German sentimentality." The same stone carver embellished each porch column with four bearded goats' heads. The porch is further decorated with wrought iron panels that are rare because they pre-date the arrival of Milwaukee's prolific and widely-known iron master, Cyril Colnik.

The "German sentimentality" described by Laura Miller may be a clue to her father's choice of an architect. Isabelle had a German governess and the family library included a broad selection of German literature. But, perhaps more important, George P. Miller had obtained the better part of his education at the universities of Breslau and Gottingen in Germany. From the latter he received the prestigious advanced law degree, *Juris Utriusque Doctor cum laude*. The requirements for this degree were said to be "among the most difficult established in the world," and he was one of only a few Americans to earn it.

George Peckham Miller became an authority on Roman Law and the philosophy of law. A contemporary, Louis Quarles, regarded him as "one of the most scholarly and intellectual attorneys that Wisconsin ever had."

One might have expected this since his grandfather, Andrew Galbraith Miller, was a territorial judge here from 1838 until Wisconsin became a state ten years later, and his father, Benjamin Miller, was a senior partner in the law firm which has evolved into the state's largest, Foley and Lardner.

Although Miller was at first less concerned about the mansion than his father-in-law, he took greater interest in it as time passed. His pride in the quality of his surroundings is revealed in a story told by Isabelle some years ago. It seems that the James E. Patton residence, next door west, had left the original family's hands and was becoming "run-down and tacky." With what we might today call a bold executive decision, Miller bought the property and tore down the old paint manufacturer's mansion. He did this, according to his daughter, for the express purpose of "keeping up the neighborhood." One might also guess that his boldness in hiring Tiffany to remodel the house was similarly inspired. Unfortunately the papers relating to the Tiffany commissions have been lost or misplaced. No one remembers why Tiffany was selected, when the

work was done, or for that matter, just how much of the present interior can be attributed to that brilliant designer-craftsman. There is, however, no doubt about the origin of many of the wall sconces, chandeliers, and leaded glass windows seen throughout the interior.

It is likely that George Miller was the one who initiated the family's long association with Tiffany Studios. He employed them not only for this house but to provide lighting fixtures for his Oconomowoc residence. And, for years, T. A. Chapman Company carried a line of Tiffany lamps — probably beginning after Chapman's death in 1892 when Miller took over management of the store. A tour of the mansion's interior today would impress even the most stubborn of critics: there is great variety in color, materials and design style. The glint of gold, the rich coloration of Orientals, the warm glow of hand-rubbed wood finishes, and the spectacular luminescence of Tiffany windows are only the beginning. Oil painting from such competent hands as Adolph Schreyer abound. In the living room is a beautiful miniature portrait of T. A. Chapman painted on a tile by F. H. Thallmaier of Munich.

Prisms of gold Tiffany favrile glass shimmer with magenta and purple irridescence against the white walls of the parlor. In the entrance vestibule a tile floor resembling a Roman opus tesselatum mosaic is played against polished marble wainscoting topped by a burgundy majolica tile panel. The influences of English Tudor, French Renaissance, Romanesque, and art nouveau are artfully entwined in a very warm and pleasing fashion.

Opposite, earliest known photograph and floor plans of the Miller house printed in the 19th Century German periodical, Architektonische Rundschau. On the left is the James E. Patton residence which Miller later bought and razed to "keep up the neighborhood." On the right is the Gothic mansion of Judge Jason Downer which is still standing. Note the round-arched window on the west (left) side of Miller's house was later replaced by Tiffany's grapevine window. Below, cross-section and two floor plans from the original 1886 design.

Abb. 1.

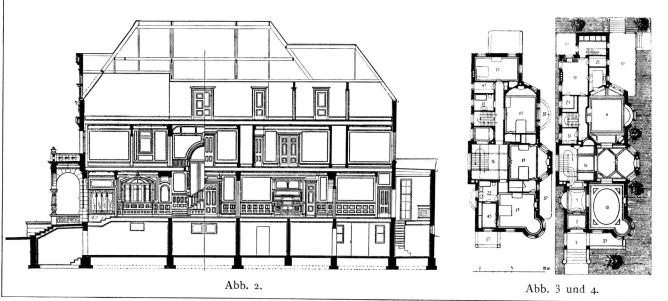

Abb. 2.

Abb. 3 und 4.

Aug. Fiedler, Arch.

MILWAUKEE.

Privat-House.
Residence for T. A. Chapmans, Esqre.

The first floor library which is the heart of the interior. Notice the finely figured mahogany paneling.

Left, Tiffany magnolia blossom window above the library fireplace mantel. This window shows the highest refinement of Tiffany's technique including built-up lead branches and thick sculptural glass. Above, detail of the fine built-in mahogany bookcases in the library. The gold-mounted vase is one of a pair which have splendid painted portraits of the Hapsburg Grand Duke and Duchess of Austria-Hungary. These came from T.A. Chapman's house and spent the duration of World War I facing the wall.

The library, which separates the front parlor from the dining room, is the heart of the house. It is paneled in finely-figured mahogany with built-in drawers and bookcases. Tiffany wall sconces and a matching chandelier create a warm glow through twenty favrile glass shades. The fireplace is flanked by a pair of massive seven foot columns which have carved rams-head capitals like those on the front porch. Between them is the room's focal point, an impressive magnolia blossom window in pastel blues, greens, and whites by Tiffany. This window shows the highest refinement of Tiffany's technique: built-up lead branch-work and thick sculptural glass.

The architecture of the library is further enhanced by bronze urns, a cloisonne clock, Oriental porcelains, framed etchings, and a splendid pair of gold-mounted vases with portraits of the Hapsburg Grand Duke and Duchess of Austria-Hungary. The latter pieces came from T. A. Chapman's house and according to the family, spent the duration of World War I facing the wall.

Opposite, the cylindrical bay window of the front parlor is in the base of the mansion's southeast corner tower. The oriental rug, oil paintings, furniture and light fixtures are all original. Left, one of the original front parlor gas wall sconces. These handsome gold-plated brass fixtures were later wired for electricity and supplied with iridescent Tiffany favrile glass prisms.

From the remote wine cellar, tucked into a corner of the basement, to the servants' quarters and high-ceilinged ballroom on the third floor, the house displays the residue of many European "grand tours." Even T. A. Chapman's steamer trunk, made by Louis Vuitton of Paris, survives in the attic. But it is a huge window, dominating the staircase, which must take the title of the mansion's crown jewel. Made by Tiffany, this depiction of grape vines in greens and violets was made to replace the original round-arched window designed by Fiedler.

This incomparable Victorian mansion is still controlled by the family through the Chapman Foundation which uses the first floor rooms for philanthropic meetings. In 1981 the foundation reached an agreement with the Wisconsin Conservatory of Music which allowed them to move their administrative offices into the second floor and to use the third floor ballroom. With a similar arrangement the Junior League of Milwaukee moved into the building in 1985.

The Miller house is now listed on the National Register of Historic Places as a part of the *First Ward Triangle Historic District*. Within a stone's throw there are twenty additional landmarks and historic sites. Together these comprise Milwaukee's richest concentration of architecture and history. Chapman would have beamed with pride. ●

Opposite, the mansion's crown jewel is this huge grape vine window by Tiffany. Added in the later remodeling, this replaces the architect's original Roman-arched staircase window. Below, George P. Miller house from the southeast.

Above, earliest known photograph of the house and its stable/barn. Notice the brightness of the new yellow brick and the darker tone of the nine-courses above the foundation which were dyed red. Left, Victor Schlitz as a young man.

Joseph Schlitz drowned in an 1875 shipwreck and, although his brewery has since made his name world-famous, he left no children to continue his family. It is a little-known fact, however, that there are still genuine, related, Schlitzes living in Milwaukee. They are descendants of Joseph's nephew, Victor Schlitz, who was a prominent nineteenth century wine and liquor merchant here. The modest mansion Victor built in 1890, is still standing at 2004 West Highland Avenue. Behind its relatively unassuming facade lies a story rich in historical associations including ties to Milwaukee's famous water tower and the royal architect to the Czar of Russia.

It all began in Hesse-Darmstadt, Germany, when Charles Schlitz established a champagne winery. In 1868 he sent one of his sons, John, to Milwaukee to represent the business and open a store here. When John Schlitz arrived, he was a stranger in a new land and he followed a custom familiar to many European immigrants — he went to live with a relative. That relative was his uncle, Joseph Schlitz, who was then living at the brewery on Chestnut Street. His address, 420 Chestnut, would now be on the north side of West Juneau Avenue between 4th and 5th streets.

According to the best (and possibly only) known view of the original Schlitz Brewery, 420 was a three-story brick Federal style building that fronted on Chestnut Street. It is likely that Joseph lived upstairs in that building. Nephew John was then given lodging next door east (418) in a smaller two-story structure with a pitched roof. The rest of the brewery's working buildings were spread out to the north of these two.

John promptly established the "Charles Schlitz & Co., wholesale wines and liquors" business at 404 East Water Street (second door north of the northeast corner of East Wisconsin and North Water Street). In 1869 Charles Schlitz is correctly noted as living in Germany. Charles never lived in Milwaukee, but there were a few local historians and newspapermen who assumed as much from the company's name.

Several "factual" references to his local residency have, therefore, crept into Milwaukee's recorded history.

In December of 1871, Victor Schlitz was mustered out of the 117th Infantry Regiment, in Darmstadt, after serving as a Lieutenant in the Franco-Prussian War. Early the next year he set out for Milwaukee to join the family's American operation as a partner. Like his brother, Victor went to live with Uncle Joseph. He

Original Schlitz Brewery

Left, front of the Victor Schlitz house as seen from the southwest in 1979. Above, the ornamental highlight of the exterior is a very uncommon terra cotta panel composed of thirty-nine pieces. Facing east from the base of a chimney stack, the design centers around a larger-than life-sized female head.

shared 418 Chestnut with John for at least three years. Meanwhile, in 1870, the brewery operation had been moved to the company's present location on Third and Walnut while Joseph continued to reside at his old Chestnut Street location.

In 1874 the Schlitz brothers built a factory and it was announced in the newspaper. This was not only described in typical Victorian rhetoric, but non-resident Charles erroneously got the credit: "That the temperance crusade has not caused Charley Schlitz to repine in despondent fear, of feeble fancies full, is evident from the fact that he has put up a large distillery and rectifying establishment on the southeast corner of Cherry and Fourth Streets at a cost of $25,000." Therein they distilled, cut, blended, bottled from casks, and otherwise modified a great variety of liquors.

Then, on May 7, 1875, on his way to Hamburg, Germany, Uncle Joseph died in the wreck of the steamship *Schiller* near the coast of England. John and

Victor then left the old brewery complex and moved into separate dwellings near their new business establishment on Fourth Street. Around 1878 John left for Cleveland, Ohio, to set up a similar establishment there. This left Victor as the only survivor of the Schlitz family in Milwaukee.

When John moved away, the name of the one-family business was changed to Victor Schlitz Company and it made one last move to 309 Third Street. In a couple of years Victor moved into living quarters above his new building. That made him a next door neighbor to the Trimmel and Mader Saloon. Today's expanded Mader's Restaurant now occupies the Schlitz site.

Victor's advertising represented him as a "Rectifier, importer and wholesale dealer in wines, liquors and mineral water." He specialized in imported Rhine wine, French red wine, Ohio, Mississippi and California wines but also stocked all kinds of whiskey, brandy, and bitters, imported and domestic. The wine labels that have survived from his business suggest that he

Above, the all oak entrance hall and staircase. Note the daisy pattern lincrusta wainscoting, the segmental arched alcove, the walnut floor stripes and the unusual door lintels capped with spindle railings. Right, the oak woodwork can be appreciated in the parlor fireplace which is both bold and delicate. Note the unusual cast iron grate surrounded by majolica glazed tiles.

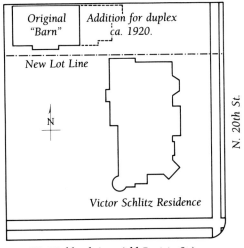

Original "Barn" | Addition for duplex ca. 1920.

New Lot Line

N

Victor Schlitz Residence

N. 20th St.

W. Highland Ave. (old Prairie St.)

Best early view of the Schiltz house looking northwest from the street corner. Note the young trees, the electric arc street light and the complex railings at the sidewalk intersection.

imported the casks and did his own bottling. Under the private label of "Victor Schlitz" he sold such names as Niersteiner, Laubenheimer, Riesling, Moselblumchen, and Concord.

By 1889, Victor Schlitz was one of ten wholesale liquor houses in Milwaukee and he employed three "traveling men" to cover the northwestern states and territories. His building was a two-story, 25' x 150' structure which had, according to an old souvenir book, this interesting feature: "at the rear of the wholesale department is a well-stocked bar, where patrons may secure liquid refreshment." Schlitz was also one of the founders of the West Side Bank and the Lakeside Distilling Co. He owned mines in Iron River, Michigan, and was once grand president of the Sons of Hermann Lodge.

Victor's wife was the daughter of Leonhard A. Schmidtner, one of Milwaukee's earliest and most prominent architects. Born of noble stock, Schmidtner's real name was Baron von Kowalski and his father had been the Royal Architect of Russia. In Milwaukee, Schmidtner drew the plans for St. Stanislaus Church and won the prestigious commission to design the Courthouse which once occupied Cathedral Square. His daughter's portrait was printed on the bank checks of the Victor Schlitz Co.

In 1890 Schlitz decided to build a new house and he purchased five lots on the northwest corner of 20th and Prairie (now West Highland Avenue). Had he been alive then, Victor's father-in-law might well have been the one to design this house. As it turned out, the man selected was Charles A. Gombert, who also was ranked among Milwaukee's top nineteenth century architects.

Gombert, a native of Koenigsberg, Germany, had done work on the old state capital in Madison and had designed houses for such local names as Pillsbury, Benjamin, and Valentine Blatz. His most famous creation, however, was Milwaukee's beloved water tower at North Point. Charles Duchow, one of the incorporators of the Milwaukee Masons' and Builders' Association, was selected as the builder.

The finished product is well crafted, picturesquely designed, and unmistakably Victorian. Gombert's seemingly random massing of shapes and eclectic use of ornamental details are very typical for the period. If it has any stylistic pedigree, the house would have to be called Queen Anne. Early photographs show that it was once even more colorful and complex than it is today.

One unusual and interesting feature is the use of a band of color at ground level. There are nine courses of cream city brick between the foundation and a limestone stringcourse which marks the level of the first floor. These show up darker in the old pictures and today, through the dirt, it is still apparent that they were once dyed a reddish color. The old views also show that the quasi-medieval timberwork was originally painted in highly contrasting colors.

The house's complexity can be appreciated by noting that there are seventy-seven windows, only a few of which are identical. Color and design were heightened by the use of terra cotta, cedar shingles, painted sheet metal work, carved and scroll-cut wood, and buff sandstone sills. The ornamental highlight of the exterior is a spectacular red terra cotta grouping on the east wall chimneystack. It consists of a larger-than-life-size head surrounded by thirty-eight ornamental squares and moldings.

The interior highlight is an all-oak entrance hall with staircase landing "room," beamed ceiling, two double and three single doors. The hardwood floor is edged with five one-and-one-half inch walnut stripes. The most unusual feature in this room, and throughout the house, is the treatment of door casings. Each lintel molding has leafwork carved *in the solid* and is topped with a turned spindle railing. The doors are fitted with high quality bronze hardware in a Romanesque-inspired basketweave pattern.

In 1915, just in time to avoid prohibition, Victor Schlitz retired from the wine and liquor business. He died in 1928, leaving the house to his six children. They sold it to the St. Vincent De Paul Society the next year and it has since served three Roman Catholic organizations. In 1975 it was purchased by Highland Community School, Inc. which still occupies the building as a private Montessori Elementary School.

Today, overlooking the side-yard playground, there is a large two-family residence which once belonged to Schlitz. It was the barn where Victor kept his four horses and several carriages. Around 1920 a few rooms and a porch were grafted on the east end and the interior was converted into a duplex.

In 1965 the Kilbourntown K-3 redevelopment project destroyed 898 buildings in a sweeping 104 acre tract right across the street. That was, conservationists hope, the last close call this historic house will have. ●

Front (south) elevation of Captain Pabst's mansion in May of 1970 when it was still occupied by the Milwaukee Archbishop. Left, Captain Frederick Pabst as a young man.

Captain Frederick Pabst's residence is the quintessential German Beer Baron's mansion. It was built at a staggering cost by a self-confident millionaire whose bold choice of an architectural style defied local tradition. It dramatically symbolizes the height to which a humble immigrant could rise in nineteenth century America. And along with City Hall, which was designed in a similar style, it exhibits a depth of European influence unrivaled anywhere in the Midwest.

Pabst was born in Nicholausreith, Germany, but his family's circumstances gave no one cause to believe that he would come into either beer or money. At the age of twelve his parents brought him to America. Frederick's father, Gottlieb Pabst, believed his friends' stories about the opportunities in Milwaukee so he came here first. Unimpressed, the family then settled in Chicago where the young boy worked as a waiter for $5.00 a month. Family tradition says that he had never forgotten the ocean voyage and, in time, decided to seek employment on the water.

At seventeen he signed on a Goodrich Line steamer as a cabin boy. By studying navigation in his spare time, and by offering to relieve pilots, Pabst worked his way up to a Steamboat Pilot's Certificate in 1857. At twenty-one he became part owner and Captain of the *Huron,* the very first boat of the Goodrich fleet.

In his largely autobiographical *Life on the Mississippi,* Mark Twain makes it clear that steamboat pilots were very proud men who were universally admired. "Commodore" Cornelius Vanderbilt made his first fortune operating ferries in New York Harbor and paddle wheelers on the Hudson River. He later gained control of the New York Central and switched to railroading, but the old title, "Commodore," stayed with him permanently. And so it was with "Captain" Pabst who left the Great Lakes in the 1860s, but proudly sported his title for the rest of his life.

According to his certificate, Pabst was licensed by the Chicago District Inspectors as a "first class pilot" for Lake Michigan and he was qualified to navigate all classes of vessels including the largest passenger steamers.

Phillip Best, the owner of a Milwaukee brewery,

got to know the young Captain while traveling on his boat. In time Pabst met Best's daughter, Marie, and, in 1862, they were married. Best was looking to retire and there was no doubt some pressure from Marie, but it may well have been a "shipwreck" that turned the tide for Frederick. In an 1863 storm he was forced to run his steamer, *Seabird,* aground off Whitefish Bay.

He was ready for a change when Phillip Best retired the next year. In 1864 Pabst gave up his marine career to accept an equal partnership in his father-in-law's brewery, Phillip Best and Company. For the next two decades he applied his talent and energy first to learning the brewing business and then to building Best Beer into a great national brand.

The year 1889 was great for Pabst: The board of directors changed the name of the company from Best to Pabst and elected him president. It was also the year when they overtook the competition in sales and could begin to advertise that Pabst was "the largest lager beer brewery in the world." The Captain chose this important turning point to announce his plans for a new residence.

In November of that year the following statement appeared in the newspaper: "Before another year will have passed Captain Fred Pabst and his family will probably have bidden adieu to the cozy little house in the triangular lot on Chestnut Street and will be domiciled in a new residence on Grand Avenue."

That "cozy little house" was actually a large, eclectic, Victorian dwelling which he had built only fourteen years earlier. It was literally in the shadow of his giant brewery complex on a triangle of land bounded by Chestnut (now Juneau), Eighth and Ninth streets and by an alley.

Many of Milwaukee's wealthy brewers lived within easy walking distance of their offices, but this must have been uncomfortably close. Pabst had once been quoted as saying, "that under no circumstances would he remove from his present home, but for the fact that he needs it as a place of business in connection with the brewery. The present dwelling house will be used for office purposes, and other buildings will be erected upon the land." Actually Pabst had been considering a new residence for two years, but there was a leased building on his lot and he "could not conveniently get possession of it."

It was worth waiting for a choice spot on Milwaukee's great street. In the old days this was a country lane which was called Spring Street because natural spring water oozed to the surface — in places making travel difficult. However, mansions began to appear here as early as the 1850s and within two decades, the street was lined with stately homes set back on lush lawns. A more appropriate name was desired for this prestigious neighborhood so Spring Street was accordingly re-named "Grand Avenue."

Finally, in May of 1890, the lease on Pabst's Grand Avenue property expired and he promptly hired contractor Val Mand to tear down the old brick dwelling which had once been the home of S.C. Scott. On May 16 the demolition was begun and by the end of the month a fence was built around the property and all the trees were boxed for protection.

On June 27 a building permit was granted wherein the cost of the new structure was estimated at a very conservative $75,000. Twenty-five competitive bids were received for the various trades involved and the largest single contract awarded was for $22,000 to C.B. Roberts & Bro. for the masonry. Val Mand received the carpenters contract with the lowest of five bids. Additional contracts were awarded to L.H. Plum, plumbing and gas fitting; Fred Andres & Co., cut stone work; Henry Weden, painting and glazing; C.H. Ross, terra cotta; N.W. Adamant Co., plastering; Greenslade Bros., architectural iron; H. Mooers & Co., steamheating; Duerr & Rohn, electrical; N.W. Tile Co., tiling, and Biersach & Niedermeyer, copper work. Brodesser & Co.installed an elevator and Johnson Electric supplied the heat regulation.

On the day that work began at the Grand Avenue site, Mr. and Mrs. Pabst were on their way to Europe for a vacation. By the time they returned in September, the new house was well underway. In fact, by January of 1891, the skylight over the stairwell was framed in

Early exterior view showing the newly erected pavilion on the east (right) end of the mansion. The stained glass dome has not yet been replaced, but it has been protected by an outer covering of clear glass.

and the final shape of the structure was already visible. The work continued until 1893 and included a pavilion, a two-story stable-barn, a brick servants apartment on Wells Street, and a greenhouse.

A remarkable amount of paper documentation has survived to give us details of the building project. On a statement dated August 2, 1892, we can see that Pabst employed a second architect, Otto Strack, to design the separate servants' apartments on Wells Street. The interesting detail is a line which reads, "50,000 old bricks taken from cor. 9th and Chestnut Sts. 5.00 pr. m. — $225.00 — to be credited to Pabst Brg. Co." Could this have been the Captain's old residence. . . re-cycled for the servants?

Another rare, and precious, sheet of paper has survived detailing "Grand Avenue Residence . . . cost of same." Here, written in what may be the Captain's own hand, is a final tally of expenses. Not including taxes or insurance the total comes to $254,614.28. This was an incredible sum in its day, especially when we can see elsewhere in the same documents that carpenters working on this job were earning thirty-five cents an hour.

At that rate, working fifty hours a week, and saving every dime of his wages, a carpenter would have to work approximately 290 years to afford such a mansion! Today, including fringe benefits, a Milwaukee journeyman-carpenter earns $19.77 per hour. If the wage-difference factor is applied to the building cost an unscientific, but interesting, comparison can be made. This simple calculation suggests that Pabst's mansion would cost $14.5 million dollars to build in 1987.

But this was only the physical plant. Furniture and decorations must have increased the total considerably. While these records have not turned up, their extent can be imagined from the inventory of oil paintings and water colors made in 1895. There are eighty-two pieces listed with a total value of $71,825. Among the painters are such important names as Ridgway Knight, Adolph Schreyer, Meyer Von Bremen, Edward Grutzner, and Eugene Verboeckhoven. Three prominent local artists — Richard Lorenz, Henry Vianden, and Robert Schade — are represented.

A good share of the canvases cost over $2,000, and there were a few that cost Pabst between $4,000 and $8,000. He purchased a substantial number at the World Columbian Exposition at Chicago in 1893. Among them was one of the most popular at the fair, "Loves Dream" by W. J. Martens. According to the inventory ten paintings hung in the music room, six in

Above, detail of the front (south) elevation showing three corbie-stepped Flemish gables. The pressed tan brick walls are lavishly ornamented with terra cotta of a similar color. The porch in the foreground is cased entirely with terra cotta. Below, the mansion's massive front doors are composed of complex oak millwork, handcarved details and wrought iron. The leaded glass panels hinge inward to allow conversation through the grillwork.

the parlor, five in the dining room, nine in the smoking room, three in the vestibule, nine in the hall, sixteen in the stairway, and the rest upstairs.

The Captain's taste for the good life also included a well stocked wine cellar, for which an inventory from about the same time survives. Of the 262 cases recorded, the greater percentage was in German Rhines and Mosels. Among these are thirty-nine cases of Schloss Johannisberger Cabinet, 1893, for which he paid $50 per case. Most of the other German wines were Spatleses and Ausleses. Also listed were 245 miscellaneous bottles including six brands of champagne, Haut Sauternes, nine bottles of Chateau Margaux-1884, sherries, and at the bottom of the list,

five bottles of Buchanon Scotch Whiskey.

Shortly after the project began, Pabst released detailed information to local newspapers, which published a copy of the architect's perspective drawing and ran large stories with headlines such as "Handsome New Residence," "A Building That Will Be An Ornament to Milwaukee," "Palatial Abode." One story described the setting, which has remained almost unchanged: "The site, on the north side of the Avenue, facing Twentieth street, is a superb one with considerable elevation above the street and a broad, sloping lawn, shaded with fine trees. The lot has a frontage of 160 feet on Grand Avenue and runs clear through to Wells Street."

The carved wooden fireplace in the ladies' parlor is as fine as French rococo design comes in this country.

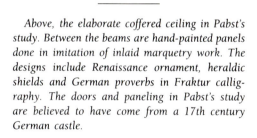

Above, the elaborate coffered ceiling in Pabst's study. Between the beams are hand-painted panels done in imitation of inlaid marquetry work. The designs include Renaissance ornament, heraldic shields and German proverbs in Fraktur calligraphy. The doors and paneling in Pabst's study are believed to have come from a 17th century German castle.

Early reports noted that the mansion was equipped with every possible luxury and convenience, including a three-story passenger elevator, an attached plant conservatory, separate parlors for the men and ladies, a billiard room, a wine cellar, and a porte cochere, or carriage porch, over the driveway. The servants even had a private dining room and separate apartments at the north end of the property. According to one published account it was also, "fireproof to a degree seldom attained in residence construction, as the exterior walls will be lined with hollow fire brick and tile and granite."

Pabst engaged the firm of Ferry & Clas to prepare drawings for his mansion. The partner credited with the actual design was George Bowman Ferry, an 1872 graduate of America's first architectural school. Ferry's front facade is a handsomely-proportioned symmetrical composition in the Flemish Renaissance revival style. Set on a Wauwatosa limestone foundation, it is executed in tan pressed brick trimmed with terra cotta in a matching color. Red "Spanish" clay tile covers the roof while downspouts, gutters and the ornamental rainwater heads are made of sheet copper.

The Flemish-style, corbie-stepped, gables and dormers are heavily encrusted with Renaissance strapwork and ornament. But the front porch and the porte cochere are even more elaborate. These two appendages, faced entirely with terra cotta, are covered with rich, sculptural, detail. When the house was completed in 1893, it had no pavilion attached to its

eastern end. The structure was already in existence, but at that time, it was doing duty as an exhibit gazebo in the Agriculture Building of the World's Columbian Exposition in Chicago. There is a rare early photograph which shows the newly-erected pavilion before the Pabst Brewery product displays were even set up. (There were many similar structures at that world's fair, including those of the Meriden Britannia Co. and the Lundborg Perfume temple.)

This all-terra cotta gem was designed by Otto Strack in the German Baroque style. Strack, who had previously done brewery work for Pabst, was also responsible for his daughter's house (Mrs. Wm. O. Goodrich — 2234 North Terrace Avenue) and the Kalvelage house at 2432 West Kilbourn. The columns and panels are appropriately sculptured with beer steins, barley and hop vines.

After the Exposition closed the pavilion was disassembled and moved back to Milwaukee where it was set on a limestone foundation and connected to the dining room by a short passageway. When it was used indoors, the entire dome and the four quarter-domes were filled with highly ornamental stained glass. As an outdoor structure these areas had to be replaced with weather-worthy copper roofing. Although no supporting documentation has surfaced, it is almost certain that Pabst had the pavilion created with this pioneer recycling in mind. His final tally shows it to have cost $11,559.62.

Opposite, a rare photograph of the Pabst beer display pavilion in the agriculture building of the World's Columbian Exposition in Chicago. Note the elaborate stained glass dome which has since been replaced by a copper roof. Left, detail of the beer pavilion as it looks today. Notice the Pabst beer trademark (a hop leaf in a circle), hop vines and sprays of barley. Brewing is also symbolized by a German beer stein on the cartouche between the two closest columns. Above, the Lundborg Perfume Temple at the 1893 World's Columbian Exposition in Chicago. This, the Pabst and the Meriden Britannia Company's pavilions shared the same basic design elements.

Above left, hanging in the dining room is the only original major chandelier to survive. Its lively rococo arms were cast by the lost wax process and then gold plated. Above right, one of several oil paintings over doors in the dining room. While many 19th century architectural paintings were only good enough for decoration, these were executed with the skill of a fine artist. During the Archbishop's occupancy these recently-restored canvases were hidden under a coat of white paint. Right, one of a pair of built-in china cabinets in the dining room. Notice how the doors, moldings, carvings and hardware follow the sinuous curves of the design with perfect precision. Opposite, the splendid rococo dining room looking east.

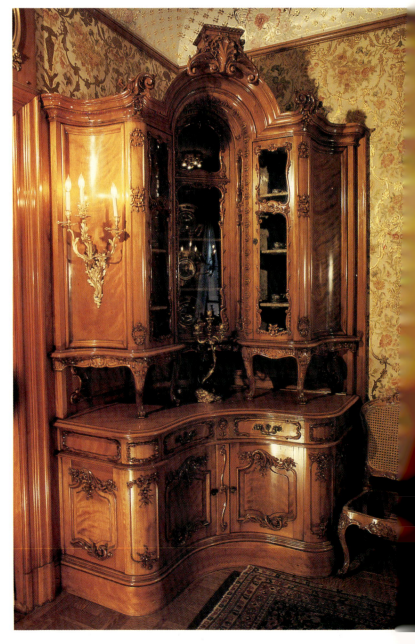

Above, the main reception hall when the mansion
was new. The large wrought iron and antler chandelier is now missing. Below, early photograph of
the Captain's study as originally furnished. Note
the gas table lamp with its flexible tube connected
to the chandelier overhead.

Above, looking southeast in the ladies' parlor when the house was new. The original gilt French rococo furniture has survived and is still in the room. Below, the mens' parlor looking east toward the fireplace. The elaborate gas/electric chandelier and the matching sconces on the twisted columns have unfortunately been lost.

The mahogany woodwork in the mens' parlor
glows through a glass-like, hand-rubbed varnish.
Beautifully executed black faux-ebony details
accent the warm red wood.

The pavilion was not the only artifact transplanted here. The Captain is said to have taken the paneling and woodwork for his study out of a 17th century German castle. The intricately crafted oak doors, casings and cabinets clearly are of German design. They could date from the 16th or the 17th century, but it must also be noted that a great deal of this kind of woodwork was being done in Germany, as a revival, in the 19th century. A very similar example appears in the 1885 dining room of Villa Hallgarten in Frankfurt, Germany.

Many of the remaining interior spaces are in the 18th century French rococo style. The most beautiful of these is the ladies' parlor which is finished in off-white enamel that originally was highlighted with gold leaf. An exquisitely carved pair of brackets flanking the window alcove and the fireplace are as fine as rococo comes in this country.

Directly across the hall is a luxury which only the rich could afford: a second parlor used as an after dinner retreat for men and their cigars. This room is appropriately masculine in design. The warm mahogany woodwork glows through a glass-like finish and is accented with black faux-ebony detailing. The fireplace is lined with dark green verde antique marble.

The rococo dining room has the only original major chandelier to survive the years of up-date lighting. Its gold-plated, lost-wax castings still look as good as new. Above the doors painted landscapes are set into carved and gilt panels. Unlike much architectural painting, which is only good enough for decoration, these canvases were executed with the skill of a fine artist. The two built-in china cabinets can also be called the work of a fine artist. As their sinuous design flows back and forth the carvings, hardware, doors and moldings follow the curves with perfect precision. Only a master furniture maker could handle a job with so few straight lines. This is probably the finest built-in cabinetry in the State of Wisconsin.

The rest of the interior is compatibly embellished with fine, carved, woodwork, marble-lined fireplaces, and ornamental plaster. The second floor consists of bedrooms with their connecting sitting rooms and baths arranged around a large central hall.

Unfortunately Captain Pabst was only able to enjoy his world-class mansion for eleven years. He died on New Years Day in 1904, and within four years his still-new Grand Avenue masterpiece was sold to the Milwaukee Roman Catholic Archdiocese. As soon as Archbishop Sebastian Messmer moved in, he built a two-story brick boiler house. In the years that followed a garage and a poultry house were added while the old three-story coach house was converted into a Chancery Office.

In one of Milwaukee's great architectural ironies, the beer gazebo, which was moved 100 miles to become an attached pavilion, was in for yet another recycling. This time it was equipped with an altar and stained glass windows and it became a chapel consecrated to the Virgin Mary.

Fortunately for Milwaukee, it was the occupancy of five Archbishops which carried the Pabst mansion through its most vulnerable years. During the decades when 19th century architecture was being carelessly slaughtered, this masterpiece was being cleaned and polished as though the Captain still lived here.

When the Archdiocese sold the mansion in 1974, a public outcry arose as the property changed hands three times. After losing the coach house in 1977, and a considerable piece of the original property to the north, the house was acquired by a not-for-profit corporation, Wisconsin Heritages, Inc. This organization now operates the mansion as a house-museum and has begun an extensive restoration program. As each year passes, Milwaukee's most important residential landmark slips a little further back into history. ●

The sixth renewal of Captain Pabst's steamboat pilot's certificate, dated March 19, 1860.

The main entrance. Notice the number, 303, below the front door. This was the original Martin (later State) Street address of the Field Mansion before the move. For sentimental reasons it has been allowed to remain on its original stone.

*D*oomed Mansion, Once Treasure House of Art." Milwaukeeans were shocked when they saw that headline in their Sunday papers. It was October of 1926, and the story announced that the great Samuel A. Field mansion was to be razed. It numbered among the nearly two dozen lake bluff homes which had to be sacrificed for the city's planned extension of Prospect Avenue. All of the land east of the new roadway was to be leveled and added to Juneau Park.

The newspaper writer continued his nostalgic lament: *"It is one of those nights when you go to Juneau Park to watch the moon rise over the lake, sitting on a bench close to the statue of Leif Ericsson, saying and thinking the things that everybody says and thinks when the moon rises over the water. . . . Let's turn around and see what the moon is doing to the old Field house. There it stands, its straight gray stone walls whitened by the moonlight, its vines black against the stone. Not a casual house with a bay window added because someone needed a sunny nook for a sewing table or to grow hyacinths. Not an excrescence of a sleeping porch built on because the high school boy grumbled that he wouldn't be able to do a thing on the track unless he had outside sleeping quarters.*

"But a 1-idea house, correct in every detail, and a building, you are convinced, that took more dollars to build and more hours of an architect to plan than many a larger house."

The city's reaction to the news was remarkable for the time. This was not the 1980s when historic preservation is a household word . . . when citizens demonstrate in front of bulldozers to halt the destruction of a landmark. This was 1926, when the other houses in this project were dispatched without the blink of an eye. This was a time when it was socially unfashionable to like Victorian-era homes.

But the exquisite detailing and the finely crafted interiors of this mansion were so superior that it could not be ignored like the others. There was a public outcry and people were begging: "Don't tear it down." "It is too good a piece of architecture." "Let it stand."

No one was more concerned than Louis Kuehn, who had purchased the house after Field's death and had been living in it since 1920. After a fruitless search for another residence, Kuehn made the bold decision to move the mansion to a new location three miles to the north.

When Field built the house its address was 303 Martin Street (now East State Street) at the southwest

103

Rare view of the Field house on Martin (now State) Street as a parade is passing in 1918. The view looks east toward Lake Michigan and is the only known rear-view photograph of the original three-story house.

Looking west across the front (north side) entrance of the mansion. Here one can see the refined moldings, exquisitely carved stone and massive iron lantern standards which have endeared this historic house to generations of Milwaukeeans.

corner of Juneau Place. And it was all of the houses on Juneau Place — as well as the street itself — which had to be removed. Only two blocks long, Juneau Place ran parallel to the high bluff above Lake Michigan. Its original name was, appropriately, Lake Avenue and it had been a prestigious location from the early days.

Field was not the first to build on that corner. When he purchased the land in 1886, he first had to tear down the old homestead of James S. Brown. Brown was a "precocious boy" from Maine who had become Wisconsin's first attorney general at age twenty-five. Later, in 1861, he was elected eleventh mayor of Milwaukee.

By the time Samuel Augustus Field acquired this lot he was sixty-eight years old. He had come here from New York State and was described as a "Yankee with a long nose, clear blue eyes and a beard that was first tinged with gray, then snowy." He made his money in real estate and lumber and was considered a wealthy man by the time he married at age fifty-seven. His bride, Miss Frank L. Bussey, was described by the press as "thoroughly accomplished and has been for a number of years the organist of Plymouth Church."

Both Mr. and Mrs. Field were cultured and well educated in history and languages. They took numerous trips to Europe and the East for pleasure and study. But the trip that was announced in June of 1887 was to be very special. Field had just purchased the Martin Street property and this was to be a two-year buying trip for the new mansion he was planning. They left on the steamer *Allen* bound for Bremen, Germany, and did not return until October of 1889.

While the common *modus operandi* was to build a house and then select furnishings, the Fields decided to reverse the process. They carefully selected pieces in the capitals of Europe and then planned the house to fit the collection. During their absence, the crates — bearing a King's ransom in furnishings — began to arrive in Milwaukee. According to one writer they contained "things which today only a Morgan can acquire — articles taken from the palaces of the Caesars, from medieval churches, a marvelous head that was a detail for a Titian masterpiece, rich velvets and tapestries and brocades, the colors of which had been quieted by hundreds of years, bronzes and carved wood and pottery."

They shipped back Florentine chairs with the upholstery bearing the coat of arms of the Medici family, Aubusson carpets, rare ivories, linens from Dresden, an ancient Roman mosaic, and fine pieces of Venetian glass. A set of spoons was attributed to Benevenuto Cellini, the master goldsmith of the Italian Renaissance. And they reportedly owned silver candlesticks from the palace of King Ludwig of Bavaria.

In 1890, shortly after the world-travelers returned, Field applied for a building permit with the stated cost of construction being $25,000. To put that figure in perspective, one must note that the builder of this mansion had just spent $100,000 on only four oil paintings for its furnishing! The man on whose shoulders fell the awesome responsibility of housing this fabulous collection was August Fiedler. A Chicago architect, Fiedler had just completed a mansion for

Left, detail of a leaded glass door leading to the solarium. This fine decorative pane was hand-painted, acid etched and silver-stained to provide the transparent amber coloration. Below left, one of the finely-detailed brass wall sconces in the parlor. Below, the built-in sideboard in the dining room. This beautiful mahogany woodwork glows through a glass-like French furniture-polish finish which was hand rubbed.

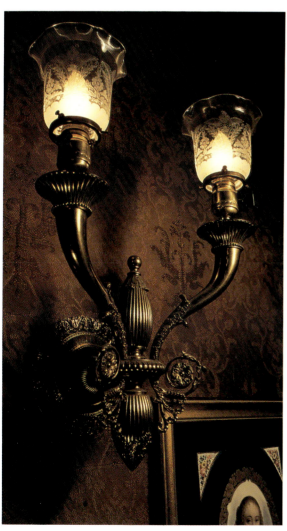

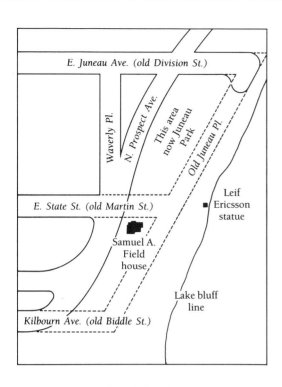

George P. Miller located only a block to the north on Juneau Avenue.

The building permit listed the style of the forthcoming house as "Norman." Its steep, hipped roof with finials and its stone walls and tall windows divided by stone mullions were, indeed, very French. The inspiration, however, might well have come from a trend that was flowering among the super-rich in New York City. Richard Morris Hunt, the first American architect to study at the famous Ecole des Beaux-Arts in Paris, was then designing French chateaux for the Vanderbilts. Those wealthy Americans who could afford it often chose to follow the lead.

Fiedler's design was not, however, a pure rendering of any specific period. There were, for instance, recognizable elements of English Tudor and of Romanesque ornament in the parapeted gables.

For all of its expense, the bulk of the Bedford limestone exterior is relatively simple in design. Where there is ornament it is understated, but of very high quality. The most elaborate treatment centers around the logical focus of the front entrance. Two stone columns, with their upper halves carved into spiral twists, support a balustraded balcony over the door. A semi-circular transom window is flanked by two carved spandrel panels. These crisply executed ornaments are delicate, heavily undercut, and rank among the finest exterior stone carvings in Milwaukee. A hanging lantern, door and sidelight grilles, and a massive pair

Opposite, the "moving print" shows the individual serial numbers which were assigned to each stone as the old house came down. This shows the north (entrance) elevation as re-built. Below, the north elevation re-drawn to remove the original third floor and recycle its stones as a four-car garage wing to the west. Above, map showing original location of Field house.

NORTH ELEVATION
SCALE — ¼" - ¶"-0"

of lantern standards are forged from wrought iron.

This impressive stone behemoth easily outclassed all of its neighbors on Juneau Place, and it handily won the public's heart when its doom seemed imminent. Its builder, however, was only able to appreciate its qualities for a short time. Field was first listed at that address in 1895 and he died at the age of ninety-one in 1909. As was customary then, his funeral was conducted from the house.

Mrs. Field died shortly thereafter and the great collection of furnishings was dispersed. By 1920 the house was owned and occupied by Louis Kuehn who was then faced with the opposite of the Fields' challenge. He had a large, empty mansion and no furnishings. For years he and Mrs. Kuehn searched far and wide for just the right pieces to match the special qualities of the house.

Just when the furnishing seemed under control, the City of Milwaukee condemned their neighborhood and the Kuehns were faced with a dilemma. In the end it seemed that the best solution might be to move the old house. Kuehn purchased a piece of property on North Lake Drive in the Lake Dells Park subdivision and obtained a building permit in May of 1928. He pleased a lot of worried house lovers with his announcement but surprised everyone with the incredible scope of the project.

To move a solid stone mansion of this size was a task of staggering proportions. It would have been next to impossible to trundle the 124,000 cubic-foot-giant

The lake (east) side of the Field house today.

three miles on wheels. So Kuehn decided to disassemble it stone-by-stone and move it north in pieces. Numerous photographs were taken and two complete sets of drawings were prepared for the move. One set, by Robert Messmer & Bro., outlined a few basic changes in the re-built house.

Kuehn decided that he needed a garage wing more than a third-floor ballroom. So when the old stones were re-laid, all of those from the top floor were assembled according to a new layout to create a four-car garage wing with servant's quarters above. The original roof design was then lowered to the second floor ceiling. This kind of major surgery would only have been possible in a total re-construction. Kuehn also added a rathskeller with an adjoining wine cellar in the new basement.

The second set of plans, by the mason contractor, showed the actual details of disassembly. These incredibly detailed drawings show every stone down to the corbels and trim moldings. A numbering system was devised which provided a separate, logical serial number for each piece. A typical stone might be designated S16N. This placed it in the 19th (S) row of stones counting up from the foundation, the 16th position in that row counting from left to right, and on the north (N) wall of the house.

With drawings in hand the masons began at the top and carefully removed all of the stones, one-by-one, affixing serial numbers as they went. The stones were trucked to a vacant lot next to the building site where they were neatly laid out in sequence.

Louis Kuehn made one more highly visible change in the appearance of the mansion. He was the president of Milwaukee Corrugating Company which manufactured, among other things, copper roofing tiles. By roofing the house with his own product he not only saved money, but he later used a photograph of the installation in company advertising to demonstrate the beauty of the tiles.

All of the ceiling beams, wood paneling, staircasing, built-in furniture, and fireplace mantels had to be removed and stored for re-installation. The original work was done by the nationally-famous Matthews Brothers Company and Kuehn was fortunate to find the craftsman who had supervised that job. Armed with his memory, he located all of the hidden dowels and pegs necessary for a trouble-free removal.

The high quality of the interior woodwork and its remarkable state of preservation belie the fact that it is nearly a century old and has been once moved and twice installed. The fine grained mahogany trim in the parlor and the dining room radiates with a rich red glow. Its hand-rubbed, mirror-like French polish literally sparkles with highlights.

Superb carved details enrich the oak, birch, and mahogany woodwork throughout the house. Light fixtures are of the highest quality and much of the hardware is gold or silver plated. Many walls are covered with fine fabrics stretched over wooden frames and one fireplace is faced with Roman opus tesselatum mosaic made from colored marbles. A number of ceilings still have original stenciled ornament which was enriched with hand-painted color tints.

Samuel Field's once-doomed mansion is still a "Treasure House." For sentimental reasons, its original address number was allowed to remain on the stone sill beneath the front door. Only the best-informed visitor would recognize that "303" as being a Martin Street address from the 1890s. And, at the original site three miles away, it would take an even greater imagination to visualize a three-story stone mansion standing next to the footpath in Juneau Park. ●

The oak wainscoted main reception hall. Notice the coffered ceiling panels. These decorative painted squares were first stenciled and then tinted with hand-applied color glazes.

The Gothic front porch is constructed entirely of buff terra cotta.

The "Yankees" and the Germans had regarded each other with suspicion for many years. So, when it was announced that William O. Goodrich was to marry Marie Pabst, Milwaukeeans were more than mildly interested. Before this 1892 wedding, newspapers carried separate columns for "Society" and "German Society." In fact, this was the first important social event in the city's history where the two groups would mingle.

The pioneers from New England and New York State had settled on Milwaukee's east side near the lake and south of Juneau Avenue. Locals had accordingly nicknamed this insular neighborhood, "Yankee Hill." German immigrants regarded the Yankees as "a class of bloodless and soulless individuals who worshiped the almighty dollar, constantly sought to practice paternalism over the newcomer, and lacked an appreciation for the higher and nobler impulses of life."

The Germans grouped themselves west of the Milwaukee River and north of Wisconsin Avenue where one of their tightly-knit neighborhoods was disrespectfully dubbed "Sauerkraut Boulevard." The Yankees viewed their clannish behavior as a threat. During the early days of heavy immigration, the growing prejudice could be seen in this local newspaper statement: "It is an injustice to draw these untutored monarchical Barbarians out of their legitimate sphere and coddle them with fine things they do not understand. Already the population is more than half foreign born. If they once gain the upper hand our liberties are lost."

But this was 1892, and the intervening years had cooled down many early prejudices. The two families involved in the forthcoming wedding were anything but unknown bourgeoisie. The bride's father, Captain Frederick Pabst, was the president of the largest brewery in the world. He had just built the city's first skyscraper (The Pabst Building on Wisconsin Avenue) and he lived in a spectacular new mansion which was second to none in the Midwest. The groom's father was a wealthy linseed-oil manufacturer from Vermont and his maternal grandfather was once president of Vassar College.

The newspapers pursued this unique match with predictable enthusiasm. Headlines called the wedding "One of the Most Brilliant Events of the Social Season." Actually, the wedding had more unique features than just the mixing of two societies. It was held on a Tuesday evening at 8:30 p.m. and the ceremony lasted only fifteen minutes. A newspaper reporter noted that it was brief, "according to the usages of the Berlin aristocracy." Another interested observer recalled the use of two rings, a custom apparently unknown here at that time.

The wedding took place at Immanuel Presbyterian Church in the center of Yankee Hill. In the middle of what must have been a very formal affair, the unexpected happened. An eyewitness said, "as the wedding ceremony was about half through, a sleek, well-fed Maltese cat, probably the property of the janitor of the church, slipped into the church from the basement stairs and walked down the aisle, as self-possessed as one of the Lohengrin swans. A young woman present said it was a good omen."

The reception offers clues that indicate the caution with which this virgin social territory was crossed. While the wedding invitation list was understandably long, there were only thirty-six invited to the reception. And Captain Pabst, whose new mansion was magnificent and potentially intimidating to his guests, took no chances with the decorations. The newspaper announced, "The reception will be a quiet affair, only immediate friends of families being present. There will be no attempt at elaborate display. The house will be decorated with flowers and everything will be as unostentatious as possible." That claim, however, did not necessarily cover the food. The story continued: "Steward Healy of the Pabst Hotel will have charge of the table and will serve a dinner of thirteen courses." All the while, Fachutar's Mandolin Orchestra was to provide music from the adjacent conservatory.

The newlyweds left immediately for an extended honeymoon trip along the Atlantic Seaboard. When they returned a month later William and Marie moved in with Captain Pabst at 2000 West Wisconsin Avenue. Two years after the wedding, a building permit was obtained for what a neighbor lady remembered as Mr. Pabst's wedding present to the Goodriches. It was to be

Opposite, an extremely rare water color produced by the architect before the house was built. The only change from this original proposal was the addition of another row of rooms across the back (left in the painting). Left and above, this chandelier carries the hand-engraved inscription, "All care abandon ye who enter here — Frederick Pabst — anno domini — 1892."

a striking Gothic mansion on Terrace Avenue, overlooking Lake Michigan from a high bluff.

Pabst's gift was designed by German-trained architect Otto Strack. In 1881 Strack came from Robel, in northern Germany, to Chicago where he opened an office and prospered. Seven years later he moved to Milwaukee and, in 1890, was appointed supervising architect for the Pabst Brewing Company. He quickly built a reputation for high quality designs in traditional European styles.

For J.B. Kalvelage he created a fine German baroque palace on Cedar Street. He took an old Water Street hotel and converted it into the spectacular Blatz Hotel and Palm Garden. And for Captain Pabst he designed the renowned Pabst Theater and the delightful beer pavilion which later was attached to his mansion on Grand Avenue.

Here Strack created a completely unique, and purely Gothic house based on 16th century French precedent. It is quite unlike the Gothic Revival which began in England in the early 19th century and swept across American before the Civil War. And it does not follow the movement, nearly a century later, which created historically accurate interpretations of English parish churches and cathedrals. This house does not fit into any convenient sub-style or movement and it may be the only design quite like it in the country.

114

Above, close-up of the north tower. The third floor level, including the dormers and top level of the tower, is faced with ornamental sheet metal. Everything else is constructed of pressed brick and buff terra cotta. Left, the built-in sideboard and a wall sconce in the dining room. All of the details in the doors, lighting fixtures, paneling and hardware are pure Gothic.

Architecture with this saturation of Gothic forms is common among churches but extremely rare when applied to a residence. The striking and completely symmetrical street facade is anchored on the corners by two three-story octagonal towers. Pressed brick walls are heavily ornamented with buff-colored terra cotta trim. The gothic-arched front porch, which is built entirely of terra cotta, is the focal point of the design. Above the second floor, hammered and fabricated sheet metal carries the ornament upward. Everywhere there are crockets, pinnacles, finials, hood molds, poppyheads and ball flowers sprouting, dripping and climbing to the sky.

Inside, the purity and profusion of Gothic continues with lavishly carved ornament and oak paneling. Most of the hardware is of gold-plated bronze in a Gothic oak leaf and tracery design. A large stairwell opens off the central entry hall and rises to a dark oak coffered ceiling. Its open space is warmed by the glow of richly-colored stained glass windows which pick up north light. The entry hall leads straight through the middle of the house to a dining room with large windows overlooking the lake.

A large built-in oak side board dominates the room with its cusped panels and glass doors decorated by geometric Gothic tracery. A hooded fireplace is lined with mirror-polished verde antique marble. The dining room's brass lanterns, wall sconces, window seats, paneling and hardware have the same well-related Gothic designs.

William Osborn Goodrich left a very personal mark on the house. The music room in the southwest corner of the first floor was created especially for him. He was an accomplished singer, so the acoustics of the room were very important. For this reason it had a ceiling nearly three feet higher than the others. This was accomplished by lowering the floor by four steps.

At an early age Goodrich discovered that he had an outstanding natural voice. After singing in local concerts and churches he was encouraged to seek refinement abroad. He pursued musical training in London, Paris, and Berlin and then journeyed to Frankfurt to study under Julius Stockhausen. A friend of Brahms, Berlioz, Saint-Saëns and Clara Schumann, Stockhausen was one of the greatest voice teachers and performers of his time. Because of his excellent training, Goodrich received a strong, personal invitation from Wagner's widow to become a principal of the Wagner Festival in Bayreuth.

Goodrich continued to participate, musically, into his 90s. In an interview he once said, "I've had stables of horses, Mediterranean yachts, stimulating business associations, years of living in Europe — but music has been my greatest pleasure." Unfortunately his beloved music room did not please one subsequent owner who felt that all floors should be at the same level. A second floor was built over the original and it remains in place today.

Goodrich spent most of his working years with the linseed-oil company that was founded by his father. After Captain Pabst's death he also served a a director of the brewery from 1904 to 1922.

When the Goodriches moved away from this, their first home, they left behind what may be the most unique "gift enclosure card" of all time. It is a six-arm brass chandelier which displays the year of their marriage and has a cast dove with its wings folded back. It hangs, as always, in the dining room. A hand-engraved inscription, which can easily be seen from below, reads: "All care abandon ye who enter here — Frederick Pabst — anno domini — 1892."●

Above left, Kalvelage's Schloss from the southeast. Set on the highest parcel of land in the neighborhood, Lake Michigan (which is fifteen miles to the east) can be seen from the upper windows. Above right, detail of the front central gable showing fine baroque ornamental work in sheet-metal and buff terra cotta. Right, section of a porch railing executed by Wisconsin's famous master of ornamental wrought iron, Cyril Colnik.

Kalvelage's Schloss would be the first of many mansions on Cedar Street. At least that's what Joseph B. Kalvelage thought in 1890, when he bought the best lot at the top of the hill. He had seen the excitement building on nearby Highland Boulevard where lots were selling briskly and fine homes were beginning to rise. So many wealthy Germans were settling there, between 27th and 35th streets, that Milwaukeeans nicknamed the strip, "Sauerkraut Boulevard."

Kalvelage judged that, if he built a mansion here at 2424 Cedar Street, (now 2432 West Kilbourn Avenue) he could trigger a similar development in this neighborhood. He selected a German architect and built a spectacular German baroque palace on a spot so high that he could see Lake Michigan from its upper windows. He commissioned the best wrought iron craftsman in Wisconsin history to embellish the exterior. It seemed as though he had done everything right.

But, as the old real estate adage goes . . . property value depends on three factors: "location, location, location." For some reason no one agreed that this was a great place to live. Or maybe it was the intimidating presence of that castle looming over the neighborhood from its high perch. Whatever the cause, Kalevlage's proud creation stood alone then, as it does today, a "castle among cottages."

Kalvelage's real estate speculation notwithstanding, his building project turned out to be an unforgettable, one-of-a-kind masterpiece. Its striking design was the work of German-born architect Otto Strack. After practicing for a short time in Chicago, Strack had come to Milwaukee where he executed a number of projects for Captain Frederick Pabst.

In October of 1896, building permit #603 was granted and the greatest project to ever grace Cedar Street was underway. The Kalvelages lived in a humble frame house located elsewhere on the property and could watch the construction as it progressed. It took two years and $40,000 (sizeable in those days) to complete the mansion.

Milwaukee had never seen the German baroque style applied on such a scale. It had a quality and density of exterior ornament which was never to be repeated here again. In the eyes of its admirers, this was truly a *castle* and it was that word in German (schloss) which came to be associated with this house ever after.

Otto Strack's design began, simply enough, as a symmetrical rectangular block with a projecting central pavilion and a convex mansard roof. The basic material, a tan pressed brick, was laid in banded rustication on the first story. The roof was covered with slate and a considerable quantity of ornamental sheet metal work was used for parapet walls, cornice moldings and trim. Stained glass windows appear at intervals throughout the composition.

But it was two of the trim materials — terra cotta and wrought iron — which gave the Schloss qualities far superior to its contemporaries. Buff-colored terra cotta was used generously to create sculptural details such as winged and crowned heads. Supported by baroque cartouches and leaf swags, these handsome heads serve as keystones in the arches and window lintels of the façade.

117

Joseph B. Kalvelage.

The focal point of the entire design, and the most imposing feature of the exterior, is the front porch. Almost entirely sheathed in terra cotta, this spectacular array of moldings and ornaments is dominated by eight life-sized half-figures called Atlantes.

The use of human figures as architectural support can be traced back to the ancient Egyptians. Words to describe them, however, came later from Greek mythology. "Alante" was derived from Atlas who supposedly held up the "vault of heaven at the ends of the earth." The female counterpart is called a Caryatid. Otto Strack grouped his eight Atlantes in four identical pairs, each consisting of two, bearded, half-figures rising out of beautifully ornamented pilasters. The left Atlante supports with his right arm while the right one uses his left.

The other crowning glory of the Schloss is its ornamental iron work. Cyril Colnik, who earned a national reputation for his fine wrought iron, was commissioned to execute balconies, railings, window grilles and a large lantern standard for Kalvelage. His superb baroque porch railings are encrusted with grotesque heads, fishtail scrolls, acanthus leaves, flowers and vine tendrils. The finest single piece is a curved balcony railing above the front porch which serves the third floor ballroom.

Colnik himself must have been very proud of this balcony. A rare glass plate negative, which he ordered taken, survives to show us how the master-work looked when it was new. Sitting on saw horses behind his forge, the just-completed balcony shines with a fresh coat of black paint. Two eagle wings sprout from

The Kalvelage mansion shortly after completion. The ornate wrought iron lamp standard, shown beside the stairs, and the original third floor ballroom window are now gone.

118

behind a life-sized cherub's head. A hammered scallop shell and numerous roses ornament the baroque grillework and the corners are guarded by a pair of fierce-looking eagles with spread wings. This is clearly the largest and finest display of Colnik's work which can still be found in its original installation.

The formal layout of the interior was planned around a central hall which bisects the house by connecting the front doors with the staircase landing at the rear. Typically German in feeling, the hall is dark and masculine with heavy carved oak woodwork on all sides. Originally a wrought iron chandelier, with antler-arms, hung from the beamed ceiling in front of the largest fireplace in the house.

To the left, upon entering, was the most elegant room in the house. Although finished in oak and baroque in design, this room was much lighter in color than the rest of the mansion. Its carved detailing, ornamental plaster ceiling and delicate chandelier were closer to French in character. The family used this parlor only one or two weeks out of the year, mostly at Christmas time.

Across the hall was the library, another dark-paneled oak room with built-in bookcases and red damask wall covering. Connecting to the north of the library was a room with a grand piano which was devoted entirely to music. Its ceiling and walls, with relief panels depicting musical themes, were appropriately hard to reflect sound. Kalvelage was an accomplished flute player and this was one of his favorite rooms.

The dining room also has dark, heavy, oak

Left, the main entrance hall looking from the front door to the back of the house. This early photograph shows all of the original furnishings and details. Above left, the "French" parlor in the southwest corner of the first floor when the mansion was new. This, the most delicate room in the house, was saved by Mrs. Kalvelage for use only on special occasions. It was completely gutted by fire in 1962 when the Schloss was a rooming house. Above right, looking north in the dining room when the Schloss was newly furnished. This, and the other early views, come from albums of professional photographers commissioned by Mr. Kalvelage when the mansion was completed.

woodwork with a beam-coffered ceiling, high plate rails, built-in sideboard and a raised breakfast nook set off from the main space by a colonnade.

There were five bedrooms on the second floor, and a ballroom with servant's quarters on the third. The groin vaulted ballroom, with its central skylight, was Mrs. Kalvelage's favorite entertaining room.

The problems of running a house this size were compounded by the "high cost" of servants (head maid-$3 per week, cook-$5 per week), and by the damaging antics of the children. A case in point was the party Mrs. Kalvelage gave for her youngest son, Clements, when he returned from duty in World War I. It was May, 1919, and he had survived two years "under bomb fire" and with the Army of Occupation in Germany. Everyone was happy and the champagne flowed freely. Clem and his buddies, dressed in their Army uniforms, marched around the music room, their combat boots badly scarring the floor's glass-like finish.

J.B. Kalvelage loved the house and he raised all four of his children here. His wife, Dorothea, was the daughter of John C. Hoffmann, founder of Hoffmann Billings Manufacturing Company. They married in 1877 and, within a year, Kalevelage was working for his father-in-law. In a short time he became secretary-treasurer of the company. Hoffmann & Billings manufactured plumbing supplies and sanitary fixtures.

While Kalvelage spent most of his active years with the family company, his business acumen led him into a number of lucrative side ventures. He was president of the Milwaukee and Hillsborough Mining Company which had its offices here, but owned land in the Las Animas Mining District of Sierra County, New Mexico. This company leased rights to explore and mine the "Copper King," the "Aurora," and other claims in that area.

Left, the northwest corner of Kalvelage's library showing how the fireplace mantel and ceiling coffers were designed to cut across the corner at a forty-five degree angle. Right, massive carved oak fireplace mantel on the east wall of the grand entrance hall.

120

From the beginning, Kalvelage's "castle among cottages" was doomed to decline. The family spent just a little over two decades in the mansion before moving to North Prospect Avenue in 1920. Four years later they sold the once-proud giant to Percy C. Day, a mechanical engineer, whose side interests were to bring the fine reputation of the old house to an abrut end. Under his ownership the property became Wisconsin Headquarters of the Ku Klux Klan.

In 1926 it was purchased by the Roger Williams Home and Hospital Association. The house was converted into a hospital and home for the aged. The kitchen became an x-ray lab, and a second floor bedroom was turned into an operating room. The hospital lasted ten years, after which the property changed hands rapidly a few times and then settled down to become a rooming house.

The rooming house years dealt the worst blow to the once stately Schloss. In 1962 a deranged tenant set fire to his room, threw all of his furniture into the blaze, locked his door, and walked out. He single-handedly destroyed the delicate "French" parlor which, for years, had been saved for just special occasions by the family. Today only the doors remain of what once was the finest room in the house.

The "Schloss" is a Milwaukee Landmark listed on the National Register of Historic Places, and recorded by the Historic American Buildings Survey. The neighborhood has continued to decline, but the dedicated present owner keeps struggling with what seems like a never-ending restoration project.

It is well worth a trip into this seemingly uninteresting area to experience the shocking contrast of a magnificent hilltop "castle" surrounded by humble dwellings. ●

The impressive staircase rises from the center of the entrance hall to a landing where it splits into two side runs. Notice the unusual baroque brackets supporting the newel posts and the overall complexity of the woodwork throughout the hall.

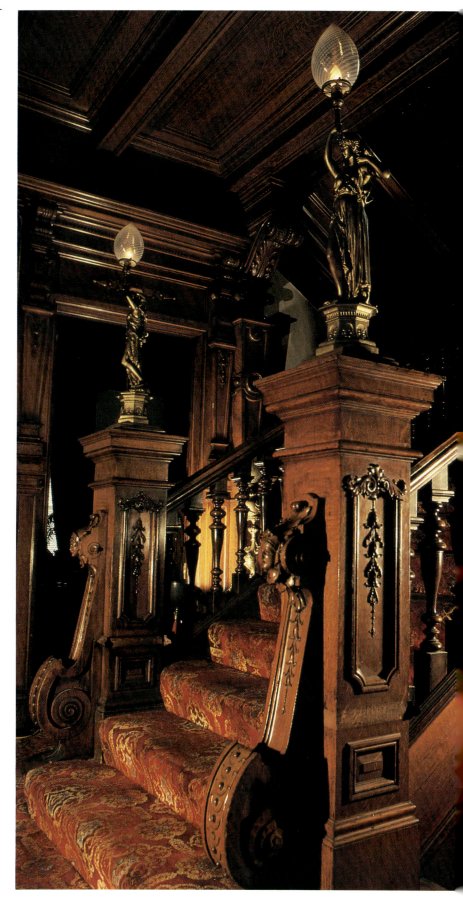

The earliest known photograph of the double house from the northeast. Note the two-story oriel window over the entrance arch to the Hawley side (left in the photo). This handsome addition to the chateau's profile was removed in 1960. The fine clay tile roof of the Bloodgood house is also gone.

William K. Vanderbilt's Fifth Avenue Chateau started the fad. It was 1881 and New York society had just been introduced to the splendors of the French Renaissance. In his bold break with the brownstone tradition, Vanderbilt had established this style as the acceptable dwelling for the wealthy. French Chateaux began to appear all over the country and for at least two decades thereafter they were considered by many to be the ne plus ultra.

The Francis Bloodgood Jr. house on the southwest corner of North Franklin and East Knapp streets, is one of only a few examples of this style remaining in Milwaukee. Built in 1896, it is actually two houses joined by a party wall. The northern half was built by Bloodgood, a member of an old family law firm founded by his father, and it fronts on Knapp Street. Mary B. Hawley (after whose family Hawley Road was named) erected the south half which has a Franklin Place address.

Both dwellings were designed by one of Milwaukee's first formally educated architects, Howland D. Russel. A number of the city's earlier architects had begun their careers as builders or carpenters and did not turn to designing structures until later in life. Russel, on the other hand, was a graduate of Cornell University and he eventually became the favorite architect of Yankee Hill.

However, Russel's rise to prominence was neither easy nor immediate. In fact, when he opened his office in 1880, James Douglas, one of the prominent early members of the profession, was "very much amused" and he called the young newcomer a "down east school architect" and predicted that he would not earn his office rent. Douglas proved to be correct as we can see in an 1883 Evening Wisconsin story headlined "Architects have all the work they can do." According to the interviews it was reported that all of the city's architects were busy but, "Howland Russel said he was doing but little and preferred not to have anything published."

The bad times soon ended and Russel found himself an interpreter of European styles for the east side's upper middle class families. His commissions were mainly residential, but on occasion he branched out and executed plans such as the Lake Park Pavilion which was erected jointly by the Electric Railroad Co. and the park commissioners. In association with A.C. Eschweiler Sr., he made drawings for the old University Club on Jefferson Street. Among his residential clients were B.B. Hopkins, F.W. Finney, and the brothers Van Dyke (John & William at 1454-1462 North Prospect Avenue, both houses now gone).

When Bloodgood bought his corner lot in 1896, he was following a family pattern. His father's home was on Marshall and Knapp, his brother Wheeler lived in a Mansard-roofed Victorian double house on the corner of Astor and Knapp, and his grandmother Colt's old dwelling was at Prospect and Knapp. Francis Jr. was just joining the lineup of Bloodgood mansions along the then fashionable Knapp Street. His lot had been vacant since its purchase by Henry Mann in 1867, the year Knapp Street was cut through from Astor to Franklin. The Manns used it as a side yard for their historic Greek mansion still standing to the south.

123

The "chateau" is personalized in this blind window panel in terra cotta. On a shield, surrounded by four fleurs-de-lis, are the entwined initials H. (Hawley) and B. (Bloodgood).

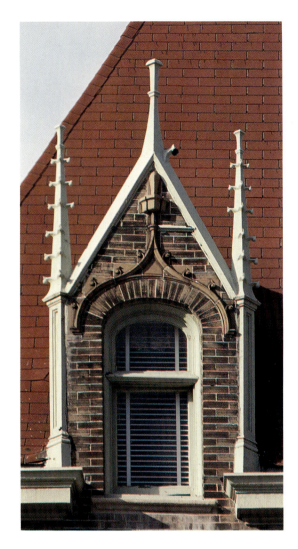

Above, one of the seven dormers which create the French chateau look of the mansion's skyline. The ogee-arched hood molding over the window is made of sculptured buff terra cotta. Right, the Hawley-Bloodgood double house as seen from the Franklin Place (east) side. Mary B. Hawley lived in the left half and Francis Bloodgood Jr. lived in the north.

Above right, the Bloodgood parlor as originally furnished. The window at the left is the east front bay window overlooking Franklin Place. Unlike much of the interior, which is made of oak, the woodwork in this room is mahogany rubbed to a glass-like finish. Right, looking west from the Bloodgood parlor (living room) through the entry hall to the dining room. This shows the original furnishings around 1900.

The Bloodgood dining room around the turn of the century.

Francis Bloodgood married Helen Hawley who had been raised by her widowed aunt on the family farm at 24th and Wisconsin Avenue. The square block between 24th and 25th streets, later occupied by Emergency Hospital, was the location of the old homestead and present Hawley Road was one of the boundaries of the farm. Cyrus Hawley, after whom the road was named, was one of Milwaukee's earliest settlers and the first clerk of courts here.

Helen's Aunt Mary bought an identical lot adjacent to the south of the Bloodgoods on the same day in 1896. And, like her new neighbors, she was remaining in the same vicinity, moving from a location only half a block to the north on the opposite side of Franklin Place.

Helen Bloodgood was well traveled, preferred French taste in architecture, and was responsible for selecting the style for her house. According to the building permit they spent $9,500 on its construction, a fact which makes it unfair to compare this modest specimen with the monumental chateaux that Richard Morris Hunt was creating for New York's "fabulous 400." It was, however, obviously inspired by the same historic models. Most of the interior and exterior design elements were drawn from the early sixteenth century transitional period between the French Gothic and the Renaissance with the emphasis on Gothic.

The Bloodgood half, like its New York cousins, is built almost to the lot line and, being on a corner, has two "fronts." The long north side is the entrance front and is divided into three bays with the two end bays, or pavilions, projecting slightly. These have steeply inclined, wedge-shaped roofs characteristic of the period. Seven dormers project from the roof and give the house its picturesque skyline. Each is decorated with three pinnacles (the small pointed spires). Each pinnacle is encrusted with small stylized leaf forms called crockets which seem to climb each side. Including those on the window lintels and gable cornices, there are 450 crockets at the roofline, a feature which is purely Gothic and which establishes the basic character of the house.

The central bay of the north facade forms an entrance with two elliptical arches made from pressed brick moldings. A limestone column with a carved octagonal Gothic capital supports the center of the opening. Sculptured ornament in terra cotta is used to complement the yellow/gray pressed brick and limestone masonry. One such piece dates the building on a ribbon in Roman numerals (MDCCCXCVI), and another signs it with a monogram on a shield with four fleurs-de-lis. The monogram has the entwined letters, B & H for Bloodgood and Hawley.

Like the New York townhouses this has a higher or "stilted" English basement only a few steps below ground. This makes for a brighter kitchen but necessitates a substantial climb to enter the first floor. The upper house was distinguished by a skylighted open well over the staircase and beautiful paneling on the first floor. The east living room was paneled in mahogany with a rubbed glass-like finish. The rest of the interior was largely oak.

The Hawley side was occupied by its builder for less than five years. Mary B. and her children traveled extensively and spent much time abroad. The house was then rented to such names as the Esek Cowens, Dr. and Mrs. H.V. Wurdemann, the George F. O'Neils, and the Orton L. Primes. William G. Herbst bought it in 1929 and remodeled the building to serve as offices for his architectural firm. Both townhouses are currently used for office rental space.

Two recent changes have altered the otherwise original appearance of the houses. In 1960 an oriel, or bay window on the Hawley side was removed. That picturesque half-octagon structure, with its chisel roof, was covered with sheet metal but its wood framing had become dangerously rotten. About the same time the handsome red clay tile roof on the Bloodgood side had to be replaced.

Of the four Bloodgoods who lived on Knapp Street, Francis Jr. was the last to arrive and his house, the lone survivor, marks the northeast corner of the most important block of landmarks on Milwaukee's historic east side. ●

Milwaukee, Wis.
Newberry Boulevard. — Newberry-Ringstrasse.

Above, Goldberg/Martin mansion from the north-east. The original coach house/stable, with its rare hand-operated carriage elevator, is on the left. Right, the Goldberg mansion was the first to be built on Newberry Boulevard. In this early bilingual postcard, printed in Germany, other houses have begun to appear across the street, but Goldberg's spire is still the only improvement on the south side of the boulevard (shown left in this view looking west from Lake Drive).

When Benjamin Goldberg began construction on his Gothic mansion in 1896, his future looked rosy. He was a prosperous lawyer and his was to be the first house on the prestigious and newly developed Newberry Boulevard. Many then regarded his as the "Finest residence that has been erected in Milwaukee since the (financial) panic of 1893."

What he could not have predicted was that, before his residence was completed, he would be disbarred from practicing law in Wisconsin, he would be forced to sell his unfinished mansion at a $20,000 loss and would end up running a mercantile establishment in Clintonville, Wisconsin.

Looking into Goldberg's background we can find two diametrically-opposed images. On the positive side there are favorable and glowing tributes such as this one, published during his lifetime, in a Wisconsin biographical history: "As a citizen of whom any state might be proud, as a man whose presence would benefit any community, and whose name would reflect honor upon any office or station, there is none more worthy whose memory should be preserved in this volume than Benjamin M. Goldberg."

This article, which placed him "in the front rank" among lawyers, called his practice "honorable" and described him as "a man of unblemished integrity and of modest mien." One wonders how such a paragon of virtue could have fallen upon those bad times. The question is answered by ten years of newspaper clippings which trace Goldberg's career and paint a picture which is more compatible with his change in fortune.

The first Goldberg notice, in the local press, describes his arrest for malicious trespassing. This was followed by such activities as "belligerent demonstrations" in court, a threatened personal libel suit against a major newspaper, and a private campaign to have a court justice's magisterial commission revoked. Then, in 1882, he made the front page when the Bar Association preferred charges against him for unprofessional ethics. At that time Mr. Goldberg was making plans to "move to Dakota" until "the whole matter would eventually die out."

Three years later he showed up in Clintonville as a incorporator of an iron mining and silver prospecting company and was elected city attorney there. But within a year he was back in the news for another dispute with a newspaper. In a rowdy street fight he blackened the eyes of two editors, drew a revolver, and was stopped just short of a shooting spree by passersby.

Goldberg's last straw seems to have been his involvement, as Waupaca County prosecuting attorney, in the sensational H.C. Mead murder trial. From a bad situation in Milwaukee, he had stepped into a controversial inferno in Waupaca. Mead, a highly respected local banker, had been brutally murdered and robbed ten years earlier. After numerous false arrests, forced confessions, and what now looks to have been a massive coverup, the murderer had still not been found. Goldberg does not seem to have done much better and apparently came away from the case with a fatally injured legal reputation.

His fortunes reversed, Goldberg was forced to stop construction on the Milwaukee mansion and put it up for sale. The builders had begun in the summer of 1896 and when they were called off the job he had already spent an estimated $50,000 on architecture. By then most of Milwaukee was aware of the spectacular Gothic landmark. In a newly improved subdivision, surrounded by saplings and empty lots, it must have been an unforgettable sight.

Goldberg's residence was not only the first to front on the subdivision's main street, but it was among the earliest to appear anywhere in the ninety acre neighborhood. Only three years earlier, in 1893, E.P. Hackett and S.H. Hoff purchased the old farm which was to become Prospect Hill. The tract was laid out with Kenwood Boulevard as the northern boundary, Park Place on the south, Downer Avenue on the west and North Lake Drive on the east. In the first year $50,000 was invested in improvements. The streets, paved in asphalt with concrete curbs, were the first of their kind in a residential area here.

After nearly two years on the market, Goldberg's lonely showplace was finally adopted. The new buyer was George Martin Jr., a prominent Milwaukee tanner. It was estimated, at the time of the sale, that an additional $6,000 to $7,000 would be required to finish

129

the mansion's interior. In July of 1898, Martin put a crew of craftsmen to work on his new purchase. By then the exterior looked much the same as it does today.

Architects John A. Moller and George C. Ehlers used the French Gothic style as their inspiration for decoration and detailing. The Bedford limestone foundation and pressed brick masonry were laid by contractor John P. Jones. Although all of the interior finish is believed to have been completed according to the original plans, there was one detail that had to be changed. Over most of the first floor doorways there was a carved wooden cartouche bearing the initials B.M.B. (Benjamin M. Goldberg). In the entrance vestibule Martin had the "B" and "G" filled and refinished. Fortunately the original "M" was not only appropriate for the new owner's name, but it was conveniently centered in the carving.

The mansion came complete with a picturesque coach house/stable which was connected to the rear of the house by an ornamental wall. This created a private carriage court accessible only through the porte cochere which spanned the western driveway. Hidden inside this unspoiled coach house is a spectacular rarity: a hand-operated carriage lift. Still in working condition, this iron-geared, wooden elevator can hoist a vehicle from the ground floor to the loft by just pulling a rope.

Martin had been able to walk to his office from the previous residence but here was forced to stable horses and commute by carriage. One of his grandsons remembered, "Grandfather liked good horses and he kept two, using them on alternate days to go to the tannery and back. Foxy, a chestnut, was a high-spirited trotter and Roy, a black and less nervous, was a pacer. On Sunday afternoons grandfather and grandmother often drove Foxy while my father and mother drove Roy. If and when they met on Grand Avenue or Kilbourn (Avenue) there would be a race. Both father and grandfather were tenacious competitors and the races would be close. The ladies were often frightened and finally succeeded in calling the races off by persuading their husbands to take different routes."

A typical day would see George Martin up at 5:00 a.m. and in his office by 6:30. At noon he drove home for dinner and would take a short nap before returning to the job. He worked a ten-hour day, six days a week.

Hard work was not new to Martin. He had come to Milwaukee with his parents from Germany in 1852. At fourteen he went to Burlington, Wisconsin, to live with an uncle and learn carpentry. Six months later his uncle died and he was back in Milwaukee working for a tannery. By nineteen he was earning $50 a week which he turned over to his mother; she would give him fifty cents for spending money.

In 1865 Martin made a big decision: He told his mother that he was going to keep all of the wages and go into business for himself. Since he was not yet twenty-one he had to include his father in the new venture so it was accordingly named George Martin & Son. By 1893 the business had been re-named George Martin Leather Company and it was turning out over 200,000 tanned skins per year. Started in a humble frame structure, the operation was then filling a five-story brick building at 538 Commerce Street.

Earliest known photograph of the Goldberg residence when it stood alone in its neighborhood. Note the saplings and open spaces around the mansion.

The main staircase looking up from the first floor.
The stairwell with its paneling, staircase, columns,
stained glass window and lavish wood carving, is
the highlight of the Goldberg interior.

Opposite page above, the ogee-arched tracery panel in front of the main hall fireplace. The fine quality of the carving and millwork, and its excellent condition, can be seen here. Below left, a typical first floor doorway with a fifteen panel sliding door. Note the flanking octagonal columns with their richly carved Gothic capitals. Above the door is one of the ill-fated builder's cartouches carved with his initials, "B M G" (Benjamin M. Goldberg). Below right, close-up of the Gothic balustrade on the main staircase. This page, the beautiful wood of the staircase is further enhanced by a very large Gothic window with stained glass in warm colors.

Left, Gothic fireplace in first floor hall. Below, friends and family gathered to celebrate the Martin's 50th wedding anniversary.

134

Martin gained a venerable reputation among tanners. He served on the Board of Trustees of Union Cemetery and was president of the Grace Lutheran Church Congregation for twenty-five years. Not a complex or flamboyant man, Martin was described by one biographer as "a quiet, respectable, honorable, dignified and useful character." After his death in 1920, Martin's four sons continued the business until the depression when it was finally dissolved. The tannery was eventually razed to make way for a new building in the Schlitz Brewery complex.

Eight children were raised in what the Martins called their "Boulevard House." The youngest daughter, Ida Marie Martin, lived there until it was sold in 1938.

The house, in which only German had been spoken before the First World War, was in for a change of language. The new owner was David Wald, who had come to Milwaukee from Hungary in 1912. He first worked for his uncle, Julius Lando, a pioneer in the optical business here. After his apprenticeship, young Wald attended a school of optometry and then opened an optometric department in a Schuster's store here. He eventually ran a chain of six optician's stores. In 1929 he married a Hungarian girl and brought her to Milwaukee.

One day a relative spotted the mansion for sale and called it to their attention. The Walds fell in love with it and bought it immediately. Over the years, his pride never flagging, Wald continued to refer to the house as "my castle." His wife, Lenke, bought lemon oil polish by the case and, six times a year, oiled the woodwork with long-handled lambs wool applicators.

Although age is finally beginning to take its toll, the mansion's interior is remarkably well preserved when compared to those which have gone the way of apartment subdivision or rooming houses. Wald once obtained a building permit to convert the house into a four-family apartment but that plan, fortunately, never materialized. The present owner purchased the house in 1980, making his only the third family to ever have lived there.

The interior is a riot of Gothic ornament. Everywhere there are crockets, oak leaves, pierced tracery, ogee arches, pinnacles, ribbons, fleurs-de-lis, and poppyhead finials. These are presented in a rich complement of materials including brass, carved cabinet woods, stained glass, majolica tile, and ornamental plaster. The highlight of the house is a fine rectangular staircase which rises in three flights and is bathed in the rich glow of a giant stained glass window.

Facing the staircase is a spectacular carved fireplace where the actual overmantel paneling, with its beveled mirrors, is only a background for the design. In front of this is a dramatic wooden ogee arch which spans the area between a pair of octagonal columns. Filling the negative spandrel areas above this arch are fine examples of pierced geometric tracery. Hanging nearby is an appropriately-Gothic gas and electric chandelier with twisted milk glass shades.

But the great chandelier is elsewhere . . . in the back parlor. This Gothic extravaganza is among the finest pieces of chandelier work in the city. Its ten arms are decorated with exquisite lost wax castings of leaf scrollwork and they are plated with gold. When one contemplates the beauty of the surviving chandeliers, it is particularly painful to remember a story once told by Mrs. Wald. She said that when the World War I brass scrap drive was underway a number of original chandeliers were "tossed on the wagon" to be melted down for shell casings.

The paneled library, with its built-in bookcases and French Gothic fireplace, has a bay in the base of the great corner tower. An attractive glass plant conservatory opens off the dining room. On the third floor is a large ballroom with an unusually high ceiling and impressive views. Many family parties took place in this room including the large and memorable celebration of Mr. and Mrs. Martin's golden wedding anniversary.

A grandson later recalled a bit of childhood mischief in the same room. "Those were the days of gas light. There was a ping pong table in the ballroom and we grandchildren quickly discovered that ping pong balls make a fine noise when they fly into a gas jet . . . chronic shortage of balls!"

Although his house holds memories for many generations of two families one cannot help but look up at all of the B.M.G.s carved into the woodwork and remember the tragic story of the man whose original dream was responsible for this opulent mansion. ●

Above, Fred Pabst Jr. house from the south. Right, Fred Pabst Jr. in his office.

The residence of Fred Pabst Jr. came very close to being sacrificed by a developer. One of the first six mansions to be built on Highland Boulevard, it has become the most important survivor of the 1960s apartment building boom.

The high population density and the activity of modern apartment living are a far cry from the lazy days when Mr. and Mrs. Pabst moved into what was then practically country. In 1870 Highland Avenue (then Prairie Street) extended west only as far as 12th Street and another six years passed before it was cut through to 27th. Shortly after 1890 the area was developed into a residential neighborhood and the road was extended west to 35th Street, this time as a wide boulevard named Highland. It was not until later that Prairie Street adopted the same name.

Before this residential development, the eight-block-long tract was divided into ten giant lots running north and south between 27th and 35th streets. These huge unimproved parcels were bounded on the south by the Watertown Plank Road (about where State Street runs today) and on the north by Chestnut Street (now Juneau Avenue).

This open field, which was to become the Highland Boulevard development, abutted the south line of Cold Spring Race Track. For decades Cold Spring Park had been the scene of cock fights and harness racing. It featured a one mile track, pavilions, and a popular hotel. In addition to its original use the property had served as the state fair grounds, a Civil War camp for the Wisconsin 2nd Cavalry, and a location for traveling shows such as Buffalo Bill's "The Wild West."

The Highland Boulevard homesites were subdivided in 1882 and the neighborhood was laid out in six blocks, three on each side of the road. The two central blocks (2 and 5) were the largest and they stretched from 29th to 33rd street. The first four mansions were built in block 2 on the north side of the boulevard and must have presented a rare sight, standing as they were in an open field on a dirt road. From the corner of 29th Street going west they were the homes of William Kieckhefer, Adolph Zinn, Charles Manegold, and Robert Krull. Next to follow were the homes of two Pabst brothers, Gustav G. and Fred Jr.

The three lots for Fred Jr.'s house were purchased in 1896 by his father, Captain Pabst. It is said that the Captain also built the house for his son. Both the property cost ($13,125, a considerable sum then) and the deed restrictions (including a condition that the front line of the house be set back 105 feet from the center of the boulevard) indicated that a neighborhood of high quality was in the making.

In the decade that followed, blocks 2 and 5 saw the coming of such distinguished names as Mrs. Fred Miller, John Pritzlaff, Fred Usinger, and A. O. Smith. It was not long before Highland became known as "Sauerkraut Boulevard" in reference to the majority of Germans living there. At least one lady remembers receiving a letter from Germany addressed to a resident of the street with that nickname.

Most of the Germans' mansions were typically heavy-handed, rough-hewn stone fortresses. Those that were not Romanesque or Gothic "castles" were bold interpretations of gentler styles. In this respect the Fred Pabst Jr. house stood apart from its neighbors with more than average grace. Its classical Grecian portico, with four fluted columns, was a pleasant contrast to the staunch medieval and Renaissance giants which flanked it.

When Fred's home was built, the Pabst Brewing Company was the largest in America. Fred, however, was more interested in stock breeding and farming than he was in the family's brewing business. His passion for this surpassed his father's well-known interest in the subject and he eventually left the brewery to pursue this avocation. He had lived in his Highland Boulevard mansion for only eight years when he resigned his post as vice president and moved to Oconomowoc, where he established a farm.

There he developed an exceptional herd of Holstein cattle which attracted breeders from as far away as South America. The Pabst Farm eventually totaled 1,400 acres and included a flourishing dairy and cheese business. Fred Pabst was at one time considered to be one of the top three men in the Holstein cattle industry.

In addition to the Holsteins, Pabst loved horses and kept as many as nine different breeds in his

137

stables. He became nationally known as a horseman and won many awards. At one time he kept a pack of foxhounds and hosted hunts on the farm.

But Fred Pabst Jr. was born to beer. After his formal schooling he was sent to other breweries to learn the business from the bottom up. He scrubbed tanks and kettles, loaded wagons and freight cars and filled kegs. When the family called, he responded.

He returned to the brewery in 1921, assumed the presidency, and the responsibility of leading the company through prohibition. In the meantime he had sold his practically new mansion to Thomas J. Neacy, president of Milwaukee Valve Company. Neacy, who lived in the house a few years before buying it in 1919, was locally known as "injunction Tom." The nickname grew out of numerous taxpayers' suits which he filed in an effort to clean up city and county government.

After Neacy's death in 1926, and while still owned by his family, the building was used as a church, the First Unity Center of Practical Christianity. It was later converted into an eleven unit rooming house.

In 1944 the $100,000 mansion was purchased by the Engineers Society of Milwaukee for $18,000. Later called "Engineers and Scientists of Milwaukee Inc.," they invested an additional $100,000 in additions and alterations. Among their projects was the building of a library on top of the old porte cochere at the west end of the mansion. This new room was executed with materials which matched the original structure and was designed in such good taste as to appear as though Pabst had built it.

At first the nearby residents viewed the society's purchase with skepticism, but they quickly realized that engineers would be much better neighbors than another fraternity or rooming house. This then became the first business-professional organization in Milwaukee with quarters of its own.

The mansion's design style was one made popular by the 1893 World's Columbian Exposition in Chicago. Now often called the Classical Revival, it was a rediscovery of the chaste and sophisticated beauties of ancient Greek architecture. The south (front) façade of the Pabst home is dominated by a handsome portico supported by four fluted Ionic columns. Each column

138

Far left, one of the beautifully proportioned first floor windows. The entire casing, including the crisply-carved acanthus brackets and egg and dart molding, is cut from limestone. Note the precision brick masonry incorporating Milwaukee's famous cream city brick laid with very thin mortar joints. Left, one of a pair of finely hand-wrought iron lanterns flanking the main entrance.

is made from a single slab of limestone and has the proper entasis (a slight swelling, or curve, in the middle).

The clean crisp lines, good proportion and artistically executed details give the house a strong and majestic appearance. Among the top quality raw materials used were pressed yellow brick, carved limestone trim, slate roofing, copper flashing, and ornamental wrought iron.

As a result of the engineers' practical demands almost nothing remains of the original interior on the upper floor. Surprisingly the first floor has remained almost unchanged and it still retains a pleasant feeling of opulence. The entrance vestibule and main hall continue the classical feeling of the exterior with white-painted woodwork and a mahogany staircase repeating the Grecian pilasters, entablatures, and moldings. In dramatic contrast, the old library and the dining room are paneled in oak and finished with wrought iron and carved wood detail in a strictly Gothic vein. The parlor or living room, has still a different character, in this case leaning to the Renaissance. It is finished with highly polished mahogany, a parquet floor, and a beautifully preserved plaster cornice which is painted and gilded. However, in quality of design and craftsmanship, the interior is considerably less important than the exterior.

The refined proportions and quality building materials for the exterior and its overall good state of preservation make the Fred Pabst Jr. house an important landmark. It is not only a splendid example of its style, but the best survivor of the few remaining grand scale mansions built by the pioneers of Highland Boulevard.

In spite of this importance, it has been threatened frequently in recent years. In 1970, when apartment developers were still replacing everything they could buy on the boulevard with low-rise apartments, the Pabst house was put on the market.

An architect stepped in and saved it to serve as his firm's offices. But this was short lived. It has since been sold twice and now seems to be safely established as a commercial property. ●

Left, looking from the Renaissance parlor into the front entry hall, note the finely finished mahogany door casing, the parquet floor and the painted and gilded ornamental plaster cornice. The hall doorway is executed in a different style. Below, the large stable and coach house also provided servants' quarters. On the right is the coach house of Fred's brother, Gustav G. Pabst.

Koenig's remodeled house from the east. This elevation now faces North 32nd Street, but before it was "modernized" it faced the old Lisbon Plank Road to the north. Left, Frederick Koenig.

*F*rederick Koenig's spectacular "farm house" is the enigma of 32nd Street. No one seems to know how old it is, who built it, or why it was moved (its front once paralleled Lisbon Avenue, but it now faces North 32nd Street with the address 1731). To further complicate the mystery, no one seems to know anything about Koenig, what he did for a living, or why he would have had such a large house, so far out of town, on such a tiny plot of land. Even his only living descendant does not have the answers to these questions and there are still fewer facts to be found in Milwaukee's historical records.

Koenig would be an easy man to forget if it were not for the house, which he enlarged and remodeled in 1897, and which now stands out like a castle among cottages in its neighborhood. However, the unanswered questions go back further than Koenig's ownership or the time when the present appearance of the house was created.

To begin with the proper historical perspective, one must go back to before the Civil War and study this area on the H. F. Walling map of Milwaukee County. This remarkable document, drawn in 1858, is perhaps the earliest map where names and buildings are shown so far from the city's center. We see that the north-south center line of section 24 was the city limits and it had not yet become a street. In later years Western Avenue was cut through along this line and eventually became known as North 35th Street.

The principal thoroughfare, cutting diagonally through the neighborhood, was the Lisbon Plank Road. It was established only eight years earlier and ran from Milwaukee, through Wauwatosa and Brookfield, to Lisbon. In 1884 it was renamed Lisbon Avenue and in another decade was purchased by the city. Walling's map shows that "Villa Uhrig" was already in existence. This nine acre "country estate" was created for a summer retreat by Franz Joseph Uhrig, a St. Louis brewer. The tract was bounded on three sides by the north-south section line on the west, the Lisbon Plank Road on the north, and the east-west section line on the south (parallel to and 173 feet north of the present present Walnut Street). Four buildings are shown on the Uhrig property and there is one on the parcel

immediately to the east. It is the latter building, without owner's name, which is of interest in the Koenig house mystery.

The unidentified structure lies directly in line with Mallory Street, one of the streets in Mallory and Kern's subdivision which dead-ended on the northern line of the Lisbon Road. Municiple Judge James A. Mallory and Assemblyman Charles J. Kern owned a large number of acres north of Lisbon Avenue and east of the present 35th Street. By the time Mallory Street was cut through to the south of Lisbon, it had been changed to 32nd and had become an important clue to the story of the big "farmhouse."

Koenig was then living in a large house on 4.04 acres which he had purchased in 1881 from Uhrig's widow. In 1863 Uhrig added 2.8 acres, which included the above mentioned "unidentified structure." The remaining 1.25 acres of Koenig's parcel were shaved off the eastern boundary of Uhrig's original 9 acre tract.

Koenig's pretty little country estate was sliced in two by 32nd Street. According to an agreement with the city, dated May 29, 1896, the street was opened by condemnation proceedings and a sewer was to be built under it. Part of a sentence in the agreement reads ". . . in addition to the further sum of $500 in payment for the destruction of a well on the line of such sewer and the removal of the house over the same."

It was at this time that the large house was moved from its original position to a spot west of the new road where it was then turned ninety degrees to face east. The earliest photograph of the house was taken from the Lisbon Plank Road looking south. It shows a large, three-story, frame barn with a cupola to the east of the house. Careful examination of the left edge of the picture reveals the judges stand and wooden fence of Cold Spring race track in the distance. Cold Spring, later called "driving park," featured a famous hotel and a one-mile trotting and harness track. It was bounded by what are now 27th, 35th, Juneau, and Vliet streets.

It was no doubt the rude surprise of the new street which prompted important decisions by Koenig. Exactly one year after the condemnation he subdivided his acreage into thirty-one lots and at the same time took out a permit to remodel the house. More than

The only known photograph of Koenig's "farm-house" before the move and the remodeling. In this view the camera is pointed south from the Lisbon Plank Road. On the left is the original stable/barn which was razed in 1938. Barely discernible at the extreme left is the wooden fence and judges stand of the old Cold Spring Race Track.

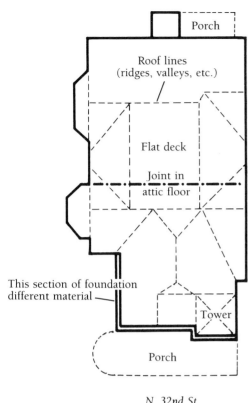

Porch

Roof lines
(ridges, valleys, etc.)

Flat deck

Joint in
attic floor

This section of foundation
different material

Tower

Porch

N. 32nd St.

This present view of the back of Koenig's house shows window and porch details which match those visible on the old photograph before remodeling.

143

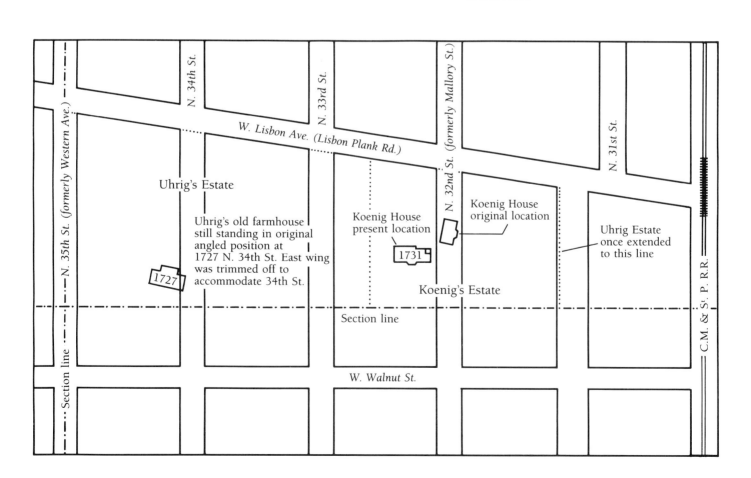

N. 35th St. (formerly Western Ave.)

N. 34th St.

N. 33rd St.

N. 32nd St. (formerly Mallory St.)

N. 31st St.

C.M. & St. P. R.R.

W. Lisbon Ave. (Lisbon Plank Rd.)

Uhrig's Estate

Uhrig's old farmhouse still standing in original angled position at 1727 N. 34th St. East wing was trimmed off to accommodate 34th St.

1727

Koenig House present location

1731

Koenig House original location

Uhrig Estate once extended to this line

Koenig's Estate

Section line

Section line

W. Walnut St.

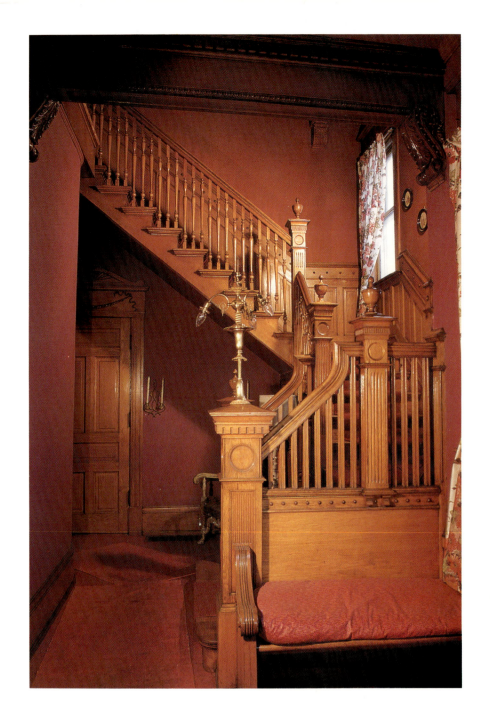

Left, the base of the main staircase. Note the typical oak millwork which was popular and plentiful around the turn of the century. Details like these were available from manufacturers' catalogs. Below, a detail of the maple fireplace mantel in the main parlor. These highly unusual majolica tiles were first fired with a clear glaze and then overlaid in selected areas with fired-on matte gold.

"just another remodeling" the project completely modernized and rebuilt the old structure. What was originally a late Victorian eclectic design in clapboard and gingerbread turned into a "modern" mansion in the Classical Revival style. The architect, F. W. Andree, preserved the basic shape of the old building, but replaced all doors, windows, porches, and trim. Rather than replace the small tower, he built a larger frame around the old one.

Inside and out the Koenig house is a splendid example of a catalog job. It shows what "wonders" could be wrought by simply picking decorative and structural elements out of a design book, such as those published by the Wholesale Sash, Door, and Blind Manufacturers Association.

Popular around the turn of the century, these catalogs listed everything from doors and stained glass windows, to complete porches and staircase assemblies with a price range for any budget.

Koenig's architect selected numerous popular details such as carved garland swags, wreaths, and acanthus leaf brackets to decorate the finished product. It is obvious that very little is custom-built, most of the woodwork being of the inexpensive machine-made type. Inside there is oak woodwork on the first floor and pine grained-to-look-like oak on the second. Many of the 1890s combination gas-electric chandeliers are still hanging and they are still piped for gas. The finest single piece in the house is a maple mantel in the main parlor with a pair of fluted Ionic columns and a set of nine unusual tiles. The white glazed tiles, with torches, urns, swags, and a ram's head, have a background of matte metallic gold.

Total cost of the face-lift, which supposedly included a twenty-four foot square addition, was $4,500. The addition brings up the mystery again, since there are many inconsistencies in the present structure. Today's front is obviously the same as that in the old photograph, but if the rear was the 1897 addition, why does it have a porch and window casings which match the old front? While it is possible that the architect could have used the salvaged front materials on the back, it seems unlikely that a project this expensive would make a new wing look old, while making the old front look new. This, plus a strange

seam in the attic flooring, and the unusual shapes among the fourteen roof segments, create a lot of room for speculation.

If the addition was not built, and the house in the old picture was as big as the present building, then why the joints and seams? Could the old building shown on the maps in 1858 and 1876 have been incorporated into the house that Koenig bought? Or did Koenig build it? Since he had only two children it seems unlikely that he would have wanted such a giant. Since this all developed before building permits, we may never know, but the complexity of the present structure will continue to tempt the historian with what looks like at least two smaller houses pulled together.

And for those who enjoy genealogical intrigue, there is the riddle of the Koenig family. There is no mention of them in the eight most important histories of Milwaukee. The only encouraging appearances of the name Frederick Koenig are in the city directories, where there are, in some years, up to four persons listed. From the first entry in 1870 until 1877 there is a choice between a drover, an ice merchant, a carpenter, and a dry goods dealer. Since there would be no address connection before 1881, the Koenig in question could be any one or none of the above.

After an eleven year absence, Frederick Koenig returns to the city directory, and this time with the address in question. He is listed as president of the Milwaukee and Brookfield Macadamized Turnpike Road Co. With the exception of three one-line mentions of "election of officers," in the newspapers, there is nothing anywhere to prove such a company ever existed. There is not even an entry in the county corporation records.

Koenig died in 1907, his widow in 1927, and the old homestead left family hands shortly thereafter. In 1938, the building inspector condemned the decaying barn and it was razed.

Much of the house's turn-of-the century character was eliminated in 1946, when it was covered with asbestos shingles. But more than just an aesthetic injustice, the siding has removed from view hundreds of square feet of clues which might have untangled the mystery of Koenig's country mansion. ●

The Goll house when newly completed. Note the fence on the right which marks the northern border of Louis Bunde's forty-foot lot. When Fred Goll was finally able to add this lot to his property it was too late to design a wider house or to center the one he built on the present 100 feet of frontage.

When Fred Goll built his Prospect Avenue mansion in 1898, many old-time Milwaukeeans thought that the bluff dwellers were recklessly exposing themselves to consumption, pneumonia and other diseases by living so near the lake. The warnings apparently went unheeded and Prospect Avenue went on to become the city's showplace. Nicknamed "The Gold Coast," that picturesque mansion-lined street was not only a favorite Sunday drive for natives, but it was, for decades, *the* place to take out-of-town visitors.

One might have expected Goll to build a large Teutonic "castle" like his neighbor, D.M. Benjamin. He was the son of a German immigrant and he married into another German family. His personal and business relations included a list of prominent Germans such as Inbusch, Stern, Ott, Schandein, Kerler, Frank and Meinecke.

But instead, Goll selected the English Renaissance for his style. This was probably due to the influence of his mother, who was described as "very English." Mrs. Margaret Stevenson Goll dropped her "H's", in typically British fashion, and only English was spoken around the house. In fact, when young Fred started in his father's business he had to take special German lessons to facilitate conversation at the office. One of his daughters remembers, however, that "his sympathies were with the English."

Fred's father, Julius Goll, was born in Württemberg, Germany. His rise to the head of the wholesale dry goods business here reads like a Horatio Alger story. After his schooling, Julius apprenticed in a yard goods store in Reutlingen. He then learned about silk merchandise in Lyon, France, before coming to America in 1848. Julius met Henry Stern in New York that year and they decided to establish a business together.

But first, the two agreed to split and travel the country in search of a good location. Stern went south, Goll went west, and in the fall they met again in New York. Then, in Stern's words, "After careful consideration Goll and I chose Milwaukee as a location, principally because the German immigration was directed there at that time."

Goll and his new partner from Bavaria had $1,600 in cash between them. They procured a loan and started buying a stock of dry goods, mirrors, clocks and other merchandise. In August of 1850 they arrived in Milwaukee and rented the first floor of a commercial building on Water Street. In the beginning, the local business was disappointing so the partners purchased a wagon to take their goods on the road. They took turns minding the store and traveling the south half of Wisconsin.

At the outset the two young men agreed that neither would marry until the business was successful enough to support two families. But suddenly, without warning, Julius Goll came in one morning in 1850 and announced that he had been married the night before. He hastened to assure his partner that he would not take any more than his single share from the company. In later years Henry Stern remembered, "The young couple lived a very quiet and economical life, and Goll spent little more than before. I often took my supper with them, and we never had anything but tea and bread and butter; still the couple was a very happy one."

In 1852, the fledgling firm of Goll & Stern broke up when Stern joined his brother in a new business. Stern sold his share of G&S to Frederick August Frank, thus forming what was to become the immensely successful firm of Goll & Frank.

Frederick Thomas Goll was raised in his father's house on Jackson Street between Juneau Avenue and Martin (now State) Street. In 1869, when he was 15, young Fred went to work at Goll & Frank. He was given a minor position and was expected to work his way up in the company to better understand all facets of the business. First he was a stock clerk, then a salesman, and finally a buyer in the textile department. Fred watched the company grow from a small commercial structure on the site of today's Marine Plaza to the huge seven-story building which still stands on the northwest corner of Buffalo and Water streets.

When Julius died in 1896, Fred was made president of the company. By then it was called "the mammoth institution" and it was the largest business of its kind in the city. There were over fifty employees

Right, the Goll house from the west. This view shows the Prospect Avenue front looking toward the bluff over Lake Michigan. Below, the south (side) gable showing the type of English Tudor detail that would not become a national norm until the 1920s. Note the cluster-flue chimney stacks, the exposed timber framework and the elaborately-carved bargeboards.

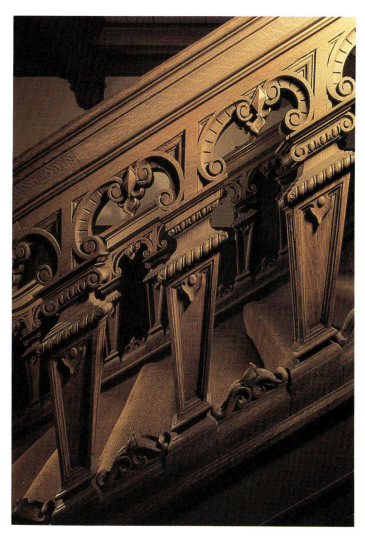

Above left, detail of the oak staircase showing the finely carved balusters. Above right, one of two eighteen-inch-high carved newel post ornaments in the form of a heraldic salient lion guarding a shield. Note the lion mask ornaments below. Left, the base of the stair well. This typically English Renaissance oak staircase is significant because it pre-dates the English Tudor mania which swept America by more than a decade.

One of the crystal and gilt-bronze wall sconces in the living room. This early photograph shows the original blue and gold brocade which was backed by flannel and stretched over wooden frames.

on the payroll and eight "commercial travelers" who sold their goods throughout the Midwest. The company also employed several hundred "outside parties" to manufacture their own line of goods.

When Fred married Eleanor Inbusch the newspapers called it "The Event of the Season in German Society Circles." Under the headline "Brilliant Social Event" there was a detailed description of the reception at the Inbusch family home on Van Buren Street and a very impressive list of gifts. Mr. and Mrs. Inbusch gave the newlyweds a Steinway piano; the groom's parents gave them a china dinner and tea set of 172 pieces. Goll & Frank employees presented the

couple with a seven-piece silver tea set. Among the dozens of other gifts listed were two oil paintings in gilt frames, two alabaster clocks, three dozen pieces of silverware with pearl handles, and a pair of magnificent vases from China. The honeymoon trip was described as a six-week tour of "all the principal cities" out east.

After Goll settled into the presidency he began to consider moving away from the old family neighborhood near the corner of Jackson and State Streets. In October of 1897 he purchased a sixty-foot lot on Prospect Avenue with the intention of acquiring an additional forty feet to the south. The later parcel was owned by Louis Bunde who, it turned out, decided not to sell. This forced Goll to change his plans and build a narrow-but-deep house on his sixty-foot lot. In 1899, when the new house was completed, Bunde looked over his narrow lot and decided it was too small for a building. He then changed his mind and offered it to his neighbor. Goll bought the lot but it was too late to change the fact that he then had a long narrow house on the north lot line with a huge side yard.

As his architects, Goll selected the firm of Ferry & Clas which had just completed the Milwaukee Public Library building. Riesen and Son did the masonry work and Louis Clas was the carpenter. The fine paneling, fireplaces, and carved staircase were built by W.S. Seaman & Co., furniture manufacturers.

The exterior is dignified, but chaste by Prospect Avenue standards. Its style is a careful blend of English late medieval and Renaissance forms executed in warm gray pressed brick and cut limestone. The front door has a wrought iron grille, the rainwater heads and downspouts are made of sheet copper, and the roof is slate. A large timbered gable, on the south, is embellished with a generous amount of carving, including a number of corbels, in the form of full-sized heads.

The highlight of the interior is a hall with nine doorways, two elliptical arches, and a grand staircase. All of the woodwork is oak and the carved details are crisp, deeply undercut and of the highest quality. Ornaments include Jacobean strapwork, convoluted scrolls, and acanthus brackets. The staircase, clearly the house's finest feature, rises to the north between two tall newel posts surmounted by eighteen-inch carved lions holding shields. At the landing it splits into two flights which follow opposite walls to the second floor. The balustrade is complex in its carving and joinery.

At one time the mansion's living room walls were covered with blue and gold brocade which was stretched over wooden frames and backed with flannel. This beautiful material disappeared in a 1947 remodeling. Another quality feature which has always gone unnoticed, is an expensive safeguard against water damage: Hidden under the tile of the bathroom floors are huge lead pans which drain directly to the basement.

The Golls enjoyed the heyday of old Prospect Avenue when there was a local law which described it as a "boulevard or pleasure way." Carts, drays, and wagons were not permitted except when making residential deliveries. Gas lights were tended nightly and the street was cleaned on a regular basis. A daughter remembers staying up past her bedtime on Wednesday evenings to watch the crew, which always arrived at 9:00 p.m., hook up their hoses to the fire hydrants and wash down the pavement. That pavement was made of six-inch cedar wood blocks laid over a one-inch plank base.

Unfortunately the good days were numbered and as early as 1921 local residents could sense a decline on Prospect Avenue. A newspaper article that year told the sad story under the headline "Save Prospect Avenue as Show Street is Plea." After fifty years as a place of beauty, the avenue was threatened by what the angry residents called "fashionable flat buildings." They observed that Prospect was virtually the "only purely residential street of its kind in the city" and that there were plenty other streets where an apartment district could be built. One mansion owner, Mr. L.J. Petit, did more than just complain — he purchased several lots adjoining his home to block a proposed seven-story apartment.

But the handwriting was already on the wall. By 1942 newspaper stories revealed the defeat with such headlines as "Prospect Avenue ponders over ghosts of its gilded past" and, "Once the pride of Milwaukee, where beauty reigned and wealth reared its elegant mansions, the old show street is fast going downhill."

Goll lived in the house with his wife and five children until his death in 1931. By then the business name had been change to Fred T. Goll & Sons. Also, in his later years, Goll had been a vice-president of the First National Bank and a president of The Milwaukee Association of Commerce. His daughter, Josephine, was the last family member to live in the house. The children sold the property in 1947 and the mansion became a rooming house.

Two years later Willard L. Momsen bought the house and remodeled the interior to become a general insurance agency for Northwestern Mutual. Goll's residence was sold again, in 1986, and today serves as offices for a large real estate firm.

Now that more than seventy percent of the elegant Prospect Avenue mansions have been snuffed out by apartments and other developments, it is good news to find one which has found the right owner. Here is a fine example of a dignified adaptive re-use which makes financial sense while preserving a vanishing species. ●

Above, the Trostel house from the southeast. The south third floor gable is executed in the style of medieval German fachwerk (timber) construction. The large pair of carved wooden gargoyles, which appear on the old photograph, are now gone. Right, one of four hand-wrought iron tie-rod ornaments on the front porch. These imaginative decorations were meant to take the curse off purely structural iron tension bars.

When Gustav J.A. Trostel purchased his lot on the corner of Terrace Avenue and Belleview Place, one critic said, "Crazy people had to move so far out of town." The newly platted neighborhood still looked like the farm land that it once was, and the beacon from nearby North Point Lighthouse would sweep across the empty landscape night after night. In the year before the Trostels came, only one building — a farmhouse on Summit Avenue — existed in the five square blocks bounded by Belleview Place, Downer Avenue, Terrace Avenue and Park Place.

When the big house was built in 1899, the land to the north of it was swampy with willow trees, patches of quicksand, and a pond. Children from the area built a raft there and used to swim in the pond which was near the present intersection of Terrace Avenue and Lake Drive.

In spite of the elegance of their new mansion, the Trostel family had the hardships of pioneers on moving day. Wagon loads of furniture came up Lake Drive and their contents had to be trundled across a field to the house. One of Gustav's daughters remembered that the wagon carrying their piano bogged down in the mud and the movers had to off-load the instrument. Trostel went to his tannery and arranged for a heavier wagon and a larger team of horses to complete the job.

The new mansion must have attracted a lot of attention standing there, with all of its finery, in the middle of a field. Terrace Avenue was later extended to Gilman Street (now Belleview Place) but Trostel had it graded just far enough to reach the new driveway. Beyond his manicured lawn, roughly-chiseled vacant lots spread out in all directions.

The money for Gustav's handsome residence came from the tanning industry. By the 1890s Milwaukee leather had become a household word in the United States and the city claimed to have the largest tannery in the world. In fact there were twelve tanneries here and, without exception, they all were owned by German immigrants and their families. The industry employed 3,000 workers and processed $7,000,000 worth of leather annually.

Albert Trostel came from Württemberg, Germany, in 1852, and founded the family tannery. He took his sons, Gustav and Albert O., into the business in 1890. For years Gustav was president of Albert Trostel & Sons, Co. which grew to become one of the world's largest producers of side leather for shoes.

The spectacle of this mansion-in-a-field was only of minor interest compared to its striking and unusual design. Although a large percentage of Milwaukee's population was German, surprisingly few chose to build in their "contemporary" national style. Called "German New Renaissance" by the family, it was a modern blend of traditional forms created from new materials and in daring new compositions. Here in one structure we can see medieval Gothic buttresses, fachwerk (timbered) gables, the jerkin-head roofs of medieval farmhouses, and the stone-trimmed ornamental gables of the Renaissance.

The story behind three architects and their complex interrelationships sheds much light on the reason behind Gustav Trostel's selection of this style. The architect of record was Adolph Finkler, who had studied in Augsburg and Munich and later practiced his profession in Chicago. He married Gustav's sister, Ida Trostel, and within three years had joined the family tannery in the sales department. He went on to become secretary-treasurer of Albert Trostel & Sons and probably earned many times the income he could have expected as an architect.

Finkler is known to have worked on this house and on an even more radical design for himself at Pine Lake (his own home followed the "Jugendstil" or German equivalent of Art Nouveau). Little else is known about the few pre-tannery years when he practiced architecture.

Hans Liebert, a German-born architect, collaborated with Finkler on the design of Gustav's house. This is the only Milwaukee project he is known to have worked on. Later he moved to Michigan's copper country and, when the boom subsided there, left for Chicago. He was a well-known pianist, but little knowledge survives of his architecture. Hans was drawn into this job through a relationship established by his brother Eugene. Eugene's first employment in the United States had been with the Trostel tannery in 1883. He later became the favorite architect of the

The Trostel mansion when it was brand new in 1900. The dirt path extends north just far enough to connect with the driveway. The rest of the block is still undeveloped and in a state of nature. The two-story porch on the left corner has since lost its wooden balconies and has been closed in to become rooms. The two fierce-looking carved gargoyles in the timbered gable are also missing.

wealthy Germans here. He designed churches for German speaking congregations, an office building for a German language publishing dynasty (Germania), and mansions for such local millionaires as Henry Harnischfeger, John Schroeder, George Brumder, and Fred Kraus.

But Eugene Liebert's greatest residential commission was a huge lakefront mansion for Gustav's brother, Albert O. Trostel in 1907. Assessed at $346,000 in 1927, that estate was once the most valuable residential property in the city. For some unknown reason Eugene stood aside while his younger brother Hans and his brother-in-law Finkler designed Gustav's mansion. He then became involved by designing the related 25′ x 35′ stable/barn.

With few exceptions, the exterior is virtually the same as it was in 1899. The two open porches on the southeast corner have been closed in and a very large pair of winged gargoyles on the south gable rotted and had to be taken down.

The crisp, clean lines of the exterior walls reflect not only the Germanic love for precision, but the rich complement of costly materials. The walls are veneered with slender brown pressed brick laid with narrow mortar joints. The front porch, and much of the other trim, is executed in precisely cut limestone. The basic materials are decorated with sheet copper, stained glass, false timber and stucco work, and a roof of red terra cotta pan tiles.

Cyril Colnik, Milwaukee's celebrated master of wrought iron, executed many of the fine ornamental details on the Trostel mansion. His hand-wrought porch balustrade closely follows the historical precedent of seventeenth century German grillework. Elsewhere on the exterior he provided artistic tie rods, chimney braces, downspout brackets, and a richly ornamented front door grille which bears a cartouche with the initial "T" for its owner. Colnik's gargoyles and scrollwork did not stop at the front door. He created an iron balustrade — much like those on the front porch — for the main staircase as well as many of the light fixtures and andirons throughout the house.

The principal rugs, predominantly in light green tints, were designed and handmade in Austria. They were complemented by a selection of more traditional orientals.

The most elaborate room in the house is the baroque parlor. Unlike the bold black iron and oak treatment found elsewhere on the first floor, this room is trimmed in enameled woodwork and ornamental

155

156

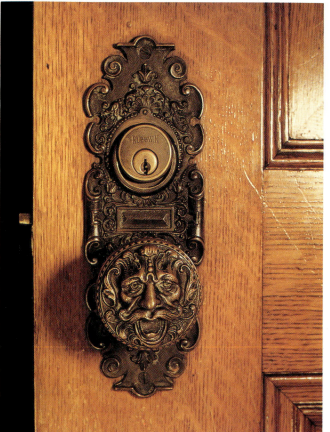

Above, an ornamental plaster decoration in the position of a keystone in a dining room arch. Note the typically rococo "C" scrolls, the shell and the two cornucopias fashioned from rams' horns. Left, the hardware on the massive oak front door. A grotesque face mask covers the knob and the bronze escutcheon plate resembles a Renaissance cartouche. Opposite, the large, painted cathedral glass window above the first landing on the staircase. This romantic view depicts Queen Louise of Prussia.

plaster. Originally, when the wall panels were filled with pink brocade and the trim was white accented with gold, the effect was even lighter. Gone, too, are the original gilt rococo wall sconces and chandelier. A ceiling height fireplace, the room's focal point, is still intact. Its firebox is framed with large onyx slabs and above the overmantel mirror is a fine, typical, rococo cartouche supported by a mustachioed man and flanked by a pair of life-sized cherubs.

The rest of the interior is more typically heavy-handed German in design. Oak woodwork, wrought iron detailing, and bold proportions are the rule.

Six-foot oak wainscoting surrounds the dining room where a pair of large carved caryatid figures decorate the built-in sideboard. A three-window complex of stained glass fills the east wall with color. The finely leaded windows are surrounded by colored roundels and include hand-painted heraldic escutcheons with Latin mottos.

The most unusual features in the house are the two large fireplaces in the main hall and the dining room. They are constructed entirely of richly colored majolica glazed tile. On the staircase landing is the strongest reminder of the house's German influence: Here is a large stained glass window which depicts Queen Louise of Prussia sitting in a garden.

The second floor includes a sitting room, three bedrooms, and an office. A large ballroom occupies almost the entire third floor. The children, however, had their own use for that room and used it as an early counterpart of today's recreation room, zooming around its fine hardwood floor on roller skates and bicycles. The tall mansion is high enough to also include a large attic space above the third floor.

The Trostel's "modern" mansion was so up-to-date that it was completely wired for electricity even though power was not yet available in that area. All of the lighting fixtures anticipated the future and were designed for both gas and electricity.

After Mrs. Trostel's death in 1944, the home was sold and in that year minor alterations were made to convert it into a two family dwelling. In 1947 a garage was added to the north side. The only other significant change was when the "barn" was moved from the northwest corner of the lot to a spot nearer to Belleview Place.

In what is now a completely filled neighborhood, it is interesting to recall the days when the lighthouse beacon shone in the second floor bedrooms of the Trostel mansion. And it is amusing that its location — once considered too remote — is now nearly eight miles *inside* the city limits! ●

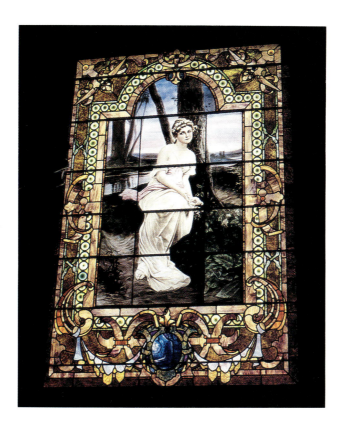

Above, view of McIntosh's mansion when it was just completed. Left, bird's-eye view of the Wisconsin Conservatory of Music today. Looking east to the marina on Lake Michigan, the two high rise buildings form a canyon around the old mansion.

For nearly a century Prospect Avenue was nicknamed "The Gold Coast." It was the street where Milwaukeeans took out-of-town guests to impress them with the local equivalent of Chicago's Prairie Avenue or San Francisco's Nob Hill. The breed of mansion responsible for that reputation is now nearly extinct. The finest survivor among the remaining examples, is the one built by Charles L. McIntosh.

Ordinarily, a residential neighborhood starts to decline when the cost of maintaining its mansions becomes prohibitive. As the buildings begin to deteriorate they turn into apartments and then rooming houses. This eventually leads to the destruction of the old houses and their replacement with lower quality housing.

Prospect Avenue, however, has not followed this traditional evolutionary cycle because of its incomparable bluff-top view of Lake Michigan. While some areas deteriorated as far as the rooming house stage, the street's ever-increasing tax base forced replacement with high quality, high density, housing. First came well-built traditional apartment buildings, then high rises, and finally expensive condominiums.

The financial pressure on old single family homes was fatal in most cases. But here, in the McIntosh mansion, we see one of the few happy endings. As a conservatory of music this house not only works for its survival, but it has an "occupation" which is pleasantly compatible with its architectural beauty. And nowhere else is the contrast between the "old Gold Coast" and new Prospect so dramatic as here where we can see a gracious home dwarfed in a canyon between two high rise apartments.

When the first fine homes began to appear on the street in the 1850s, Prospect was considered country and the dwellings were called summer houses. In the '80s and '90s a new crop of even more elaborate mansions began to supplant the original buildings. This residential replacement continued with considerable frequency until World War I. Since those days of the idyllic residential lane another, third, generation (mostly apartments) has permanently removed the gentle aspect of the street.

The McIntosh house is second generation, having replaced an earlier home on the same lot. The property was purchased by McIntosh in 1903 for $57,500. His deed reveals there was a large home already there, built by the previous owner, Robert C. Spencer.

Charles L. McIntosh had come to Milwaukee the previous year and was in temporary residence at the then-new Pfister Hotel. Originally a native of Jamestown, New York, he had been general manager of the Jewel Belting Company of Hartford, Connecticut, and later was a banker in Denver. In 1895 he moved to Racine, Wisconsin, where he bought a controlling interest in the J.I. Case Threshing Machine Company, which was in the process of reorganization. It was during the Case years that McIntosh became affiliated with the Milwaukee Harvester Company as a director. This relationship was responsible for luring him to Milwaukee.

While visiting his son in Boston, McIntosh was impressed with the new Boston Public Library, patterned after the Bibliothèque Sâinte-Geneviève in Paris. According to tradition, McIntosh sold the directors of Case on the idea of having their office building follow the same design.

A well known Chicago architect, Horatio R. Wilson, was commissioned for the job and the limestone building which resulted can still be seen at 700 State Street in Racine. At almost the same time, McIntosh engaged Wilson to draw the plans for his splendid mansion in Milwaukee.

Construction was begun in September of 1903 and the architect's superintendent, P.M. Adams, stayed on the site continuously for fifteen months until the job was completed.

Only the finest and most permanent materials were used throughout. The exterior is built with Galesburg paving brick trimmed in Michigan raindrop brown stone. The cornices and roof balustrade are made from sheet copper and the roof is covered with tile. Although the design was then called "colonial," it is now considered to have been inspired by the 1893 World Columbian Exposition in Chicago and is called *the* Classical Revival.

As a rule, if a newspaper story were written about the mansion when it was new, it would be next to

159

impossible to find it today since there is no local index covering that period. Such a story *was* written and we are fortunate today that, on October 29, 1904, one thoughtful person snipped it from the daily paper. This wonderfully detailed account takes the reader on a room-by-room tour through the house. At the time of writing it was estimated that the building would be completed in four weeks.

The 6′ x 9′ entrance vestibule was described as "wainscoted with mahogany to the ceiling." The floor was mosaic and both the front doors and the marble-lined radiator niches were covered with wrought iron grilles. This led to a 9′ x 15′ vestibule from which one could go north into Mr. McIntosh's den. Rosewood trim and an African marble fireplace framed the room's tapestried walls. A special storage area for cigars was provided.

Across the vestibule to the south was the French rococo sitting room finished in green and gold. Wall sconces and hardware were gold plated and the ceiling was to be hand painted (a plan which, if executed, has since been covered with numerous coats of paint). From the inner vestibule the tour passed into the huge main hall which served all of the other first floor rooms.

To the south opened the library, finished in Circassian walnut and tapestry. To the east was the dining room with its mahogany woodwork, hand-rubbed to a glass-like finish. Since the dining room was centered on the first floor, it was possible to look from the front doors through two vestibules, the main hall, and out to the lake through its giant 10′ x 18′ circular bay window. The walls were covered with tooled and hand-painted leather.

The 25 x 50′ music room serves as a ballet studio and recital hall today. The semi elliptical transom windows are decorated with pastel roses in the manner of Art Nouveau.

Above, the superb stained glass window on the first staircase landing. This gold and lavender master-piece is almost certainly a magnolia blossom design from Louis C. Tiffany's New York work-shop. Left, a view looking up through the three-story open stairwell.

162

Above left, a corner of the ornamental plaster ceiling in the French rococo parlor. Above right, detail of the delicate carved scrollwork on the dining room fireplace. Below, the beautifully detailed mahogany fireplace mantel in the dining room.

The largest and most beautiful room in the house was reached by descending three steps at the north end of the main hall. Called a "veritable paradise" by the reporter, this 25′ x 50′ giant was the music room and dance hall. An elliptically vaulted ceiling ran the length of the room which terminated in a large bay window at each end. Although the room's design was essentially eighteenth century French, the unmistakable mark of Art Nouveau, then at the height of its popularity, was clearly interwoven. Gilt and crystal wall sconces are mounted on large mirrors and the mirrors are placed opposite each other to create a visual labyrinth.

A graceful mahogany and enamel staircase, with delicate turned spindles, wound through an open well to the third floor. The first landing was illuminated by a five-sash stained glass bay window in shades of gold, lavender and blue. Although no proof has been found, these beautiful windows are almost certainly magnolia blossom designs by Louis Tiffany's studio in New York, a fact which today would make them the mansion's greatest treasure.

The reporter's tour continued to describe each room in the house, from the billiard room in the basement to the commodious, tapestry-lined bedrooms upstairs. Since no expense was spared, the interior was incredibly elaborate and all possible conveniences were installed. There were silver-plated jewel safes for the ladies, marble tables and German silver sinks in the kitchen, a trunk lift, a built-in telephone system and a wine cellar.

It is hard to imagine better floors than those McIntosh walked on: rough underfloor, a layer of deafening quilt, two inches of mineral wool, another deafening quilt, a second rough floor, and finally a finished top surface of 7/8″ quarter sawn oak. And this was no ordinary oak . . . it was specially kiln-treated with ammonia fumes to give it a uniform lustre throughout, thus eliminating the usual effects of wear. Considering the wear and tear of more than eighty years, a surprising amount of the home's original elegance can still be seen.

The McIntoshes hosted many lavish parties in their new home. Elegant dances and receptions took place in the spacious ballroom. Gustav Pabst Jr.

remembered that it was here that "the curtains were taken down every Christmas and banks of candles set in every window on both floors."

But McIntosh's enjoyment of this house was unfortunately short-lived. He was returning from a trip to Egypt when he was taken ill in Naples, Italy. His son made a "sensational" trip to New York and managed to catch up with a steamship which had already put out to sea. He arrived at his father's bedside in April of 1910, in time to see him die.

Effie McIntosh, his widow, sold the house to William Osborne Goodrich in 1921. The Goodriches had just moved out of their wedding-present Gothic mansion which can still be seen at 2234 North Terrace Avenue. They in turn sold the Prospect Avenue gem to the Wisconsin College of Music in 1948. From that time until the present the building has been used as a school of music. (The name has since been changed to Wisconsin Conservatory of Music.) The dining room is now a general office; the library is still used in its original capacity, and the beautiful dance hall is serving admirably as a ballet studio and recital hall. The fact that this Gold Coast gem has been spared, and has a sympathetic owner, cannot be taken for granted. Two major threats to its existence have occurred during the last half century. A 1921 newspaper headline begged, "Save Prospect Avenue as show street is plea." Apartment buildings were threatening to change the character of the street and old-time residents were so angry that one wealthy homeowner (L.J. Petit) purchased several lots adjoining his home to block a seven story apartment.

Again, in 1924, there were ominous rumblings about widening Prospect and destroying everything on the east side of the street from Juneau Avenue to Kane Place. This plan was designed to create a long and spectacular lakeview park. Since then, a major widening of the pavement has destroyed the ancient trees which once formed a shady cathedral-like arch over the street. The relentless march of developers continues to narrow the odds against the survival of a mansion like this. At least, for the moment, we can continue to relish this tangible link to the days when Prospect Avenue was *the* place to live. ●

Above, the Pabst mansion from the southwest. This earliest known photograph shows the house in almost new condition. Note the sheet metal canopy hanging from the columns (now gone). Each of the columns was cut from a single block of stone. Left, looking west from Lake Michigan. The Pabst mansion has an incomparable view of the lake from its bluff-edge site. Notice the various terraces, staircases and gardens as they step down the incline.

Around the turn of the century, a popular pastime was driving through Milwaukee's posh neighborhoods to look at mansions of the beer barons and their families. While the "Sunday tour" is still popular, the supply of brewers' palaces has unfortunately dwindled. In fact, most of the early homes of the Blatzes, Millers, and Uihleins have disappeared within the last decade. Only the Pabsts seem to have had any kind of luck at survival, their family being represented today by at least five major mansions.

A reminder of the age of elegance is the Gustav Pabst house at 2230 North Terrace Avenue. Built in 1906 of the finest materials, it has hardly been "broken in" and could weather another century without revealing its age. It stands on a beautiful street which has a history of fine homes dating back to 1855. Terrace Avenue begins on the lake bluff at the northernmost corner of Milwaukee Bay and has one of the city's finest views of the lake.

Gustav and Fred were the two sons of Captain Frederick Pabst, who built what became for years the largest brewery in the world. "Gus," as he was called, had the personality and the talents of his father. In addition to his involvement with the brewery, he held directorships in local companies such as the Wisconsin National Bank and Allis Chalmers. He was a horseman, an excellent shot, a hunter, and a fisherman. On his "hollyhock" farm in Oconomowoc he raised nationally famous holstein cattle. In 1904, when his father died, Gustav was elected president of the brewery and he gained the respect of his employees who came to regard him "just the same like the Captain." More than just the chief executive, he was the brewmaster and spent a great deal of time personally judging quality.

His first mansion was on Highland Boulevard next to the home of his brother Fred. Both of these are still standing. In 1906 the lot on Terrace was purchased and Gus and Hilda Pabst planned the most elegant home on the street. They were again to be neighbors of the family, this time next door to Gustav's sister, Marie. When Marie married W. O. Goodrich in 1894 Captain Pabst built the picturesque Gothic house at 2234 Terrace Avenue as their wedding present.

The Pabsts began in the proper manner by first selecting one of Milwaukee's greatest architectural firms, Ferry & Clas. It was this famous office which designed St. John's Cathedral tower, the Milwaukee Central Library, Northwestern National Insurance Co., the Forest Home Cemetery chapel, and the Matthews building (S.W.corner 3rd and Wisconsin Avenue and now part of the Grand Avenue shopping mall complex). Their finest residential masterpiece was the incomparable mansion at 2000 West Wisconsin Avenue, which was built for Gustav's father in 1892.

It is apparent that no expense was spared in the construction of Gustav's house. Its classical façade is replete with the finest and most expensive materials: limestone, sheet copper, wrought bronze, and glazed tile. Even the four Corinthian columns of the portico, which at first look like any other limestone columns, are in fact very special. When they were first delivered, each came in three "drums," as had been the custom since the days of the Parthenon. But Hilda Pabst was disappointed and she had them taken back. In their place, a new set was ordered, each column to be chiseled from a single block of stone. While the building permit lists the mansion's cost at a conservative $75,000, the true bottom line has been estimated at nearly half a million dollars.

The grilles on the front door and the balconies were hand wrought from solid bronze. Although more difficult to work than wrought iron and considerably more expensive, bronze has the advantages of longer life and a desirable green patina which develops with age. The third floor dormer windows, projecting from the mansard roof, are fabricated from sheet copper. This material, which was cut from flat stock, folded, and hand soldered, also acquires a characteristic green appearance as it ages. The ornamental details were made by hammering sheets into hollow molds and then trimming off the excess material with hand shears.

When entering the front doors, the beauty of the first floor layout becomes apparent. From the marble-floored vestibule, one has a striking view through the reception hall, "the long room," the east porch, the terrace, and out to Lake Michigan. This handsome open space slices through the first floor dividing it in

The highly dignified main entrance is framed in carved limestone and trimmed with bronze. The two glass-paneled doors and matching transom window are guarded by exquisite hand-wrought grilles. Above is a wrought bronze balcony serving the French doors on the second floor.

two. Halfway down the hall a great eliptical staircase rises along the north wall to a stained glass skylight which illuminates the area from above. The balustrade which sweeps gracefully upward with the stairs, is made of wrought bronze. Unlike the similar bronze grilles outside, which have acquired a sixty-five year patina of green, these great balustrade panels still have the mellow bronze-sculpture look that they had on the day of installation.

North of the hallway, through a fine pair of glass doors, is the largest and most spectacular room in the house. This 18′ x 25′ drawing room is partially paneled in Circassian walnut. The door casings, in the same wood, are richly carved and still have the crisp look of newness. Originally the non-paneled wall spaces were covered with silk damask. The room is generously illuminated by four sets of tall, glazed, French doors, each of which leads to a bronze-railed balcony. The doors are fitted with the most expensive hardware money could buy. These gold-plated bronze espagnolette bolts have cam hooks, top and bottom,

which lock when an ornate handle is rotated horizontally. They appear to have been made by Fontaine et Cie of Paris. The drawing room is further illuminated by a spectacular pair of Lalique chandeliers and four gilt acanthus-leaf wall sconces. The chandeliers' gold plated castings are rococo inspired and extensively hand finished. Each fixture supports five large scallop shells made of the translucent satin glass that became Rene Lalique's trademark. A spectacular Italian Renaissance coffered ceiling crowns the drawing room. Its ninety-one ornamental plaster wells are complemented by an oak parquet floor in the herringbone pattern.

Standing out from all this elegance is a superb fireplace which is 8′ wide and 7′ tall. Exquisitely carved in Italian marble, this piece is the highlight of the house. No finer marble carving can be found in Milwaukee: there are cherubs, dragons, chimerae, acanthus leaves, eagles with serpents, and griffins carved into the mantel.

Left, the half elliptical main staircase. Right, detail of the wrought bronze staircase balustrade. Gracefully flowing coils split, overlap and intersect in one of the Midwest's finest examples of bronzework.

Looking east in the drawing room toward the lake terrace. This room is wainscoted and trimmed with Circassian walnut.

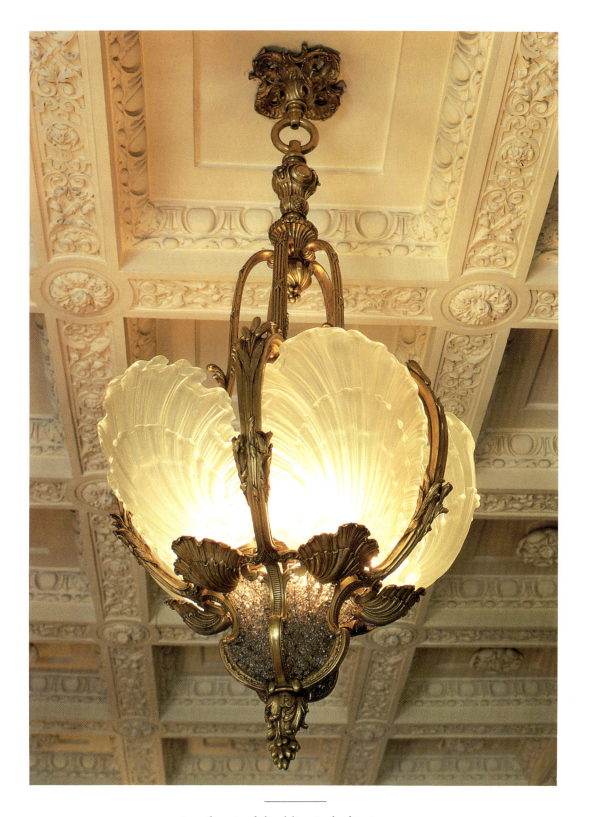

One of a pair of chandeliers in the drawing room by Rene Lalique of Paris. The rococo-inspired framework consists of hand-finished brass castings plated with gold. Each fixture supports five large scallop shells made of translucent satin glass.

Across the entry hall to the south is the library which also has an interesting fireplace. Its mantel slab is made of white marble with an inlaid Greek key pattern in yellow marble. Two bronze cherubs, holding torches, supply lighting.

At the rear, overlooking the lake, the dining room features still another style of marble fireplace. This specimen, in two inlaid black varieties, boldly dominates the 18′ x 25′ room. Ebony woodwork, finished to a glass-like shine, complements the blackness of the mantel. Overhead, between the glistening beams, glows a ceiling of gold.

The so called "long room" stretches across the lake side of the house to connect the drawing room with the dining room. A carved marble fountain on a pedestal decorates one wall and light is provided by wall sconces like none other in the city. This house is rich in quality lighting fixtures, but special mention must be made of these sconces. Their bodies consist of heavy, carved, marble cherub's heads on cartouches with two electrified bronze torches springing from each.

On the second floor are five large bedrooms and four baths arranged around a central hall. The third floor is occupied by a cedar room, a trunk room, and six servants' chambers. At one end is a giant room, running the full depth of the house, which in most cases would have been a ballroom. Here, however, the original architects drawing indicated it as an "amusement hall." In use it became the playroom for the three Pabst boys and was outfitted like a gymnasium. It never saw the gala parties and dances that its size suggests.

The plaster Italian Renaissance coffered ceiling decorates the drawing room.

Above, the carved marble Italian Renaissance style fireplace mantel in the drawing room. Left, detail of the carving. This heavily undercut pilaster is among the finest examples of marble carving in the state.

Above, the entry hall as it looks today, facing west to Terrace Avenue. The present owner removed a wall which divided the house into two units. At right, the earlier view taken facing east to Lake Michigan shows the dividing wall.

Although they were obviously concerned with the aesthetics of their surroundings, the Pabsts did not overlook the latest in modern conveniences. The all-tile kitchen in the basement was equipped with one of the first electric ranges and a dumb waiter. The servants had separate rooms for laundry, ironing, and drying as well as different cellars for wine and vegetables. Central vacuum cleaning was installed throughout the house, along with the latest in servant call systems. The largest basement room was set aside for billiards.

The last year of occupancy by the Pabst family was in 1951, and for a few years only a caretaker lived in the big old house. In 1955, Bernard Dziedzic and Ashur Wetherbee bought it jointly and invested more than their purchase price in remodeling. Numerous subdivisions and changes were executed to convert the mansion into a two family dwelling. This helped to turn what might have become a white elephant — headed for destruction — into a financially practical project. Unfortunately, one of the finest first floor spaces was sacrificed in the subdivision. A wall was built through the middle of the reception hall to divide the first floor in half.

The present owner, only the fourth in the mansion's history, has removed that wall and restored the hall's long-hidden elegance. Today, with a Mediterranean villa on one side, and a French gothic "chateau" on the other, the venerable Pabst mansion stands among friends. Together these three wildly diverse designs form one of Milwaukee's most important architectural groupings. ●

One of the Circassian walnut door casings in the drawing room. The crisply executed leaves, flowers, and cartouches rank among Milwaukee's finest wood carvings.

Early photograph of the Emil Ott mansion from the northeast. The street in the foreground is Lafayette Place.

One of the finest architectural interiors in Milwaukee is hiding behind sober gray walls at 2127 East Layfayette Place. Although its plain limestone façade is obviously expensive, the Emil H. Ott mansion offers few clues to prepare a visitor for the grandiose surprise inside. Even the interiors of the MacLaren house at 3230 East Kenwood Boulevard, which is a far better example of the English Tudor style, pale by comparison.

The Otts were not the first to build a stone mansion on Lafayette Place. Another very similar one was erected in 1903 by Ferdinand Schlesinger. By 1911 that short street had grown into a row of great houses and could boast of such names as Fitzgerald, Gallun, Brumder, and Uihlein. But this was only a late development in a neighborhood which has a long and interesting history.

In the beginning the whole area was a part of Glidden & Lockwood's addition and John Lockwood's great mansion was the only residence in that subdivision. When the streets were laid out in 1854, they ran north, 35 degrees east and were numbered (2nd, 3rd, 4th, and 5th avenues became Prospect, Summit, Lake Drive, and Terrace Avenue respectively). The only exception to this grid was Park Street which ran due east-west and which later became East Layfayette Place. By 1877 Lockwood's mansion had been remodeled into a resort-hotel called the Sherman House and fine homes had begun to appear on Terrace Avenue. The building up of the area continued until the turn of the century when the greatest boom got underway and such names as W. O. Goodrich, Gustav Pabst, and A. O. Smith started to appear in the neighborhood.

It was in August of 1906 that Emil Ott purchased the lot on the southwest corner of Layfayette Place and Terrace Avenue. By this time the original lot had lost a generous strip along its eastern border. That parcel, as wide as Terrace Avenue and extending to the lake, was taken by the city in 1886 "for public use for the purpose of a street." The street, however, was never cut through.

Emil H. Ott was married to Ida Steinmeyer, daughter of the founder of a wholesale-retail grocery firm here. Ott later became president of Steinmeyer's and his three sons, Irving, Walter, and Harvey, held executive positions in the company. After eighty-two years in the business, Steinmeyer's closed its doors forever in 1947.

The Steinmeyer building can still be seen on the southeast corner of North 3rd Street and Highland Avenue. It is probably no coincidence that Ott selected the same architectural firm which had designed the family business building to plan his house. The celebrated office of Ferry & Clas. had already executed commissions in the Ott's new neighborhood, i.e., the Fitzgerald house (2022 East Layfayette Place) and the Otto and Frank Falk houses on Terrace Avenue (both now gone).

Alfred Charles Clas, the partner who was directly responsible for Ott's design, had been awarded a gold medal at the World Columbian Exposition for his work on the Milwaukee Public Library and Museum. He had received similar commendation at the St. Louis Exposition of 1904 for the State Historical Library in Madison, Wisconsin.

Clas prepared drawings for Ott in the English Tudor style. This particular variation — based on the square plan Elizabethan country manors of the sixteenth century — was distinguished by the parapeted gables which rose above the roof and the hood moldings which crown the window openings.

Mr. and Mrs. Emil Ott.

176

Top, detail of a carved wood lantern, gessoed, gilded and polychromed. Above, base of the central staircase showing the fine, carved and pierced, oak balustrade with its Jacobean strapwork. On the landing is a custom made grandfather clock which was designed to match the rest of the interior. Right, the spectacular English Jacobean oak staircase looking up to the east landing. Notice the typically-geometric ornamental plaster ceiling.

Above, a carved limestone fireplace set in a recessed inglenook facing the staircase. Note the re-refined quality of the stone carving and the unusually large wrought iron andirons. Right, St. George slaying the dragon is depicted in the wall sconce.

The expansive limestone façades are embellished with occasional panels of carving and all gutters, downspouts, and rainwater heads are fabricated from sheet copper. The roof is covered with the rarest and most costly of slates. Of all the colors available from American quarries, red has always been the scarcest. In fact, it is now so rare that suppliers will not ship enough to a single customer for a complete roof. The Ott house is one of the few places where this luxury can still be seen.

Beneath the pedimented entrance porch is the first clue to the elegance inside. A pair of massive doors and two matching sidelights are fitted with wrought bronze grilles. The solid impression of the grillework is heightened by the heavy bronze plates laminated on the outside surfaces of the three-inch-thick oak doors. Both for the security of talking through the door without unlocking it, and to facilitate cleaning, the plate glass panel can be unlatched and swung inward on hinges.

On the other side of the marble-floored vestibule is a second pair of doors with clear leaded glass accented by colored oak leaves. Beyond these is an inner vestibule, illuminated by an unusual Gothic-styled ceiling fixture in silver plate and onyx.

This humble area flows into a great hall which expands upward to the second floor ceiling. Here is one of the largest and most spectacular rooms to be found in a Milwaukee home and it is certainly the highlight of the Ott house. Beginning in the center of the floor, between a pair of six-foot carved newel posts, the staircase rises to the east, spreads out on a landing, and doubles back in two flights along the outside walls. At the second floor level the stair balustrades sweep back over the hall, turn, and eventually meet forming a large open well.

The entire area is illuminated by a great expanse of windows in a tall bay on the landing. The windows, covering a 12′ x 15′ area, are of leaded glass with colored oak leaves in the upper transoms. What originally was intended as a hall seat was later converted into a plant conservatory with the addition of large sheet metal pans.

The landing is further enhanced by a nine-and-one-half foot clock with a choice of Westminster or Whittenton chimes. Its carved oak case appears to have been custom made for the house and in particular this landing.

The staircase is a masterpiece of craftsmanship without equal in the city of Milwaukee. In typically

Below, the original oak hall bench is still with the house, located, as always, in the stair hall.

English fashion it is constructed of oak and has many large, square newel posts. Instead of a succession of spindles or balusters, the handrail is supported by a series of pierced panels hand-carved of Jacobean strapwork.

The strapwork theme is repeated in the square and quatrefoil design of the ornamental plaster ceiling. From this arched ceiling, which is nearly twenty-five feet above the hall, there hangs a carved wooden lantern finished in polychrome and gilt.

On the main floor, opposite the stairs, is a fine limestone fireplace flanked by two inglenook niches into which the Otts placed carved English chairs. A magnificent pair of andirons guard the fire box. This huge four-foot-tall pair is hand hammered from wrought iron bars. Each standard terminates in the head of a fierce gargoyle with an open mouth and extended spoon-shaped tongue. Between them hangs a Maltese cross on chains and a heavy poker. The most impressive piece of original furniture in the house is a large Italian Renaissance hall seat which is heavily carved in oak. It has lions-head arms, claw feet, and a tooled leather seat. The piece was almost certainly made in Milwaukee by F. L. Montelatici, a wood carver who specialized in just such "Florentine" styled parlor furniture.

Equally worthy of mention are the splendid light fixtures in the great hall. On the floor-to-ceiling oak paneled walls are four silverplated Gothic wall sconces with pierced work and each has a relief of St. George slaying a dragon.

Over the fireplace is a silver repoussé sanctuary-type lamp with three winged angel heads supported on silver chains. The two sconces on the overmantel are nickel plated and display oak leaves, a lion's head, and a medieval man holding a wineglass.

The remaining first floor spaces are no less splendid. To the left of the entry hall is a paneled library which is finished in olive lacquer with antiquing over-glazes. The overmantel panel is surrounded by a lavish fruit and flower garland in the manner of the great English wood carver, Grinling Gibbons. The living room has a plaster coffered ceiling from which hangs a chandelier with a hand-carved, translucent, alabaster bowl. The doors and wainscoting are made of costly Circassian walnut and the walls, now plain, were once covered with silk damask.

The spectacular living room mantel slab followed an interesting old stone setting tradition. Rather than trust the movers and masons with a fully carved stone,

179

Delicate stained glass doors reflecting the influence of Art Nouveau grace the dining room.

Opposite page, looking east from the dining room into the living room. Note the richly-carved door casing, the high wainscoting and the richly embossed and polychromed leather wall covering. The leaded glass insert panels below and at right reveal the strong influence of Art Nouveau.

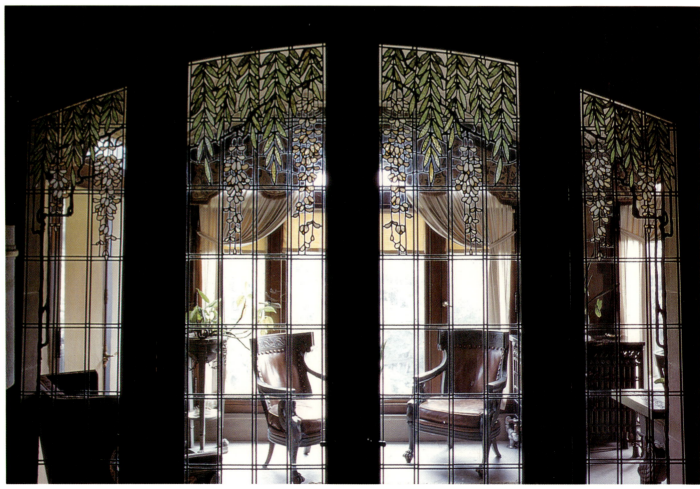

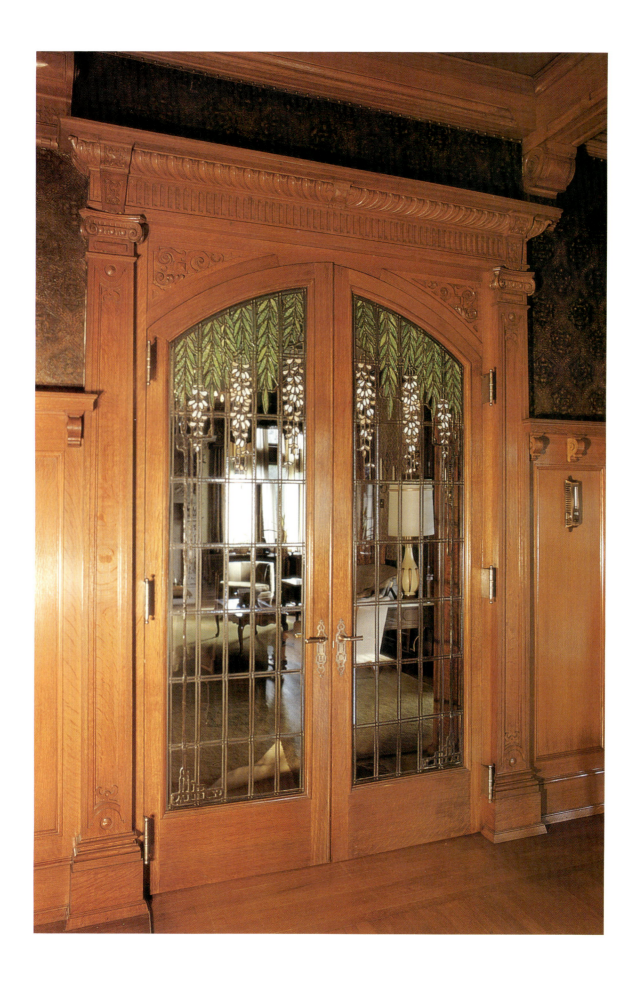

the quarry sent only a rough slab to the job site. When this was safely mortared into place the artisan was summoned. In this case the stone carver spent around four weeks in the living room hand chiseling eagle heads, flowers, and strapwork into the 2-1/2' x 7' block. Two rococo carved and gilt wood sconces are mounted on the fireplace.

The dining room has all of the literal earmarks of the English Jacobean style, but there is an unmistakable precision and hardness that leans more to the German Renaissance. All of the oak woodwork is precisely fitted, beautifully finished, and equipped with mechanically perfect hardware. The walls above the high wainscoting and plate rail are covered with tooled and polychromed leather.

Hanging from the ceiling is a crisply detailed twelve-arm chandelier in pewter and gold. Its light is reflected back down by glazed dutch leaf on canvas which fills the spaces between the oak beams.

Stretching across the entire south wall of the house is a long, marble-floored solarium with a vaulted, ribbed, ceiling. To separate this from the living and dining rooms there are three arched double-doorways filled with some of the most delicate stained glass in the city. These beautiful panels of hanging willow branches and flowers are created with tiny pieces of glass and very intricate leading. They reflect, more than anything in the house, the fact that this was not really built in the sixteenth century but near the turn of the twentieth century when Art Nouveau was popular. All of the solarium furnishings are quasi Grecian or Egyptian and have antique green patinas.

On the third floor is a large ballroom with a coved and beamed ceiling. Two wrought copper Art Nouveau fixtures hang from the birch beams.

In the basement is a tile floored billard room and rathskeller. Heavy ironwork, large beams, stag's heads, and carved wood and antler chandeliers create one of the finest rooms for this purpose in the city.

Opposite page, the limestone fireplace in the living room. The carver was summoned after the rough block of limestone was safely set in place. He then worked on the slab, in the room, for over four weeks. All of the master carver's chisel and tool marks can still be seen in the close-up above. At right, detail of the fireplace sconce.

184

*The long solarium stretches across the entire south
wall of the Ott house.*

Antiquity and Old World customs were not employed to the exclusion of modern technology. Ott equipped his mansion with the latest in labor saving devices. An annunciator servants' telephone system was installed and a large permanent gas clothes dryer was built into the basement. A second floor bathroom was fitted with a fancy shower which sprayed warm water from all sides and levels out of four circular rings. In 1930 an elevator was added to travel from the basement to the third floor.

After Emil Ott died in 1935, his son Irving continued to live here until his death in 1952. Ten years later Mrs. Irving Ott donated the mansion to Concordia College, which allowed its president to live there for a number of years. In 1971 the house was sold to a man who attempted to convert it into an art museum.

All plans were cancelled when a two-alarm fire raged through the third floor in July of 1977. While the actual burned area was confined to the third floor ballroom and nearby servant's garrets, a flood of water rained down through the splendid lower rooms destroying plaster and damaging woodwork. But worse yet was the residue left by heavy smoke. It looked as though a team of commercial painters had gone through the house with spray guns loaded with flat black paint. Paneling, oriental rugs, oil paintings, furniture, ornamental plaster, stained glass . . . all were pitch black.

Today, after a decade of cleaning and repairing, only a few scars remain to tell that sad story. The magnificent interior has been brought back to life. Once again it glows with the warm colors and rich woodwork which first delighted the eyes of Emil Ott in 1907. ●

Emil Ott house from the west (side). Under the limestone porte cochere is the side, or carriage entrance. Note the rare red Vermont slate roof with its shingles in graduated sizes from eaves to ridge.

The earliest known view of the Uihlein house taken before any changes were made (sometime before 1914). Note the porte cochere on the left before a room was added on top. Note the south end (right side) conservatory out in the open before it was hidden by the huge playroom and its connecting passageway.

When Ilma Vogel Uihlein died Milwaukee lost more than just the matriarch of its most famous brewing dynasty — it lost the last opportunity to observe a style of life which today's generation will have to read about in books. Here, in her one-owner Lake Drive mansion, Mrs. Joseph Uihlein resided until 1983 with live-in servants and surrounded by museum quality antiques and furnishings. Her dinner guests were often treated to fresh vegetables from the family's Port Washington farm and the orchids floating in their finger bowls were raised in a greenhouse on the grounds.

A turntable in the garage floor enabled the chauffeur to drive in front-first, and then turn the car around to exit the same way. Years ago the Uihlein children were provided with an in-ground swimming pool and a "play room" so large that they were able to play football in it. Outside, the formal grounds were kept in immaculate condition by a gardener.

Joseph E. Uihlein, the man who was responsible for these things, might well have been expected to live like this. He was the oldest son of August, who was the oldest of the four Uihlein brothers who took control of the Joseph Schlitz Brewing Company after the untimely death of Mr. Schlitz in a shipwreck. August was the dominant brother and his sons, Joseph, Robert and Erwin, continued to be the controlling influence over the brewery.

But Joseph, who never shirked his responsibility in the family business, was different from the rest. He never seemed to complain about having a generous supply of money, but he often was outwardly critical of the family fortune. He once proclaimed that the Uihlein family's accumulation of wealth should not have happened. Similarly he blamed the long-term unrest in Europe on the concentration of so much wealth in the hands of so few.

In 1949 Mr. Uihlein said, "A lot of these people of wealth are not deserving of what they possess." He found "something was wrong with the wealthy class" and believed, "a whole lot of them would be better off if they had to work." For a man of such inherited position and wealth he was an unusually outspoken rebel. And this all happened in what we now view as extremely conservative times.

Joseph Uihlein was different from the rest of the clan in another important way. He had highly developed aesthetic and historical sensitivities and he possessed the strength of character to pursue these interests in the face of criticism. According to one of his sons, he returned from an 1897 trip around the world and got off the train with a quantity of prized red damask fabric. He was greeted by his no-nonsense father, August, who said something like "What are you going to do with them rags?" While this hurt young Joe, he went on to use this material in his future mansion.

And it is in that mansion — Milwaukee's quintessential Jacobean manor house — that we can see evidence of Joe Uihlein the connoisseur. This is a house that was built not only with a relatively unlimited budget, but with taste and a lot of love for detail. He could easily have followed the precedent of his peers by just placing orders and paying the bills, but everything here points to a man who personally supervised all of the details and relished every minute of it.

In 1904 Joseph married Ilma, the daughter of Fred Vogel Jr. of the Pfister & Vogel Tannery. Early on one could see that this branch of the family was going to be different. For one thing, they elected not to live on "Uihlein Hill," a neighborhood centered around 5th and Galena streets which had long been the tightly-knit province of the Uihlein family. It was so named because, at this time in history, the city directories listed no less than twelve Uihleins there. This location, of course, made it easy to walk two blocks down the hill to the brewery.

Joseph and Ilma, on the other hand, chose to become pioneers on Lake Drive. When they built this mansion in 1907 the neighborhood north of Kenwood was still mostly country. They were probably the first to erect a twentieth century house in that vicinity, but there was already a Victorian house on the next property north. By an interesting coincidence it was the summer home (called "Ferny Brae") of another brewer, Valentin Blatz.

It is probably no coincidence that Kirchhoff & Rose were selected as architects for the Uihlein mansion. They had a well established relationship with the brewery and had created, among other things, the Schlitz Palm Garden which was known then as the most elegant "saloon" in America.

To put the selection of a style in perspective, one must realize the depth of the country's love affair with the architecture of Renaissance England. It is easy to understand the educated and well-traveled people who wished to duplicate some of the beauty seen abroad, but the English Tudor craze was bigger than that. In the first two decades of this century, it seemed like everyone preferred English. The extent of this desire is clearly demonstrated by the appearance of Tudor furniture in Sears and Montgomery Ward catalogs of the period.

Architects specialized in the style and companies were created to supply authentic casement windows, leaded glass, carved oak furniture, wrought iron, and other appropriate fittings for the room. A small industry developed to remove ancient paneled rooms from English castles and manor houses and to sell them in America. For those unable to afford these rare treasures, there were specialists, here and in England, who made reproduction paneling in the time-honored fashion.

Countless books were published on the subject of English house design and decoration and the magazines of the period ran a continuous stream of articles on the history and details the public wanted. One could (and many did) put an entire English house together with standard designs and furnishings offered in catalogs.

It was into this English milieu that Joseph Uihlein stepped with a love of architecture and history and a large budget. He was able to select the best of all offerings and had the resources to custom make the rest. He selected the style generally associated with the reign of King James I (1603-1625) and which was so named "Jacobean." On the interior, however, are additional influences of the earlier, Elizabethan period.

Opposite, the Lake Drive view of the house showing the greenhouse addition. Above, the front entrance as it appears today.

Above, close-up of the ornamental plaster ceiling in the dining room. At left, brass wall sconce with cherubs. Opposite page, details of the handsome oak-paneled dining room.

Uihlein bought only the finest materials from the best houses and employed top-drawer professionals to do the work. One particularly fortunate alliance seems to have been with Charles J. Duveen of London. One of the most influential men in the English Renaissance Revival, he maintained showrooms in London and New York. Under the name Charles of London, he widely advertised his stock of "Old English paneled rooms, old English furniture," and "tapestries."

Under the pseudonym C.J. Charles he authored a large, expensively printed book entitled *Elizabethan Interiors*. (On March 20, 1917, he presented an autographed and inscribed copy to Mrs. Uihlein.) In the introduction he reveals his passion for the period: "With the aid of carved oak, stained glass, paneled walls, beautiful tapestries and splendid pictures, the lordly manor houses and princely mansions reached the height of magnificence and comfort . . ."

The book was illustrated by perspective renderings of rooms he had executed in England and America. In addition to the Boston and New York clients, he did work in Lake Forest, Illinois, and the interior of the spectacular Charles S. Pillsbury house in Minneapolis. He sold five Elizabethan paneled rooms to Marshall Field & Company of Chicago.

So, without specific documentation, we might reasonably assume that Duveen was the supplier of the vast majority of the paneling and woodwork in the Uihlein house. We do know, from Joseph's own description, that "the living room ceiling was in the home of Charles Duveen of London. He made wax squeezes of his ceiling and installed it (plaster casts) for many of his valued friends. It was he who put the ceiling into this room."

Both that and the dining room ceiling, which is a cast from the world-famous Bromley room in London's Victoria and Albert Museum, have very special patinas. In Uihlein's words, "It took one man seven weeks to paint the ceiling to get the effects of antiquity in the original. The colors produced in the English ceilings are said to be due to fruits, vegetables, meats, sausages that were dried in the garret of the old English houses and the mischief caused by cats. The leaky roofs of the old houses brought the rains through these ceilings and produced the colors in question."

He was so proud of the patina that he warned that no one should "ever allow the ceilings to be painted . . . that would ruin them."

The ceilings are beautiful, but the true elegance of the first floor comes from the warmth and rich color of the oak paneling. Some is genuine old material and some is well designed and well executed in-fill to complete the composition. Most of it is Elizabethan in style and is composed of solid stile and rail construction joined with wooden pegs.

One enters this exquisite manor house through a carved stone doorway and a pair of wrought iron gates. Straight through the entry hall is the back entrance with its view of the terrace and lake bluff. A handsome, heavily carved, Jacobean dog-leg staircase rises over four landings to the second floor. To the left is a paneled den with a carved stone fireplace where both the chandelier and wall sconces are made of antlers.

Opposite the den is the dining room with its bright three-sided stone bay filled with leaded glass.

This is the best-proportioned room in the house and its floor-to-ceiling paneling is the most attractive.

A right turn at the entrance leads into the huge living room. Over fifty feet long, this impressive space is lit at both ends by leaded glass bays facing the front lawn and Lake Michigan. The full height paneling and fireplace are near-perfect copies of the living room in Chequers Court, the country home of British prime ministers. Described by English historian H. Avray Tipping as "one of the very best of Buckinghamshire's old houses," Chequers was begun in the late sixteenth century.

Adjoining the living room on the south wall, is a five-sided plant conservatory with a carved marble fountain. When this bright room needs light it is provided by a pair of bronze sconces depicting cherubs riding giant dolphins. The floor is paved in travertine

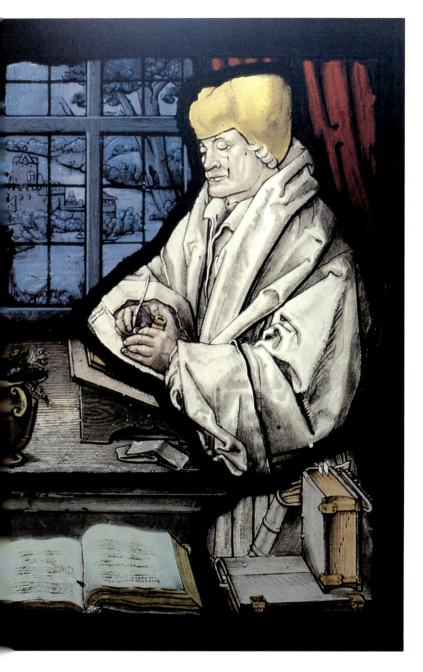

Allegorical and heraldic figures, some dating from
the sixteenth century, comprise one of the finest
collections of stained glass in the state.

Right, the elaborate hall fireplace. Far right, the bronze chandelier which hangs in the two-story high "play room." Below, the Jacobean dog-leg staircase which rises over four landings to the second floor.

marble which is inlaid with lead border patterns.

One of the highlights of the house is the superb wall of glass which separates the solarium from the living room. In the great expanse of clear leaded glass there are included nineteen extraordinary stained glass panels executed with opaque pigments, flashing, silver stain, and acid etching. The subjects are mainly allegorical and heraldic and some date back to the sixteenth century. There is, perhaps, no finer such collection in the state.

This was the original south wall of the house and the solarium extended out to the sunlight. But, with the coming of five children, a major addition was planned. The "playroom," as the family called it, was built as a separate structure south of the solarium and connected to the living room via a long, low, passageway. Even the building permit lists this as a playroom, but when one first walks into its two-story 24′ x 52′ space the words that come to mind are *immense baronial hall.* On its hardwood floor is an inlaid shuffle board game.

Kirchhoff & Rose are again listed as the architects of record for this 1914 addition. But the "room" itself was designed by Sir Charles Allom, a man described as the "foremost English decorative artist." The room's highlight is a 14′ high half-octagon bay window which faces northeast to the lake bluff. At the west end is the mansion's largest window: a two-story cut-stone complex of twenty-one openings.

The original architect was called back again in 1917 to add another room over the north end porte cochere. When two of the Uihlein children contracted polio in the 1920s Joseph followed the doctors' advice and excavated an old duck pond on the front lawn to create a free-form swimming pool for their benefit.

As the years passed, Joseph & Ilma's bold move to the "country" began to look more and more sensible. By 1912, four more members of the family had moved into the neighborhood. Joseph's sister, Paula Uihlein, lived directly across the drive at 3319. Forever the dedicated historian-builder, Joseph also played a leading role in the planning and construction of that twenty-six room English mansion.

No one could have been prouder of his houses and their furnishings than Joseph Uihlein. He relished conducting tours through both the town mansion and his Port Washington country estate. On one occasion, in 1950, he hosted thirty members of the Wisconsin Centennial Committee of Museums and served them baked ham and beer in the playroom. Another time he wrote a five-page description of the architecture and furnishings to be passed out to his guests.

195

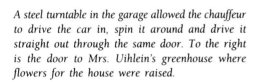

A steel turntable in the garage allowed the chauffeur to drive the car in, spin it around and drive it straight out through the same door. To the right is the door to Mrs. Uihlein's greenhouse where flowers for the house were raised.

In 1957, at the age of eighty-two, Uihlein announced that he would will his precious mansion to the University of Wisconsin-Milwaukee. He also promised a substantial number of the original furnishings which included three Renaissance tapestries. Joseph died in 1968 and his widow Ilma continued to live there until her death in 1983.

When the University took possession of its prize, the mansion's rehabilitation and operational expenses were analyzed. It was determined that no reasonable adaptive use could be justified, so the great Jacobean manor house was sold back to two members of the Uihlein family.

After a short skirmish with critical neighbors, the house and garage were converted into six condominium town houses. Although this was not the ideal fate for such a landmark, it was done in such a manner as to leave the exterior largely original and to make only minimal changes to the spectacular first floor rooms.

One would like to think that Joseph Uihlein might approve of this practical solution to saving what he once described as "One of the three finest English country houses in the Midwest." ●

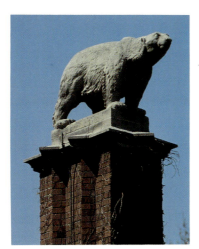

Top, the sundial gracing the garage. Above, a carved limestone polar bear caps one of the typically English brick chimneys. Right, a view of the backyard and fountain from the northeast.

Looking northeast across the beautifully landscaped terraces behind the mansion. In the distance the land drops off abruptly to Lake Michigan which is far below.

Schlesinger mansion from the east. The front (North Lake Drive) façade looks over a spacious lawn. The rear (North Marietta Avenue) is now the street address and the principal entrance.

Mansion is hardly the word for it. Armin Ardery Schlesinger's impressive residence is a *collossus* set on one of the largest lots on the west side of Lake Drive. Its interior, unlike those of its contemporaries which follow the English Renaissance preference for oak, is almost entirely fitted with costlier walnut. The house fronts on three streets: North Lake Drive, East Hartford Avenue, and North Marietta Avenue. Ironically, the present owner's name for the building and its address come from the rear entrance. "Marietta House," as it is called by the University of Wisconsin-Milwaukee, is numbered 3270 North Marietta.

Begun in 1911, Armin's house was built by the Foster Construction Company for a contract price of $144,461.22. It is, however, only one of a succession of landmarks left behind by Milwaukee's wealthy Schlesinger family. The mansion building began in 1890 when Armin's father, Ferdinand, built an impressive Victorian residence at 1444 North Prospect Avenue. Designed by architect Charles D. Crane, of Crane & Barkhausen, this was one of the Gold Coast's showplaces. It was said to have had the first elevator in a Milwaukee home and the marble fireplace mantels were imported from Italy. A "Chinese pagoda" (gazebo) was perched at the edge of the lake bluff in the back yard.

The Prospect house met with an inglorious fate after a fire swept through it in the late 1950s. Until a decision was reached on the property, the once-dignified mansion stood boarded-up and continued to deteriorate. It was finally razed to make way for a part of the Jewish Community Center complex. Only a few pieces (terra cotta sculpture and the front door escutcheon plate) remain in the hands of private collectors.

Ferdinand Schlesinger later built a much finer mansion at 2045 East Lafayette Place. This time he chose Alexander C. Eschweiler Sr. as his architect and English Late Tudor for the style. The imposing structure, described then as "one of the most elegant private residences on the east side," was built in 1903 of gray Bedford limestone with carved detailing. Asked by a *Milwaukee Journal* reporter to describe his newly finished mansion, Schlesinger replied "I have nothing

whatever to say for publication about my house, and I see no reason why it should be paraded in the papers." It was, in fact, beautifully finished with much wood paneling and carving and it deserved its popular reputation for elegance.

Ferdinand died in 1921 but one of his sons, Henry J., continued to occupy the house until his death in 1955. Henry was once characterized as a "millionaire club man and horse owner." He was married to Mona Strader, a "horsewoman" from Lexington, Kentucky, who was later named among the ten best dressed women in the world. They were divorced in 1920 and Mona went on to marry Count Edward Von Bismarck, a grandson of Germany's Iron Chancellor.

After Henry's death there was some talk of converting the big stone house into luxury apartments, but in 1957 it was purchased by Milwaukee County for park development and it was razed. Today the McKinley tennis courts occupy part of the original estate.

Henry's sister, Gertrude Schlesinger, married Myron T. MacLaren in 1918 and a mansion was built which survives today as Milwaukee's finest example of English Tudor architecture. This, the crown jewel of the Schlesinger mansions, was also the most expensive. At one time it was valued at over one million dollars with its antique furnishings. The house's spacious grounds, at 3230 East Kenwood Boulevard, once sported the largest private swimming pool in Wisconsin.

As might have been expected, Gertrude's father played an important role in building the house. He is even said to have personally transported a spectacular crystal chandelier in suitcases from Paris. This now hangs in the paneled dining room.

There are a number of interesting parallels between the houses built by Armin and his sister Gertrude. They were both designed by Architect Fitzhugh Scott, whose son married Armin's daughter Eileen. Both are English-inspired and both were eventually purchased by Milwaukee State Teachers College to be used as women's dormitories. The purchase price in each case was the same: $80,000. Now part of the University of Wisconsin-Milwaukee, they serve in different capacities: Gertrude's house is an Alumni Center; Marietta is used

A secret two-door safe hidden behind the paneling of the dining room. The interior is fitted with highly-polished mahogany shelves and drawers lined with green felt. The individually locked drawers still bear original labels such as "bouillion cups-gold," "sherbert glasses" and "butter spreaders."

for offices of Outreach and Continuing Education and as graduate student studios for the School of Architecture and Urban Planning.

When Armin Schlesinger built this house he was only twenty-eight. Considered to be among Wisconisn's most promising young businessmen, he was already secretary-treasurer of the Newport Iron Company, treasurer of the Milwaukee Coke & Gas Company, and vice president of Vera Chemical Company. At age twenty-two, the year he graduated from Harvard, Armin organized the Milwaukee Solvay Coke Company and became its first president.

By this time his father, Ferdinand, was already working on his second fortune. The first was lost in 1893, when his substantial speculation in the Gogebic Range iron ore boom collapsed. A newspaper headline of the time foretold of the the "Mining King's Utter Ruin." It listed Schlesinger's unpaid notes and pegged his indebtedness to the Marine Bank at $799,760.31. The Marine sued to foreclose on his mortgage and sold his Prospect Avenue residence to tannery owner A.F. Gallun. Originally costing $150,000, the French Renaissance mansion was sold in "virtually new" condition for $80,000.

Schlesinger rebounded quickly and in 1904 formed the Milwaukee Coke & Gas Company. At the time of this death in 1921, he had purchased the Northwestern Iron Co. of Mayville, Wisconsin, and was involved in numerous mining operations throughout the country. Armin blazed his own business trail but he was closely related to his father's dealings and eventually inherited control of the family companies.

On April 21, 1911, architect Fitzhugh Scott Sr. completed the drawings for Armin's new residence. Now that the building has undergone so much remodeling, it is interesting to study these original plans to see how the house was first laid out. In the basement, for instance, were three separate cellars — one each for wine, vegetables, and preserves. A 19' x 40' laundry was not enough so another room was set aside for drying.

One can better appreciate the grand style of living and understand the present cut-up spaces by studying the original room descriptions. On the first floor, for example, a spacious 22' x 29' room was designated "living hall." It was obviously intended as the mansion's entry room, but its great size, massive fireplace, and numerous leaded glass windows indicate its use for more than just traffic. The huge, 127' long, first floor plan also included a 26' x 35' living room, a billiard room, dressing room, kitchen, butler's pantry, and two dining rooms (one for servants).

Two main floor rooms were planned to take advantage of sunlight. At the south end is an unusual nine-sided conservatory with a two-color marble floor. The room's eighteen leaded glass sash are framed in sheet copper and the semi-circular bay is framed in the same metal. The other walls are covered with glazed tile accented with nine square relief panels of peacocks in blue and cream. The original drawings show that a fountain once splashed in the center of the room.

On the northeast corner of the first floor is the other sun room. This appears on the plan as a "breakfast porch." Here on a brick and stone floor is a cheerful room with two walls of leaded glass. Through the twenty-four sash and two doors is a view of the spacious east lawn.

The kitchen-pantry complex consists of three rooms with floor-to-ceiling white glazed tiles. The most unspoiled and certainly the most impressive feature of the present interior is the three-story open stairwell. The Tudor/Gothic design is executed in walnut and rises through four flights and two landings to a timbered ceiling at the third floor level. The upper floors originally contained nine bedrooms, four sleeping porches, three baths, sitting and sewing rooms, and numerous closets and storerooms.

Five fireplaces on the first floor provide focal points in their respective rooms and display the finest wood and stone carving in the house. It is in these features that one can best date the house stylistically. We can see here that the design is basically English-inspired, but it follows no single period with any accuracy. There are elements of pure cusped-Gothic tracery, late Tudor oak leaf carvings, classical scroll brackets with acanthus leaves, and touches of then-modern Art Nouveau.

In like fashion, the exterior is an odd blend of different English centuries tending toward Tudor. All materials are of the highest quality and where timber work is used it is made believable with honest 4″ x 8″ timbers. The red brick is laid Flemish bond trimmed with complementary wine-colored sandstone, red tiles, and sheet copper. With wrought iron grilles and leaded glass, the overall effect is one of great quality.

When William and Thekla Brumder purchased the property in 1927, they became the only other single family to occupy the house. When Mrs. Brumder died in 1946 the Board of Regents of Normal Schools passed a resolution authorizing the purchase of this house for the Milwaukee State Teachers College. Since it was to be used as a dormitory to accommodate the rapidly expanding enrollment, an additional $35,000 was authorized for alterations and furnishings. Again Fitzhugh Scott was given the job, but this time his son (Armin Schlesinger's son-in-law) was also in the firm.

Since that first major remodeling there have been numerous alterations and additions, each of which has robbed the structure of a little more character. There are, however, still a number of happy little surprises that remind visitors of the lavish lifestyle that once existed here. In one office there is a five-inch-thick walnut door with a built-in billiard cue rack. Behind another door, in the old dining room, is a large safe lined with highly polished mahogany and green felt. The lockable drawers inside carry such labels as "bouillon cups-gold, sherbet glasses, butter spreaders," etc.

While the interior has suffered from adaptive use, there are few clues on the exterior that would lead a stranger to suspect that this is not still the residence of wealthy industrialist, Armin Schlesinger. ●

Looking up through the spacious three-story stairwell to a beamed ceiling on the third floor. This is easily the most important surviving feature of the original interior.

The wrought iron gates at the Lake Drive entrance
to the Thompson estate. This fine example of Cyril
Colnik's masterful ironwork is now gone. Taken
shortly after the mansion was completed, this
photograph shows the original 910 Lake Drive
address on the posts. Today the number has become 3288. In the background is the well-built
coach house/garage.

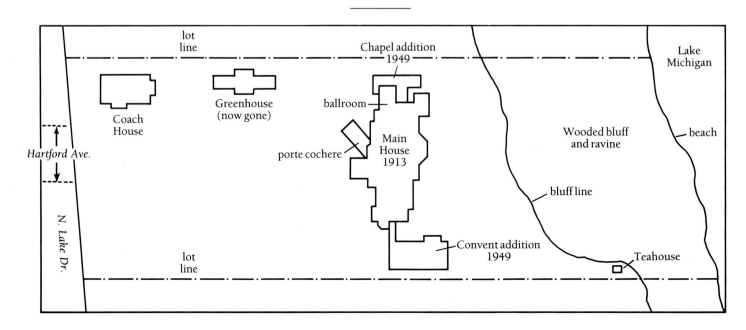

A Mosinee lumber baron's daughter, a Civil War surgeon, and a rising young architect figure prominently in the story of Henry M. Thompson's mansion. Perched at the head of a spectacular wooded ravine on the bluff overlooking Lake Michigan, this impressive stone residence now serves as a parochial college-preparatory high school. Since it was built in 1913, the Thompson house, at 3288 North Lake Drive, has been occupied by only three owners. Its architect, A.C. Eschweiler, used ornament sparingly on the exterior, but the interior comes as a surprise, with its rich complement of materials and craftsmanship.

Henry Thompson came to Milwaukee with his mother in 1868, when he was seven years old. His father, James H. Thompson, arrived a year earlier and was already working at his new job. He had been appointed surgeon to the National Soldier's Home here and was already beginning to build a reputation as one of Milwaukee's most distinguished early physicians. The appointment to this position followed his exemplary tour of duty as surgeon in the twelfth regiment of the Maine Volunteer Infantry during the Civil War. He had been promoted to lieutenant colonel for "meritorious services" in August of 1865. Dr. Thompson received his M.D. degree from Bowdoin College in his native Maine.

After three years at the Soldier's Home, Thompson resigned and began what was to become a very successful private practice. He purchased a double-house on the north side of Wisconsin Street (now East Wisconsin Avenue) between Van Buren and Cass. Residing in one half, he set up a physician's and surgeon's office in the other. Dr. Thompson shared his practice with two of the most prominent names in Milwaukee Medical history: Dr. Erastus B. Wolcott and Dr. William Mackie. Mackie was married to one of Alexander Mitchell's nieces and at the time of his alliance with Thompson, was living in the Mitchell mansion on 9th Street (now the Wisconsin Club).

Young Henry Thompson lived with his parents on Wisconsin Street and was educated in Milwaukee schools. At age eighteen he started his business career with a $4-a-week grocery clerk job. Four years later he was a messenger at the Marine National Bank. He stayed with the bank in a clerical position until he was twenty-seven, all the while studying "every phase of the banking business."

The turning point in Henry's life came in 1888 when he married Stella L. Dessert of Mosinee, Wisconsin. Lumber was the principal industry in Mosinee and Dessert was the principal name in lumber. Stella's father, Joseph Dessert, was the owner of one of Wisconsin's greatest lumber businesses. A look at a turn-of-the-century property atlas reveals the extent of his control over Mosinee. Every scrap of land on all sides of the town and the island in the Wisconsin River were owned by the Dessert Company. There were few settlers in the towns of Mosinee, Castle, Marathon, and Wien who were not Dessert Mill or Lumber Camp employees at one time or another. Even the name of the town was Joseph Dessert's suggestion: When it was incorporated in 1856, he urged adoption of the name of a Chippewa Indian chief, Mosinee.

Henry Thompson promptly moved to Mosinee and began his career in the lumber industry. With his father-in-law he reorganized the company under a new name, Joseph Dessert Lumber Company, and became the secretary and treasurer. Dessert was president and Henry's new bride was a major stockholder. By this time the business was already a giant, cutting over 6,000,000 board feet a year and manufacturing shingles, lath, pickets, etc. It employed 100 men.

But things were not always so. When French-Canadian Joseph Dessert came to Marathon County in 1844, the Wisconsin wilderness was considered an uninhabitable place where one might remain a few years to make money and then return home. Dessert once said that he would not have promised to become a permanent settler then even if he "had been offered the whole country as a gift." He became one of the earliest lumbermen on the Wisconsin River and he had one of the longest continuous careers in the business. He saw the industry develop from hand-work with the whipsaw in a trackless wilderness to the high-speed steam-operated bandsaw in a bustling lumber community.

In addition to his lumber interests, Joseph Dessert built a grist mill, developed a 150-acre farm and owned a tannery. In 1898 he erected a public library for Mosinee and paid its first eight years of operating costs. In the meantime, his son-in-law, Henry, was expanding his horizons. He was, for six years, a village supervisor in Mosinee and then a Republican assemblyman. He learned the lumber business so well that in later years he became, simultaneously, president and director of three other lumber companies in Zenda, Walworth, and Elkhorn, Wisconsin.

But, in 1902, after clearing 43,000 acres of pine, hemlock, and hardwoods, the end of the Dessert Company was finally in sight. The timber supply was exhausted and the big mill was eventually dismantled. That year Henry and Stella Thompson moved to Milwaukee where they spent the rest of their lives. In anticipation of this move, Mrs. Thompson purchased the choice Lake Drive lot in October of 1900. They were, however, to live in two other locations before

deciding to build. The first was on Juneau Avenue near Astor Street and the other was at 913 Cambridge Avenue.

The house at the latter address, between Oakland and Bartlett, may have been the deciding factor in the selection of an architect for their Lake Drive house. The Thompsons had purchased a then-almost-new mansion from Col. Howard Greene.

Built in the 1890s, its stone and timber English Tudor design was by architect Alexander C. Eschweiler Sr. At that time no one recognized its importance as a landmark or a milestone in the history of Milwaukee architecture. It was, in fact, the first large residence to be designed by the founder of an important Milwaukee firm. It was job number 27 in the Eschweiler office which was eventually responsible for 3,253 commissions. Included among their Milwaukee jobs are the Milwaukee Downer College buildings, the main

Opposite, the masterpiece of the house is this heavily-carved oak staircase with pierced balustrades in the style of the Jacobean strapwork. Left, one of the superb stained glass windows on the staircase landing. These delicately designed and beautifully painted windows are believed to be from England and are characteristic of the work done by William Morris and Edward Burne-Jones. Above, detail of a landing window showing the delicate painting, extensive silver staining (in yellow) and subtly variegated squares of hand-blown glass.

Left and below, heraldic shields carved into the marble fireplace in the main entry hall.

206

offices of the Wisconsin Telephone Company, the Wisconsin Gas Company, and numerous residences such as those for Charles Allis, Elizabeth Black, and Charles Albright.

It is likely that their nearly ten-year experience in Col. Greene's house left the Thompsons with a favorable impression of the rising architect's potential. Whatever the reason, they commissioned Eschweiler to create an even more ambitious Tudor mansion on their Lake Drive lot. Only the finest materials and craftsmen were employed on the project. The wrought iron work was executed by Cyril Colnik; the general contractor was Samuel J. Brockman, regarded as one of the city's greatest authorities on building construction.

The Thompson mansion is set deep on the lot and is planned to take advantage of the views in both directions. In the front (west) is a large coach house built of the same materials and with trim similar to the house. Between was a large cruciform greenhouse on a stone foundation, but this has since been razed. To the east is a nicely landscaped, walled garden with stone balustrades and terraces. Beyond the garden is a dense woods which rolls over the lake bluff and continues down to the beach. The back lot is bisected by a picturesque ravine through which a foot path has been cut. On a narrow strip of land — the easternmost extension of the high ground — the Thompsons built a glassed-in teahouse. Perched at the very edge of the bluff, it commands a spectacular view of the lake.

The house's design, not a pure example of any style, has a strong leaning toward English Tudor. It is primarily constructed of rock-faced limestone with a minimum of ornamental trim. The roof is gray-green slate in graduated sizes with sheet copper ridging, downspouts, and rainwater heads. Two of the rare ornamental touches are the carved wood bargeboards at the port-cochere gable ends and the carved stone detail around the main entrance. Both are characteristically embellished with English oak leaves and vines.

Although it is obviously a mansion in scale and expensive in finish, the exterior is cold and does not prepare a visitor for the interior's warmth. A fine door with a wrought iron grille opens on a marble-floored vestibule. Beyond this is a large central hall with floor-to-ceiling stile and rail oak paneling. The ceiling is ornamental plaster and at one end is a finely carved marble fireplace mantel.

Opposite the mantel is the grand staircase which is without a doubt, the masterpiece of the entire architectural composition. Rising from the hall's center,

One of two repoussé sanctuary-lamp chandeliers in the living room. These silver-plated, sheet copper fixtures were made by hand hammering, filing, chasing and scroll-sawing the originally flat metal sheets.

it is flanked by a pair of pierced and heavily-carved oak balustrades in the style of Jacobean strapwork. At a wide landing it splits into two flights which double back with a continuation of the fine carved woodwork. Above is an L-shaped hall which wraps around the stairwell and, on one side, provides an open arcade from which to look up and down into this pleasant open space.

The stairwell is illuminated by a spectacular set of stained glass windows which easily rank as the finest pieces in the mansion. They appear to be from England and are obviously influenced by, if not actually from, the school of William Morris and Edward Burne-Jones. Their designs include beautifully painted full figures and heads in subtle and tasteful colors. Their backgrounds are carefully chosen squares of variegated clear glass painted with ornamental outline forms and liberally colored with yellow silver stain. The windows are superb examples of the late nineteenth century arts and crafts movement.

Among the first floor rooms is a very unusual feature — a ballroom. Most ballrooms in the previous century were assigned to the top floor, but this one is the house's main floor north wing. Opposite its five double-hung leaded glass windows is a musician's balcony ornamented with a pierced and carved balustrade. This room has since been converted into a chapel.

The living room is very large and has a beamed ceiling from which hang a pair of sanctuary lamp chandeliers made of thin repoussé work. They appear to be silver plated copper and each is supported by four winged angel-head brackets. Light is also provided by a superb set of four large wall sconces in the Italian Renaissance style. Each is about three feet tall, made of finely cast bronze, and each supports six electric candles. The carefully hand-finished castings include grape bunches, putti, garlands, gadrooning, lambs tongue and other ornaments.

The dining room is fully oak-paneled and has a carved fireplace, but its real beauty comes from the attached breakfast room which is a half-octagon bay extending to the east. Here, with a great expanse of leaded glass, is the best view in the house. It overlooks the garden, the woods and the lake. The adjacent kitchen is walled, floor-to-ceiling, with white glazed tile and trimmed with blue lines of the same material. Even the large hood over the range was sheathed in tile — inside and out!

Next to the main entrance is a partially paneled library with hand painted flowers and vines decorating the upper wall. In the basement is a vegetable cellar, billiard room, laundry, store room, and a bowling alley. Upstairs are five bedrooms, six baths, two sitting rooms, five servants rooms, and linen and sewing rooms.

Henry Thompson died in 1947 and his funeral was held in the ballroom of this house (Mrs. Thompson died in the previous year). In the following year their daughter, Edith Thompson Montgomery, sold the property to the convent of Our Lady of the Cenacle, which was founded to conduct retreats for women and "to foster, promote and preserve the faith, teaching, principles, law and discipline and religion of the Roman Catholic Church." Immediately the firm of E. Brielmaier and Sons was retained to adapt the mansion to their needs. A large wing was added to the south to become a convent dwelling for the Cenacle sisters and the ballroom was enlarged and altered to become a chapel.

In 1973 the Cenacle sold their specialized facility to another order which had such parallel needs that no additional modifications were necessary. The new owner, the Western Province of the Community of Saint Mary, was a religious order within the Episcopal Church. They, too, used the mansion as a convent home and retreat center. Eleven years later The Wisconsin Institute for Torah Study purchased the building and adapted it to function as a fully equipped boarding high school for Jewish boys.

The old mansion's future seems secure and, unlike so many large residences of its vintage, the Thompson house is being well maintained, used to capacity, and appreciated for its special qualities. ●

Perched at the very edge of the bluff, the glassed-in teahouse commands a spectacular view of Lake Michigan.

The west (Marietta) elevation showing the main
entrance and the drive-through "tunnel" which
leads to an inner courtyard. Above the "tunnel"
is a bedroom, and to the left, the garage with
quarters above and boiler room below. The heavy
paneled oak door was built to replace the original
which was stolen after the fire.

3000 East Newberry Boulevard

As the fire gnawed through the big house it reduced carved oak paneling to charcoal and made powder out of the ornamental plaster ceilings. Rivulets of molten lead trickled down from the leaded glass windows and splashed onto the tile floors. It was Christmas Eve, 1970, and no one doubted that this would be the end of Albert Gallun's thirty-six room mansion. When the flames burned through the living room and dining room their cut-stone arches almost glowed from the heat. Firehoses were freezing on this bitter cold night, and when the ice water hit those hot arches the stone literally exploded.

At daybreak, after a five-hour battle, the firefighters left and the curious began parading by to look at the damage. No one then would have wagered that this sorry-looking, ice-covered hulk could ever come back to life. But it did, and it stands today — fully restored — as a monument to its fortress-like construction. The eighteen-inch-thick exterior walls consist of a heavy layer of limestone over fireproof hollow tile. Inside walls and floors are made of poured concrete and the roof is covered with heavy Vermont slate, up to one-inch-thick at the eaves. All the fire could do to this solid shell was to burn furnishings and woodwork.

When Albert Frederick Gallun built the mansion in 1914, he obviously had permanence in mind. And he was wise enough to select an architect who was not only well educated in historical styles but who could combine authentic details with "modern" thinking. His method of garbage handling, for instance, was absolutely state-of-the-art. The Gallun blueprints reveal a deep sump was buried in the courtyard and that it had an overflow connection to the sewer system. A garbage can rested on a grille located halfway up in this pit, but low enough that its top was under the pavement. Covering the pit was a heavy metal lid with an edge flange that fit into a groove in the pavement. Servants kept this moat-like groove filled with water to completely seal the odors inside.

Another hygenic luxury unnoticed by most visitors was an elaborate bathroom exhaust system. Specially made toilets, with built-in air channels, were connected to ducting in the walls. When one flipped the appropriate switch, a large blower in the attic would turn on and pull air through the rim of the toilet bowl. Three heavy-duty blowers served the mansion's eleven bathrooms and vented through the roof.

Rather than trust even the best plumbing job to be reliable, all water supply pipes were routed through sheet lead tunnels. If there was a leak for any reason, the water would surge safely through the upper house and dump in the basement. Waste pipes were packed in cork so no gurgling sounds would be heard on the first floor.

The entire house was supplied with clean, fresh air through an extensive system of ducts cast into the concrete walls. An "air scrubber" sprayed water across the direction of flow and its drive motor was mounted on a concrete pier in the basement to keep noise from entering the system. All halls and major rooms were connected to a central vacuum cleaning unit in the boiler room.

A post-top detail of the fine wrought iron fence made by Cyril Colnik. Note the riveting, collaring and hot-forged fishtail scrolls. This is the finest iron fence remaining in Milwaukee.

211

Originally heat was generated by two large coal-fired boilers, either one of which could have handled the mansion's needs. One was supposedly intended as an emergency backup. Later, a third boiler was added to burn natural gas while one of the coal units was converted to oil. With three perfectly capable boilers, the Galluns were free to use the one which burned the most readily available fuel.

In a day when insulation "R" factors are on most homeowners' minds, the construction of this 1914 roof seems nothing less than amazing. The top layer is up to 1"-thick Vermont "unfading" green slate. Under this is a layer of tar paper, a layer of sheet copper and then another layer of tar paper. The supporting deck is made of tongue and groove planks a full one-inch-thick resting on 4"x6" rafter beams. A layer of wood lath and plaster covers the inside of the rafters. Then a secondary set of 2"x4" under-rafters is attached to the above and finished off with another complete lath and plaster wall. The resulting massive roof traps two separate pockets of air (one 4", and one 6") between the top and bottom layers.

The designer of this remarkable structure, which looks old and traditional at first glance, was Milwaukee

The Marietta Ave. (west) entrance pavilion. Note the slate roof, leaded glass windows, timber gables, copper roof ridge, wrought iron railing and cut Bedford limestone trim.

architect Richard Philipp. Unlike many of his contemporaries, Philipp rose to prominence in his profession without a formal education. After high school he joined the distinguished firm of Ferry & Clas as an apprentice. During his early years there he was able to look over the shoulders of his superiors and watch the drawings take shape for the splendid Milwaukee Public Library project.

He remained with Ferry & Clas for ten years and became one of their chief designers. In 1899 Philipp decided to broaden his experience and he went to Europe to study architecture. He returned with

snapshots, commercial photographs which he had purchased, and clippings from architectural periodicals. Back home, he arranged these into several large scrapbooks with titles such as "French Work," "English types," "Italian details." These scrapbooks, which still exist, served as inspiration and reference for his work to follow.

The "English types" which he later produced, rank among the largest and finest Tudor mansions ever built in Wisconsin. In Kenosha, he produced one for W.H. Alford in 1928, which now serves as national headquarters for the S.P.E.B.S.Q.S.A. (Society for the

The all-limestone main staircase is remarkably light for stone. Its intricate details flow gracefully around corners as if made of a more easily carved material.

Preservation and Encouragement of Barber Shop Quartet Singing in America). He designed another very large one in 1924 for Frank J. Sensenbrenner in Appleton.

According to historian Richard W.E. Perrin, "In 1914 Kohler and Richard Philipp, close personal friends, had toured Europe and together absorbed the atmosphere and charm of great English and French houses which were to be translated into a house for Walter Kohler back in Wisconsin. The two also visited and studied the industrial garden cities of England and Germany, later incorporating their findings and ideas into Kohler Village, a model American industrial community."

But it was not until 1921 that Philipp began the construction of Kohler's "Riverbend Farm." Albert Gallun, then, may have been the first to recognize Philipp's potential in this style. Gallun's 1914 Tudor is an excellent and perhaps the earliest surviving example of Philipp's monumental "English types."

It took a tremendous amount of money to build like this, but Albert Gallun was prepared. He was the president of the highly successful A.F. Gallun & Sons Company, one of Milwaukee's largest tanneries. The business had been founded in 1858 as a partnership between his father, August Gallun and Albert Trostel. Both had come from Germany and Gallun was the third generation of a long-standing family of tanners in

Osterwieck a Hartz. Trostel & Gallun split in 1885, with each taking a share of the business and starting a new company. Trostel took the two small tanneries and parlayed them into a giant, while Gallun took their largest and continued to build on it. Because of this re-organization Gallun's eldest son, Albert, was assigned heavy responsibilities at an early age. He handled the pressures well, and in the late 1890s, his father turned the business over to him.

In his early years of running the company, Albert Gallun lived in an English-styled house overlooking the Milwaukee harbor from Lafayette Place. When he decided to build his own mansion, he purchased what was, arguably, the finest lot in the then-new subdivision called "Prospect Hill." The parcel was bordered on three sides by streets: Marietta Avenue on the west, Newberry Boulevard on the south, and North Lake Drive on the east. Newberry was the finest street in the development and Lake Drive was (and is) one of the city's most prestigious residential addresses.

A building lot of this importance and exposure required a house which was not only impressive, but three-faced. Richard Philipp created an admirable solution which attracted a six-page spread in *The Architectural Review* and the comment that he had produced a residence that, "is well suited to its location and that is dignified, substantial and homelike in appearance."

Looking through the living room doors from the sun room. The molded, cut limestone arch is a replacement, the original having been almost completely destroyed when the cold water from the firehoses hit the glowing stone.

*Looking west from the dining room to the main
hall. The floor-to-ceiling oak paneling in this room
was reduced to charcoal in the fire. The fine Gothic
chandelier is mercury-gilt and made for candles.
When it was added in the restoration, matching
wall sconces were designed and they were wired
for electricity.*

Left, looking west in the living room. The ceiling was damaged beyond repair and has been replaced with a cast plaster reproduction of a ceiling out of Sir Paul Pindar's London townhouse. Right, northeast corner of the restored living room showing the new leaded glass doors leading to the sun porch (right) and the entry hall (left).

The basic plan is a "U" shape in which three wings are folded around a private central courtyard. All street frontages are edged with a tall wrought iron fence set on a limestone curb wall. This hand-wrought beauty is one of southeastern Wisconsin's finest fences. A car can be driven through a large pair of iron gates on the Marietta Avenue side and into a tunnel from which passengers can enter the main hall under cover. The driver can then turn to the left, enter the rear garage door and drive back out to the street.

The first impression this exterior makes is usually one of size and stone: its 18,000-square-foor plan is indeed large and almost the entire exterior is covered with stone. The basic material is limestone from Waukesha County which is variegated from gray to buff with a large percentage of the pieces orange-stained from rust. All of the carved and molded trim is executed in cool-gray Indiana limestone. And the roof is covered with green slate (with a little purple mottling) from Vermont.

Size is also a factor inside. The living room is 20'x35', and on the third floor is a huge 24'x46' ballroom. Even the prosaic boiler room is a generous 21'x38'. One enters the house from the west and can look down a long, tile-floored hall, through the dining room and out to Lake Park on the east. The principal rooms on the first and second floors are arranged to the east and south of the central hall to take advantage of sunlight and the best views.

The mansion was decorated with carved oak paneling, English black walnut millwork, inlaid ceramic tiles, stained glass "bulls eye" windows, ornamental plaster ceilings and numerous fireplaces in carved stone, wood and tile. An especially fine piece of craftsmanship can be seen in the all-limestone main staircase. Its carved balustrade appears remarkably light for stone and its intricate details flow gracefully around corners as if created from a more easily carved material.

After Mr. and Mrs. Albert Gallun died in the 1930s, their daughter Elinor began to occupy the house with her husband, John C. Pritzlaff, and their family. In 1953 the then-widowed Elinor Pritzlaff decided to donate her mansion to the University of Wisconsin-Milwaukee. The gift was structured so the University would acquire a percentage of ownership each year for eight years, during which time Mrs. Pritzlaff could continue to occupy the premises.

In October of 1970 it was announced that the Gallun/Pritzlaff mansion would be open to the public

Above, a vignette in the library showing some of the leaded glass taken from the Victor L. Brown mansion and adapted to this room's limestone frames. Below, looking into the reception room from the entry hall. Before the restoration the carved walnut, limestone and inlaid tiles of the fireplace were hidden under a coat of white paint.

218

The sunroom looking south to Lake Drive and Lake Park. This room suffered the greatest fire damage to its stone openings.

during a tour of homes sponsored by the women's league of the university. After fifty-six years as a private residence the impressive stone house was at last available to the curious public. It is ironic that this first view would also turn out to be the last view of the house as originally built and furnished. The fire hit exactly fifty-four days later.

And the fire was only the beginning of the mansion's troubles. Since the university and Mrs. Pritzlaff were co-owners at this stage of the transfer, a dispute ensued over liability between the two insurance companies. After a disappointing court settlement, the university boarded up the structure and pondered the alternatives.

For three-and-one-half years the Gallun's splendid Tudor home stood vacant while grass went to seed and the bushes around it grew into a jungle-like thicket. Rain poured in through the roof and caused the ballroom's hardwood dance floor to heave up nearly a foot in places. The huge boiler room turned into a lake four-feet-deep while its three giant boilers turned to rust.

At the same time, vandals were adding insult to injury. Despite attempts to secure the building, large groups of young people found their way into the ghostly hulk behind the protective cover of the thicket. They came to have parties, and according to the neighbors, some of these groups were quite large. They built bonfires on the floors and littered the place with garbage. The walls were defaced with large and often obscene graffiti. The thieves began to loot the house. One by one, chandeliers, wall sconces and lanterns began to walk out. The carved oak front door vanished, a wrought-iron grille was pried out of a stone jamb and hardware started to disappear. When there were no more things of beauty to steal, opportunists began to eye the value of scrap. Fine cast bronze radiator grilles went to the junkyard along with copper gutters,

downspouts and flashing. The ultimate insult was the smashing of leaded glass windows. After the stained and clear glass was pulverized, the narrow lead cames were squashed into balls and taken away to be sold by weight.

By the end of 1972 the university could see that the old shell was going to cost more to repair than they could reasonably expect to raise. The mansion was sold to two attorneys for $41,000. Both the attorneys and the developer to whom they subsequently sold it tried to secure a multi-family zoning variance. Their attempts were repeatedly blocked by the neighbors in spite of arguments that compared a future well-maintained apartment building to what everyone agreed was by then an eyesore. On August 8, 1973, the city issued a demolition order, effective within thirty days if no rehabilitation was commenced. The owner delayed the death notice with a court-issued restraining order, but the mansion's real salvation was assured when John Conlan purchased it with the intention of restoring the structure as a single family home.

Having no experience with such a project, Conlan walked in with optimism and confidence. He quickly discovered that because of the fire and vandals, almost every window in the house needed replacing. This turned out to be a very costly order of 377 leaded glass sash. Another surprise surfaced after an inventory of lighting fixtures was completed: almost every fixture in the house was gone. When all the garage, utility room, closet and vanity fixtures were added, the total came to almost 400.

In the end, the restoration really amounted to building an all-new house in the old shell. By doing so, the owner was able to bring plumbing, electrical and heating up-to-date. Richard Philipp's fine Tudor essay, however, is still present everywhere on the surface, and his beautifully engineered structure is still as good as new. ●

The Lake Drive front of "Craigmore" from the southwest looking toward Lake Michigan.

When the Herman Uihleins moved into their Italian Renaissance palace in 1919, it was just like camping out. Their magnificent lake bluff estate, at 5270 North Lake Drive, was then situated among farms without roads or sidewalks; the mansion was run on bottled gas. They were the first to build in the newly platted "Pabst Whitefish Bay Subdivision" which replaced the once-famous pleasure resort of the same name.

The Pabst Whitefish Bay Resort, which rivaled the Schiltz Palm Garden as one of the great places to drink a beer in the Midwest, was established three years before the village of Whitefish Bay. An eighteen acre park, which extended north from what is now Henry Clay Street, it was built on a narrow strip of spectacular lake bluff property by Captain Frederick Pabst in 1889. For a quarter of a century Milwaukeeans made the five-mile trip by horse and carriage over the Lake Avenue Turnpike, or on the steamboat *Bloomer Girl* from the Grand Avenue dock in downtown Milwaukee to a pier at the foot of Henry Clay Street. The most popular route, however, was the "Dummy Line" railroad which operated trains every forty-five minutes to the resort gate.

The famous Blue Ribbon Beer could be sipped at mushroom-shaped tables along the bluff, or at the giant circular bar in the pavilion. Looking like an Atlantic City hotel, the gingerbread-encrusted, 250-foot-long pavilion offered lounging parlors and dining rooms where a planked whitefish dinner featuring fish caught the same day in the bay could be ordered. Throughout the day, band concerts provided a delightful ambience. In later years, when Ferris wheels became the rage, a fifty-foot model was installed at the northern end of the park.

But as time passed, a less genteel clientele began to frequent the place, bringing their own lunches and not buying anything. This and the automobile, which extended the daily travel radius, made the annual maintenance of the property unattractive to Pabst. So in 1914 the great resort, which had once been Milwaukee's "farthest north," was closed and the buildings were razed.

When Mr. and Mrs. Uihlein toured the property in 1915, the only remains of the old complex were a few tables, pieces of the concrete walks down the bluff and the passenger pier jutting out into the lake. The lot they purchased was a few feet north of the spot where the pavilion stood and if the bandstand were still there today, it would be right in front of their house.

Mrs. Uihlein had seen a house design which pleased her very much and she took it to Thomas L. Rose of the architectural firm Kirchhoff and Rose, the same firm that designed the Schiltz Palm Garden and that would eventually create residences for Paula, Joseph E., Robert, and William B. Uihlein. The firm designed the Palace Orpheum Theater in New York and several Milwaukee cinemas including the Riverside, Palace, Majestic, and Alhambra. Other familiar commissions included the Second Ward Savings Bank (now the County Historical Center), the Cudworth Legion Post, and the new Milwaukee Police Administration Building.

221

Detail of the projecting west entrance pavilion showing the precision limestone masonry and a wrought iron balcony.

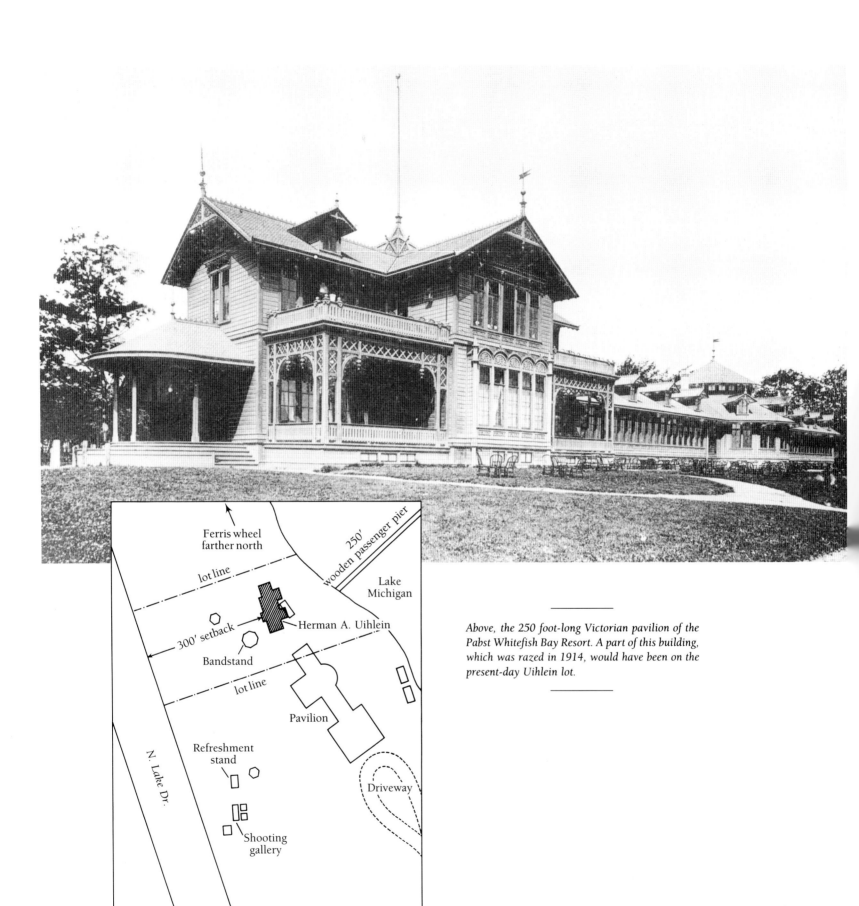

Ferris wheel
farther north

lot line

250'
wooden passenger pier

Lake
Michigan

300' setback

Herman A. Uihlein

Bandstand

lot line

Pavilion

N. Lake Dr.

Refreshment
stand

Driveway

Shooting
gallery

Henry Clay St.

Above, the 250 foot-long Victorian pavilion of the Pabst Whitefish Bay Resort. A part of this building, which was razed in 1914, would have been on the present-day Uihlein lot.

The plans for the home were drawn for Mrs. Uihlein in 1917, and construction was begun the next year. Cyril Colnik, it is said, spent three years creating the wrought iron balustrades, wall sconces, door grilles, and balconies for this job. The famous Matthews Brothers woodworking firm got the contract for all of the paneling, doors, and wood carving. F. J. Staunton, of Milwaukee and New York, was the interior decorator.

The finished mansion was so stunning that it was made the subject of a four-page picture story in *Town Topics* magazine published in New York. The reason for the excitement can easily be seen in the quality construction, the work of the artists and craftsmen, and in the lavish selection of materials used throughout. In fact, its imposing stature caused it to be dubbed "the Whitefish Bay Library" by villagers.

The superb craftsmanship and attention to detail can be appreciated by reading the 134-page book of specifications which were written for the job. The attention to detail begins to show on page one when the architect specified that trees be protected by plank boxes during grading, and that all garden quality topsoil be set aside for later use. All of the buff Bedford limestone used on the exterior was ordered to be taken from a single quarry and from only one level within the quarry. Possible damage to stone carved ornament during shipping was avoided by this directive: "carving of all ornaments shall be done at the building, sufficient rough material being left for this purpose."

Other stone included Bedford blue limestone for base course and sills and Illinois limestone for terrace and entrance steps. The lavish treatment, however, came in the great variety of imported and domestic marbles called for. Among those used were Italian Travertine, Tinos Green, Old Convent Sienna, Verde Antico, Numidian Pavonazzo, Westfield Green, Gray Tennessee, and White Sanitary.

The painters were warned not to use mineral thinners, but only genuine well settled and aged linseed oil. Pigments had to be permanent and non-fading and everything received at least three coats of paint. Many areas called for five coats of "first class finish" and in one case a canvassed wall required one coat of filler and six coats of enamel, sanded and rubbed. All glass was specified as American polished plate, at least one-quarter inch thick, of the best silvering quality, with no blemishes.

Although the house was richly finished and historically designed, it was at the same time built with up-to-the-minute technology and filled with modern

The front doors and transom grille by wrought iron master Cyril Colnik. Note the carved bracket-keystone above with an upturned cornucopia on each side.

223

224

Base of the main staircase. This beautiful example of wrought iron and stone masonry is the master-piece and focal point of the interior.

conveniences. There were sixteen telephones (five city and eleven annunciator), a central vacuum cleaning system, and a plate-warming cabinet in the butler's pantry. Rainwater from the roof tiles was conducted by pipes to the basement where it gathered in one side of a double cistern. Between the sides there were two brick walls separated by an eight-inch space. These bricks were laid with close-mortared horizontal joints, but *no mortar was used for the vertical joints* and the two walls were tied together with slate strips. The eight inch space between them was crammed with "selected clean willow charcoal." Rainwater seeped through this giant charcoal filter into the other side where it was drawn off for use in the laundry.

During its heyday, the Uihlein's house was the scene of much entertainment and for a time there were musicales held every Sunday afternoon. An Aeolian two-manual pipe organ was installed in the main hall and was played by many nationally important artists, including the organist of St. Patrick's Cathedral in New York, who was a regular visitor. Singers would assemble on the great staircase and Mrs. Uihlein, who had studied opera in New York, would join in.

Mrs. Uihlein remembered that it was not unusual to serve fifty to seventy-five dinner guests on short notice. In peak years it took a staff of ten servants to run the house: two cooks, two waitresses, an upstairs maid, six laundresses, two nursemaids, a chauffeur, and a gardener.

Detail of the carved walnut transom over the inside front doors. This beautifully drawn and executed grille ranks among the finest wood carving in Milwaukee.

The main hall as documented by a commercial
photographer shortly after the house was
completed. This photograph was one of many
taken for Town Topics magazine published in
New York.

The dining room which was adapted from the
Forde Abbey banquet room in Dorchester, England. This photograph was taken when the mansion was young. The paneling and fireplace were
later removed and given away.

Left, detail of a carved oak pilaster in the paneled library. Mounted on the pilaster is a complex wall sconce made from many individual lost wax castings. Below, the rear (Lake Michigan) elevation. Mrs. Uihlein remembered catching her sons in the act of tightrope walking between the facing second floor windows of the two projecting bays. Between these projections is the large arched window which illuminates the grand staircase. Opposite, the Uihlein mansion had such an impressive façade that it was nicknamed "The Whitefish Bay Library" by locals. Its stately exterior has always attracted photographers. In this case a commercial photographer used it as a background for an automobile advertisement.

The central stair hall is the masterpiece of the interior. One enters the house through front doors mounted with a pair of handsome wrought iron grilles. The inner pair of doors, and its matching transom, are exquisitely carved in walnut and open to the great hall. The hall's ceiling is a geometric coffered design in ornamental plaster. Flanking the inside front doors are two closet doors and two pipe organ grilles in matching walnut. These carved elements are among the very finest pieces of wood carving found in the city.

On the south wall of the great hall are two walnut double doors with magnificently carved acanthus-scrolled pediments. Between them is an Italian Renaissance-styled fireplace mantel carved in buff Amherst sandstone. The masterwork of the house is the great staircase which sweeps up to a landing under a giant round-arched window then splits into two flights, along opposite walls of the stairwell. Between the walnut handrail and the Travertine marble steps is a beautifully flowing wrought iron balustrade by Colnik.

Here can be seen a very special relationship which once was common between architects and craftsmen. A note on one of the staircase elevations requests that Colnik provide appropriately designed iron grille work in that location. Only the handrail and stair treads were drawn by the architect . . . the rest was entrusted to the man who executed the work.

Also on the first floor are the solarium, with murals of a formal garden, statuary, and fountains; the drawing room in French baroque style; the library in English Jacobean style with oak paneling, and a large dining room which was adapted from the banquet room of Forde Abbey in Dorchester, England. The original room was designed by Inigo Jones. Unfortunately the Uihlein's dining room paneling and fireplace have been removed, but the original ornamental plaster ceiling is still in place.

The mansion's architectural shapes and monumental scale created special opportunities and challenges for growing boys. Mrs. Uihlein remembered her shock when she discovered that her sons had strung a rope between the two projecting rear wings and were planning to tightrope walk.

Herman Uihlein, a manufacturer and a one-time director of his family's Schiltz Brewing Company, died in 1942. Mrs. Uihlein left the big house four years later. In 1953 the mansion was purchased by the Milwaukee vice-province of the La Salette Fathers for about $45,000. The Catholic order, founded near Grenoble, France, in 1851, served three homes for the elderly and substituted for any parish in the Archdiocese. They used the building as a mission house for five priests and two brothers. It has since been returned to a single family home.

Mrs. Uihlein's pipe organ is now in use in the Whitefish Bay First Church of Christ Scientist and the marble mantel from the drawing room has gone to one of her daughters.

Otherwise this exceptionally well built mansion, dubbed *"Craigmore"* by the family, is still as good as new. ●

*View of the main entrance to the north from the
arcaded porch.*

When the English Tudor rage swept America in the 1920s, Milwaukee was left with a generous share of homes designed in that style. Of the hundreds still standing, the Myron T. MacLaren home is the finest. Located on the lake bluff at the end of Kenwood Boulevard, this mansion enjoys one of the most impressive views in the city.

What makes it so important is the refinement of its design, the building materials, its good state of preservation, and the location. Tudor homes can be found in great abundance along Lake Drive and in the Washington Highlands. Most of these, however, were detailed under a limited budget or were "loosely adapted" from the pure style. The inevitable result was a standard builder home of the period embellished with a handful of "Tudoresque" details. In contrast, the design of the MacLaren house adheres closely to the historical precedent. The excellence of its ornamental detailing and proportions make it stand apart from most of the nation's Tudor homes. No expense was spared in obtaining the finest hand work and materials.

Not even the generous supply of Tudor homes remaining in Milwaukee could accurately indicate the extent to which this country once loved English style. In the decade before the depression, architectural and decoration magazines were replete with offerings of wrought iron, oak furniture, tapestries, leaded glass and other English, late Gothic, and early Renaissance furnishings.

One firm, Charles of London, with offices in New York and London, specialized in importing authentic paneled rooms taken from castles and manor houses in Britain. Almost every business, including Sears Roebuck and Montgomery Ward, carried lines of Tudor-styled goods.

From this melange of quasi-English there emerged only a few houses and mansions which could be considered important or significant from the standpoint of design. The MacLaren house is one of these. In England the style from which it was derived spanned the years of transition from the late perpendicular Gothic (last part of the fifteenth century) to the end of Queen Elizabeth's reign (1603).

Why such an expensive-to-maintain mansion should have survived in almost original condition is a question with a complex answer. The structure itself is built like a fort with imported Plymouth stone and roofed with green and purple slate shingles. Rainwater heads, gutters, and downspouts are custom-made with lead sheet.

Four of the more than one dozen hand-painted heraldic crests said to have come from old English castles and manor houses. This group is in the large oriel window above the main entrance.

231

Above, the west front of the MacLaren mansion from the southwest. Below, detail of the variegated Vermont slate roof. This very authentic English roof begins with large and thick (some over 1 inch thick) slates at the eaves and tapers down to smaller and thinner slates at the ridge.

Details of hand-wrought rim locks. These, and all of the other hardware pieces, are said to have come from English castles and manor houses.

These and other materials, along with the high quality of workmanship, have reduced the amount of deterioration that one might expect in a building this age. The house is located closer to the bluff than was usually considered safe and were it not for the thousands of square feet of drainage tiles imbedded in the slope, it may well have fallen to the beach by now. The hardest earned of its many reasons for survival, is an economically feasible adaptive re-use. This condition has been met by the present ownership under the University of Wisconsin-Milwaukee.

Officially known as the "UWM Alumni House," the mansion is presently used in a number of capacities. The impressive first floor is rented to paid Alumni members for such events as weddings and birthday parties. Some campus organizations also use the former living spaces for meetings. The second and third floors are occupied as offices.

It is difficult to imagine this spacious behemoth as the single family dwelling of the Myron T. MacLarens. The plans were drawn during the last of the great mansion building eras by Fitzhugh Scott Sr. and MacDonald Mayer. At least one member of the firm traveled to England to study the stone houses of the

Cotswold District for this job. Construction was begun in 1920 and not completed for three years. More than just a beautiful mansion, the total plan included a sunken garden, a garage with connecting underground tunnel, a swimming pool, tennis courts, and a private beach at the foot of the steep bluff.

The tennis courts are now gone and the pool has been filled with soil. What was once called the "largest private swimming pool in Wisconsin" can still be visualized by looking at its huge 110′x 33′ concrete outline in the grass. Footings were constructed for a garage which was to have reflected the style of the house. This project never materialized but the matching Plymouth stone for it had already been purchased. Anticipating the possible future use of that stone, the MacLarens decided to store it underground. Just north of the house, at the end of Hampshire Street, they excavated a large hole and piled in the costly stone.

It is still there today, and its presence is an un-recognized luxury that perhaps no other landmark can claim. Here, on site, is a generous, cost-free supply of a rare, original, building material with which restorations could be continued for centuries.

South half of the west (front) elevation in March of 1969. Taken with a telephoto lens, this flat-on view best shows the richness and texture of the materials and the carefully studied asymmetry of the design.

When the English craze swept America, authentic
and reproduction paneling was used to furnish
homes in the style of castles and manor houses.
The living room walls shown above are a reproduction of typical Elizabethan oak paneling
assembled with wooden pegs on a framework of
stiles and rails.

DIEU·EST·MA·FORCE

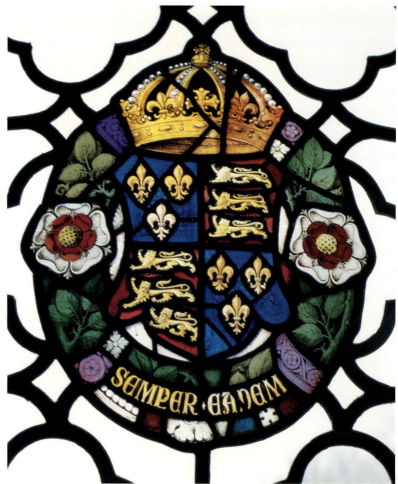

SEMPER·EADEM

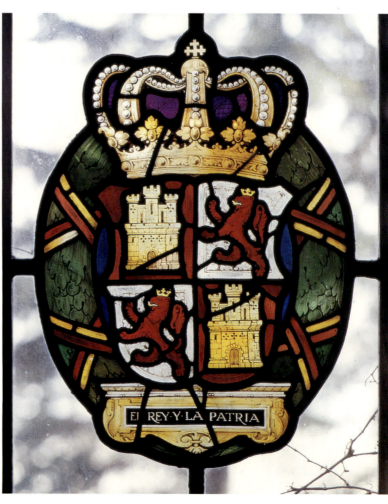

EL·REY·Y·LA·PATRIA

An underground tunnel, which was to connect the house to the garage, was built and still survives. This eight-foot-high gravel-floored passage was to have doubled as a heating duct for the garage. Today an air vent, near the "temporary" frame garage, marks the end of that tunnel. The once beautiful sunken garden can be recognized only by the outline of its shrubbery and the great low area in the front of the house. Until a couple of years ago, it was surrounded by nearly a hundred elm trees.

Although the landscape has lost much of its beauty with age, the house has gained a mellow patina and a charm which only half a century of weathering can bring. Its continued permanence is ensured by the expensive combination of building materials which include Plymouth quartzite, Brian Hill sandstone, Vermont slate, copper, lead, wrought iron, and oak. Almost all of the exterior ornament is made of carved sandstone. With the exception of a large heraldic escutcheon on the main oriel (bay window), most of the carved details are small pieces which are worked into the stone masonry. In unexpected places one might find a reclining lion, a porcupine, or a squirrel.

The authenticity and general effect of the interior falls considerably short of the exterior. There are, however, a number of redeeming features which are so fine that they eclipse any compromises in the general design. These stained glass and hardware details are said to have come from old castles and manor houses in England. Perhaps most valuable are the more than a dozen hand-painted heraldic crests in stained glass which embellish the leaded windows of the house. No finer glass painting can be seen in a Milwaukee home. Equally beautiful are the rim locks, door pulls, and latches which are made of hand-wrought iron. All are different and they show a great variety of English design in forged, filigreed, and chased metal.

Cast iron firebacks, (one of which is dated A.D. 1588), and some of the lighting fixtures are also said to have been imported. The Hayden company of New York furnished the twenty-eight-room house with a fine blend of antiques from many nations. Among the original inventory were such museum pieces as an Italian Renaissance trestle table, an early Chippendale sofa, and three Queen Anne pieces (a secretary and two desks). A $6,000 oriental carpet and two pairs of crewel-embroidered linen drapes, which originally cost $3,500, are still in the giant living room. Two seventeenth century French tapestries originally hung on the paneled walls of the first floor.

The living room walls are a reproduction of typical Elizabethan oak paneling assembled with wooden pegs on a framework of stiles and rails. The handsome large-panel walls, which surround the dining room, are typical of a later century and are made of walnut. The spectacular crystal chandelier in the dining room was supposedly transported here from Paris in suitcases by Ferdinand Schlesinger, a wealthy industrialist and the father of Mrs. MacLaren. He played an important part in the building of the house. His daughter Gertrude divorced her first husband, Oskar Roller, and married Myron T. MacLaren in 1918. Myron, a stock broker, was the only son of William MacLaren, a former manager of Gimbels department store here.

The great mansion and its furnishings were once considered worth over a million dollars. Although the cost of the building has been quoted at $600,000 through the years, the architects records prove the total to have been $335,000. In either case it was a bargain, when in 1949, the state of Wisconsin purchased the estate for $75,000. It became a women's dormitory for the (then) Milwaukee State Teacher's College. An additional $5,000 was authorized to retain certain of the MacLarens' furnishings. When filled, the facility was able to house fifty girls in its eighteen bedrooms.

The Alumni Association has made restoration of the house an on-going priority project. In 1983 the University took possession of the Joseph Uihlein mansion on Lake Drive, along with a large collection of its furnishings. Many of these fine English pieces have since been added to the MacLaren interior.

Mary Pickford and Douglas Fairbanks once visited the MacLarens and were so impressed with the mansion that they reportedly returned to California and fashioned their own "Pickfair" estate after its design. ●

237

Opposite, heraldic crests showing the refinement of hand painted detail. Collectively these beautifully executed panels are the treasure of the mansion.

238

*The Chamber of Commerce building around 1940.
This rare flat-on view was taken with an extreme
wide angle lens from across the street and in the
position of the center point of the building.*

When President Taft was given a sightseeing tour of Milwaukee in 1909, he stopped to inspect only two buildings: One of them was the incomparable Chamber of Commerce at 225 East Michigan Street. Built at a time when Milwaukee was the largest primary wheat market in the world, this venerable structure housed the Grain Exchange and had always been an object of civic pride. Today, the 108-year-old landmark has garnered nearly every form of recognition available. It has been recorded by the Historic American Buildings Survey, listed on the National Register and designated an official landmark of both the city and the state. In Smith's two-volume book, *Architecture in America*, the Chamber of Commerce building is featured in one of only two photographs representing Milwaukee. It is clearly among the most important commercial landmarks in Wisconsin history.

The building's birth, however, was not without pain. The Chamber had discussed the idea of erecting its own building for years, while it moved from one rental location to another. In 1873, a newspaper reporter penned this complaint: "The public will think it is about time the Chamber of Commerce did something besides *talking* of a new building." Even when the "talking" was over, and the decision to build was firm, new "hot" controversies arose which would delay the construction for years.

The story of this famous giant is laced with ties to Milwaukee high society, a world-famous invention, a disastrous fire, a hidden room, "cheap cigars," a missing statue, and what would today be considered a flagrant abuse of natural resources.

It all began in 1858, when the local "Corn Exchange" members met and decided to restructure themselves as the "Chamber of Commerce of the City of Milwaukee." This new organization was dedicated to providing an "equitable mercantile tribunal" to settle differences among its members. On November 1 of that year, the new Chamber signed a lease with Sherman M. Booth to obtain a meeting space in the Free Democrat Building located at #1 Spring Street. (Marshall Field's downtown store occupies the lot today.)

Booth's original proposal for this lease has miraculously survived. According to its handwritten script he was to "fit up" the first floor of the building with the proper furniture, restrict its access to ticket holding members, and charge each member $4.50 semi-annually in advance. Booth further agreed . . . "to put on file daily, for the use of members, the daily papers from the principal cities of the Union & Canada . . . to put on the bulletin at half past one o'clock each day the market reports, by telegraph, of New York and Buffalo; to register also the receipts of produce daily by the different railroads, and shipments, and the receipts of lumber and merchandise by lake." Such was the humble beginning of the Chamber of Commerce.

Only two years had passed when the rapidly growing organization began its long battle for a building. While some members wanted to stay put, others proposed moving to Michigan Street on the east side of the Milwaukee River. A number of offers were declined. Finally, a fire paved the way for a major move. On March 1, 1862, historic Albany Hall was destroyed in a blaze and Chamber member Alexander Mitchell made a proposal they couldn't resist. He, and two others, agreed to rebuild the Albany to the Chamber's specifications, and in 1863, a move was made to a new building on the southwest corner of Michigan and Broadway.

Ten years later the Chamber had grown to include the who's-who of Milwaukee business giants and the city's grain volume was attracting national attention. With this in mind, an 1873 newspaper story summed up the city's embarrassment: "Milwaukee has long been in need of a building suitable to the wants of her business men, and in this respect has been far behind sister cities making less pretensions than ours in respect to the volume of business annually transacted. To say the least it has been a shame that the largest wheat mart on the continent should have remained without this necessary adjunct so long."

A committee, which included C.F. Ilsley, John Johnston, and Guido Pfister, was appointed to plan the erection of a new building. But this was only the beginning of another six-year period of loud speech-making, gavel-pounding, sarcastic slashes, and personal aspersions which attended the seemingly endless controversy. No one could agree on location, size of

239

building or timing of the project so the votes kept postponing things indefinitely.

In the meantime Alexander Mitchell had completed his spectacular bank building to the west of the Chamber's quarters. This necessitated discussions of remodeling the Albany, "so that it will not appear so out of place in that quarter of magnificent buildings."

Finally, in 1879, the Chamber of Commerce membership came to its senses and agreed that a major new building should be erected. By then a number of divergent proposals were in hand and one had to be adopted. The three hottest contenders were Alexander Mitchell, John Plankinton, and the Market Square Group.

Plankinton's offer would have meant moving back to the west side of the river to the location of the present Plankinton Arcade Building. His tempting $250,000 plans were based on "The Grand Opera House of Paris, compared to which the other plans presented dwindle." Described as "undoubtedly the finest site in the city," this just re-kindled a long time east side/west side rivalry.

The Market Square Group offered a clear title to the triangle of land where City Hall now stands. The group's local businessmen had pledged to donate nearly $100,000 toward the construction of a building. Mitchell's proposal was to raze the Albany, erect a new office building on that lot, and construct an exchange room therein for an annual rent of $5,000.

The final days of squabbling were so spirited that "certain members had threatened to secede from the Chamber of Commerce." When the smoke cleared, Alexander Mitchell was the winner with nearly three times the votes of all the other contenders combined. He had won in spite of having the most expensive proposal. But then he *was* the richest man in Wisconsin and he had just proven that he could produce a splendid building on the lot next door.

Mitchell was so confident of victory that he had already negotiated to buy out his partners, Thomas L. Ogden and the heirs of James S. Brown, for the Albany property. He had also commissioned several building sketches from his architect, Edward Townsend Mix. Having just completed Mitchell's great bank, Mix was probably an important factor in winning the final votes.

Left, the re-built Albany Hall erected in 1863 after a fire destroyed the original in 1862. Built by Alexander Mitchell and others, this is the site of the present Chamber of Commerce building. Above, earliest known photograph of Chamber of Commerce and Mitchell buildings, 1883-1885, taken after the tragic Newhall House Hotel fire across the street (note empty lot). This rare view was only possible for two out of the Chamber's 102 years, since Northwestern Mutual built on that lot in 1885. Their office building is still there today.

According to contemporary descriptions, the design for the new building was called "modern conventional Italian . . . plain in treatment," and it was to "embrace the results of Mr. Mix's recent observations in the east." On July 22, 1879, the old building was gone and a crew of sixty workmen were on the site to drive the first pile and begin construction. Gray Minnesota granite was laid for the foundation and Haldeman sandstone, from Cleveland, was ordered for the upper stories. The "L"-shaped cornerstone was delivered by Milwaukee contractor Cook & Hyde and was laid by the Grand Lodge of Free Masons after a parade through the downtown streets. In addition to the usual documents and articles, wheat was enclosed in the stone which bears the date, "OCT. 30 A.L. 5879."*

As the new Chamber of Commerce continued to rise, the press commented that "the architects have been lavish in their designs and ornamentations and builder, Alexander Mitchell, has spared no expense in carrying out the details of these plans." A local art expert called it "a masterpiece of architectural beauty" and claimed that "nothing in America will compare with it."

The two-story entrance arch was framed by four polished Scotch granite columns above which stood a fifteen-foot pewter statue. This female allegorical figure, called "Commerce," was the work of local sculptor Gustav Haug. Flanking her were two carved heads representing the bull and bear of the trading pit. According to plans, the contractor first installed them looking away from each other. Some complained that the antagonistic bull and bear should "wildly eye each other," so they were removed and switched to their present positions.

Elsewhere on the exterior, stone carvers produced date panels, the Great Seal of Wisconsin, giant grotesque heads, a name tablet, and transportation symbolism. Compared to its heavily carved neighbor to the west, this building was plain and simple. Both were created by the same man and the same architect but the three-year difference in their age could be seen in this thoroughly "modern" design. It was built using the Wight fireproof process which featured a veneer of clay baked with sawdust surrounding the iron floor beams.

The exterior was dominated by a campanile, or clock tower which loomed 150 feet over the pavement and contained a 2,050-pound bell. But the real focal point of the building was the great three-story-high exchange room inside. Through a twenty-four-foot corridor and up a marble staircase, was the most glorious room Milwaukee had ever seen. The huge 60' x 115' cavern was truly the heart of the Chamber. Its walls were a riot of rich colors and gold leaf. Beautifully painted murals, stained glass, and eight brass chandeliers combined to create an awe-inspiring work space.

Interior of the great Chamber of Commerce exchange room showing members examining grain samples.

* A.L. stands for anno lucis (in the year of light). Ancient masons believed the world began in 4,000 B.C. and accordingly added 4,000 to the calendar year.

Above, the only known photograph of the grain exchange room as it looked in the early days before any changes were made. Note the original octagonal trading pit. Below, the first known representation of the grain exchange room. This stone lithograph appeared in the Chamber's annual report shortly after the building's completion.

INTERIOR VIEW OF THE
NEW EXCHANGE ROOM
OF THE
MILWAUKEE CHAMBER OF COMMERCE.

SIZE OF MAIN HALL 60 BY 114 FEET.
HEIGHT OF CEILING 46 FEET.

Opposite above, a view looking east from the spectators' balcony. Below, the restored grain exchange room looking north to the main entrance. The oil painted frieze near the ceiling was cleaned and restored; the lower scenes had to be repainted from the crumbling originals. This page, a view looking northwest to the main entrance and spectators' gallery. The plaster-covered columns are painted faux-marble. New oak bases were designed for them.

Architect Mix was described as "particularly happy" with the Queen Anne style of the room's ornamentation. A Chicago fresco painter, Almini, spent two months on the scaffold creating a spectacular array of ornament and symbolism on the ceiling. The Bay View Rolling Mill, Milwaukee Water Works, City and State seals, shipping and railway symbols, the four seasons and, of course, lots of wheat and barley were to be seen there in bright colors.

Two large (12' x 14') oil paintings on canvas were executed in New York and applied to the north wall flanking the entrance. One showed sailing vessels in the Milwaukee River and the other was an agricultural scene. Then, as though the original scheme were not enough, Mitchell had an afterthought and hired Milwaukee artist, J.S. Conway, to create a large allegorical painting above the main entrance. The resulting forty-five-foot mural was divided into three panels representing agriculture, mining, and the commercial wealth of Milwaukee.

"Several young society girls" had the honor of posing for Mr. Conway's masterpiece. Alexander Mitchell's niece, Bella, became the figure representing harvest; Ethelinda Thorsen (later Mrs. John Johnston), became the figure in mining. Milwaukee's nationally famous china painter, Susan Frackelton, posed for the coal industry allegory.

By an interesting coincidence, the timing of the Chamber of Commerce project happened to straddle the dividing line of the lighting revolution. Thomas Edison received his famous lightbulb patent in 1879, but the first practical electric lighting system did not come until 1882 in New York. So, a few months before the cornerstone laying, someone wrote, "the matter of artificial lighting is yet uncertain. It is hoped that the electric light will be perfected before the building is completed; should it not be, gas will be brought into service." All of the chandeliers and wall sconces finally had to be gas.

Electricity *was* used, though, for the official clock over the door to the exchange room. Another up-to-date marvel was the hydraulic elevator which made 300 trips daily. Today, conservationists would scream if they heard the proudly announced fact that the elevator consumed 3,163,770 gallons of water every 29 days. Offices in the building were supplied with fire-proof vaults, open fireplaces, magnetic bells, telephone and telegraph attachments, and wires for stock and gold tickers.

To escape the workaday world, a Japanese-styled smoking room was provided with a sky-blue ceiling. Almini decorated this with "patches of cloud, bright-hued butterflies and birds, [and] flowers and sprays of verdure." He painted the tobacconist's shop with tobacco leaves and ornamental groupings of cigars. But it was his telegraph office decoration which prompted the building's only negative reaction. The telegraph poles and wires and eagles were not objectionable, but according to the commentator, "the eighteen naked human arms hurling thunderbolts, are simply horrible."

The completion of the Chamber was no ordinary event. In a day when newspapers were only eight pages, and the average story only a couple of column inches, the opening ceremonies here occupied the whole front page and most of the paper. Trains brought honored guests from far and wide and all of the city's hotels were crowded. The November 19, 1880, event was called "one of the most remarkable epochs in the city's history." The Newhall House Hotel across the street was the scene of a thirteen course banquet which included eighty-six items such as Turtle Steak Sauté with Truffles, Potted Quail with Mushrooms, Loin of Antelope, Broiled Jack Snipe, Boned Prairie Chicken a l'Anglaise, and Charlotte Imperial.

When the glow finally faded it was back to Grain Exchange business as usual and the first sale in the new room was made by Alexander Ray for 1,000 bushels of No. 2 spring wheat for January delivery. The traders quickly geared up and within 15 minutes 300,000 bushels had changed hands at between 1.07¼ and 1.09. The actual business of buying and selling grain was conducted in an arena which has strong ties to Milwaukee and this Chamber.

In his 1922 *History of Milwaukee* William George Bruce wrote, "A fact that is not generally known, even among the traders themselves, is that the pit — the octagonal trading platform, with steps on the inside and outside — which is used by the traders as a convenient device for their particular purposes, was first used in the Milwaukee Exchange, and was planned by Wm. J. Langson, the Secretary of the Chamber." In 1883 Secretary Langson recalled the history of his important invention:

"For a long time it was a puzzle to the floor committee of the Chamber of Commerce and to myself to conceive a means of enabling members to transact their business in comfort during periods of active trading. One of the first expedients resorted to in the old Chamber was a circular table with a hole

Left, the present front door hardware, enlarged 30% from antique originals to be in proper scale with the huge 12' high door. Below left, the original balcony which had no staircase. Only a hole remained from a later staircase addition, so a new one was designed from scratch. This oak, Eastlake-styled newel post is hand-carved and has inlaid bas-relief in cast brass. Below, the pair of 12' high oak doors designed for the restoration in the Queen Anne/Eastlake style. Not a single photograph has survived to show what the original doors looked like. The ornamental plaster is original.

in the middle. It was thought that by standing around this table all the operators could see one another and carry on transactions in an orderly manner. In practice, however, it was found that the operators were too far apart, and the device failed to give complete satisfaction. The table was sold to the proprietor of the Milwaukee Garden who used it for a bar. On picnic days a man stood in the middle, with a keg at his elbow, dealing out beer to the thirsty crowd. It was in 1870 that I got up the first trading pit. It differed from the present one in not being circular. The objection to it was that when it was crowded the men at the ends of the steps were in constant danger of being pushed off. The present modification followed in the course of time and brought the device to perfection. The principle of the thing is very old — it is the Roman amphitheater over again, but on a smaller scale. In 1878 a man in Chicago applied for a patent on the device of a trading pit with steps, and had the cheek to serve us with a notice that if we didn't pay him a royalty he'd sue us. Of course we laughed at the preposterous attempt to obtain money. If he should take his case into court we could produce hundreds of witnesses to testify that our pit was in use ten years before he applied for his patent."

The original trading floor was too badly damaged to restore. A medallion, designed in exotic hardwoods and inlaid brass, commemorates the building's original creator, its restorer, and the two dates. A parquet dance floor was added to help the building pay its way.

Milwaukee's original pit has since been adopted throughout the world as the standard appliance for this purpose.

Historian Bruce summed up the importance of this pioneering association in 1922: "Being one of the oldest and most progressive exchanges of the middle western states, the Milwaukee Chamber of Commerce has been in many respects a pioneer in grain exchange methods. The rules in effect in this organization have served as the patterns after which the structures of other and more recently created trading associations have been built." In fact, the rules of numerous exchanges organized since 1860 contain entire sections copied word-for-word from the rule book of the Milwaukee Chamber of Commerce."

Through the years the great Grain Exchange Room saw not only trading business but concerts, parties, the ritual smashing of top hats, flour-throwing celebrations and such trivial activities as a campaign to ban the smoking of "cheap cigars." By 1889 the room had become so dirty that the walls had to be re-painted. According to an exuberant newspaper writer, "The dinginess of long growth in that modern Babel has given way before the decorator's brush and has emerged a comely Nile Green." In retrospect, it can be seen that the so-called "comely" paint job obliterated most of Almini's fine Eastlake ornament and substituted what the members felt was a more acceptable Renaissance scheme. Fortunately for the future, the directors decided not to re-paint the incomparable ceiling. An additional oil painting of an Indian harvest was added to the north wall.

In 1909 the pewter statue of "Commerce" was taken off the building and re-erected in Jackson Park by the South Division Civic Association. Still standing on a block of Montello granite, the old statue is now known as "Lady of the Woods." By 1935 the wheat market had shifted away from Milwaukee and the Chamber of Commerce moved out of the building. New owners all but gutted the historic structure in a massive remodeling project. Only the Exchange Room was spared. The building was then re-named "Mackie" in honor of Alexander Mitchell's grand-nephew, Mitchell Mackie. But the ultimate insult to Milwaukee's greatest room was yet to come. The new owners later asked forty-one "prominent Milwaukeeans" if it should be remodeled. Although they said "no," a Chicago architect reversed that decision with scary stories about heat losses. So, with little sensitivity for the aesthetic or historical importance of the room, contractors descended upon it with orders to reduce the massive indoor cavern to a one-story office floor.

To accomplish this, hundreds of anchors had to be callously punched through Almini's fine painted ceiling. Then a forest of steel wires was dropped down three stories to a framework which held a new ceiling of acoustical tile and fluorescent lights. For decades, office workers moved about under this false ceiling completely oblivious to the magnificence which towered forty-five feet above their heads. Only an interested few knew what was then-called "the city's best kept architectural secret." Only by opening a window in the fourth floor men's room and peering through a broken skylight was the long-hidden chamber visible.

In 1978 the building's owner, Mrs. Elenore P. Ashley, made the decision to restore this historic room as a memorial to her late husband. The ceiling could not be cleaned, so it was repaired and re-painted according to the original design. The bottom ten feet of the room had been completely destroyed by office remodelings so new design work was required in the carefully researched style of the period.

For the room to earn its keep, instead of just existing as a museum, one major concession had to be made. An elaborate parquet dance floor was created to replace the old working surface which had been abused for a century by traders walking over spilled grain samples. This provided an opportunity, in an ornamental medallion, to commemorate the original builder, the date of construction, the restorer and the date of restoration.

But more importantly, the dance floor contains the outline of Milwaukee's famous trading pit. During the demolition of offices, sections of an old sub-floor were uncovered. On the badly worn wood, scars revealed the shape of an old octagonal pit measuring 23'-8⅞" across. The exact position and accurate outline of this shape was then cut into the new floor. The depression was inlaid with brass to permanently mark the historic spot where world wheat prices were once set.

The restored grain exchange room sparkles now, recalling a time when world grain trading was conducted in a surrounding of fresco, marble and oak. The exterior of this venerable landmark is still 95% original, and its bull is still "wildly eyeing" its bear. This stately giant remains one of Milwaukee's most magnificent architectural treasures. ●

The Library/Museum building shortly after its completion.

Well thought-out design and exquisite craftmanship have given a kind of *aesthetic immortality* to the Milwaukee Public Library building. Although it has been on the scene for nearly a century, its Neo-Renaissance façade is never tiring. There are so many levels of complexity in its design that one can study it for years and still discover new subtleties.

It is an early and important example of the nineteenth century movement which attempted to pull America away from Victorian eclecticism by reviving the classical styles. But behind the dignity and elegance of its classical façade lies a turbulent story of angry architects, worried librarians, reneging politicians and name-calling newspapers. From the time when it was first discussed, in 1889, until it was fully occupied a decade later, this building was a constant source of controversy and aggravation.

It all began when Milwaukee's Library, and its independently governed Museum, complained of insufficient space and high rents. Both institutions were located in high fire-risk areas and were paying heavily for insurance. To find a solution, the two boards of trustees appointed a joint committee to "consider and report" on a site for a new building. The committee first met on January 8, 1890, and sifted through numerous offerings from property owners city-wide. They finally settled on the present site on Grand Avenue (now W. Wisconsin) between 8th and 9th Streets. According to the committee's report, the decision was unanimous and all were pleased with the site. City Librarian K. August Linderfelt observed, "It is doubtful, whether another place could have been selected, so eminently suitable for this purpose, situated as it is on high ground, at the beginning of one of the choicest residence portions of the city, on one of its most beautiful streets and still within a few minutes walk of the business center, while it is almost the exact geographical center of the city within the corporate limits."

He further suggested an attitude of civic pride in the upcoming building project which would soon infect the citizens of Milwaukee. Library board president Matthew Keenan said, "We feel confident that in time our municipal government will erect a building in every way worthy of the location."

In November, 1890, Linderfelt and Adolph Meinecke, of the museum, traveled the country visiting library and museum buildings from Michigan to Connecticut. They took notes and prepared a report of their findings which would later become the basis for the Milwaukee project. Among their published conclusions was this key statement: "The most satisfactory solution of the problem would be the erection of two practically independent structures, connected only toward the street, so that they may present the appearance of a uniform whole." The lengthy report included detailed descriptions of buildings visited, general specifications and a number of suggested floor plans drawn by an architect from their own sketches.

It was then the responsibility of the trustees to select an architect. Instead of making an outright appointment, they elected to offer this splendid opportunity to all the architects of the country. An open competition was a popular way to handle public building projects. Among its advantages was the chance it gave minor architects to develop major projects under realistic competitive conditions. Such contests were even more popular in Europe where, during the same decade, a monthly periodical was published on just that subject: *Duetsche Konkurrenzen* (German Competitions) featured the winning and losing drawings submitted for that country's building projects.

There was also a bad side to the practice of open competition which caused many architects to regard them with suspicion or avoid them altogether. Many scandals had been uncovered in the past and bribery of public officials was common in some areas. But the trustees had made their decision and on September 7, 1893, the public call for entries was made by advertising in newspapers and a national trade journal. A twelve-page pamphlet, *Instructions to Architects*, was published and distributed to potential applicants.

Architects were warned that the total cost, including their own fees, was not to exceed $500,000. Plans were to be drawn to the scale of eight feet to the inch and were to be supplemented with type-written specifications. The instructions called for two pen-and-

251

ink perspective drawings, "without shading or landscape embellishment except a single human figure six feet high to indicate the scale." Five exterior building materials were given from which to choose and a plat map of the site was included.

Aesthetically, the only restraint imposed on contestants was a single sentence: "The building should be of a pure style of architecture, befitting its uses, and impressive to the eye by beauty of proportion and harmony of lines rather than by showy ornament or eccentric features."

The competition deadline was noon on November 15, 1893, and at that time sixty-one sets of drawings had been received. Since others were shipped in time, but delayed in transit, the final count of legal entries reached seventy-four. Everyone was pleased with the size and quality of the response, especially in view of the recent Milwaukee City Hall competition which drew only fourteen entries. (The attractive Eiffel Tower project, in Paris, turned up just a few more than 100 proposals.) The excitement was so high that, as soon as the drawings were unpacked and enough easels could be gathered, a public exhibition was set up in the Builder's Exchange.

The greatest number of entries, fifteen, came from Chicago and, as might have been expected, fourteen of Milwaukee's firms responded. But the rest came from as far away as Nashville, Atlanta, Denver and Toronto. Among the cities to submit three or more entries were Boston (six), New York (five), St. Louis (five), Duluth (four), Detroit (three) and Minneapolis (three). The applicants included numerous firms with prestigious reputations as well as newcomers still struggling to be recognized. Included among the latter names was young Frank Lloyd Wright, whose name meant so little then that it was misspelled in all the official listings as Frank *H.* Wright.

One of the most common first-reactions to the exhibition was that the Chicago World's Fair (World's Columbian Exhibition — 1893) had made a deep impression on the country's architects. Some went so far as to say that a few of the designs were merely adaptations of specific buildings at the fair. There was, however, no doubt that the majority of them were classically oriented. A Milwaukee architect bet "a box of good cigars" that at least ten plans would feature towers, but he apparently lost since the remaining evidence shows comparatively little interest in that feature.

253

Three views of the south (front) façade showing the crisp, carved stone detailing and the finely proportioned Neo-Classical design.

Left, view from high scaffolding during construction. The crew of stone carvers is working on Corinthian capitals at the top of logia columns over the entrance. According to the architect's specifications, all stones were to be roughed-out and set in the masonry before carving. (Note the roughed-out wreaths above the carvers' heads.) Above, the view looking southeast toward the dome during construction. Notice that the eagles had not yet been erected at the front corners.

About a dozen entries were immediately disqualified for incorporating too much "showy ornament or eccentric features." Another dozen were discarded because their "interior arrangement was so wretched that their serious consideration was out of the question." John A. Moller, of Milwaukee, flirted with disqualification by submitting illegal colored drawings. His plan was described as bearing "the most marked traces of the World's Fair." Two Milwaukee architectural firms, Ferry & Clas and H.C. Koch, had their designs compared to the similar Leipzig Library in Germany. Chicago's Henry Ives Cobb was accused of only slightly modifying his design for the Newberry Library there.

One of the most analyzed designs was submitted by H.C. Koch. In addition to the Leipzig allegation, there were those who thought his entry closely resembled the exterior of Milwaukee's city hall, which competition he had only recently won. It also looked like Strassburg architect Joseph Muller's second prize design for the Bremen Library competition in Germany that year. Koch claimed his building was "no direct copy from any existing building, although the central feature bears some similarity to that of the technical high school of Berlin."

Above, looking across the rotunda at the third floor level. Note the Sienna marble balustrade. All of the other ornament, including the large spread eagles, is in plaster. Right, detail showing the fine match between the real Sienna marble balustrade and the imitation (scagliola) plaster columns. Far right, three circular windows on the south (front) elevation at the third floor level.

Although there were a few Greek and Romanesque designs, the overall impression of the entries was one of the Italian Renaissance as interpreted in the World's Fair which was, in turn, inspired by the principles of the Ecole des Beaux-Arts in Paris. It was not long before the seventy-four entries had been narrowed down to around ten serious contenders. The Board of Trustees received letters from competing architects suggesting the employment of a professional advisor and they did, in fact, hesitate to delegate such an important selection to a group of laymen. In answer to the board's invitation, Professor William Robert Ware of Columbia College traveled to Milwaukee to aid in making the big decision.

After three days of intensive study, Professor Ware returned to New York with a handful of the better drawings for further analysis. Milwaukee waited in suspense for the results and finally, on January, 1894, his report was presented at a joint meeting of the trustees. The five finalists announced were Andrews, Jacques & Rantoul of Boston, Boring & Tilton of New York, Ferry & Clas of Milwaukee, H.C. Koch & Co. of Milwaukee, and Nettleton & Kahn of Detroit.

But a day before the report was officially presented, the deliberations had already eliminated all but the two Milwaukee firms, Ferry & Clas and H.C. Koch. After a free discussion on Professor Ware's report, the boards voted on the issue and Ferry & Clas won nine-to-six. Ware commented on the winning design: "The elevation is, to my mind, one of the best, if not the very best of them all, elegant and sufficiently dignified, and a great improvement upon the library at Leipzig, which it notably resembles."

Not everyone agreed. In fact, a group of architects appeared at the board meeting to protest what they felt was an "indiscreetly conducted" competition. Their protest was ignored and put off until the next meeting. The runner-up, H.C. Koch, sought an injunction to stop the Board of Trustees from, "Rewarding the unfair practices of the said firm of Ferry & Clas." Koch, and ten other Milwaukee architects, claimed the winners had produced a revised plan after the deadline and that the additional drawing figured prominently in Professor Ware's decision. The complaint further alleged that there were "other underhand, illegal and fraudulent means used for and on behalf of said Ferry & Clas to obtain the reward." The protest caused a lot of grief, but eventually failed.

George B. Ferry and Alfred C. Clas were young architects, but they had already made an impressive mark on the community. By the time of the library/ museum project, they had completed the Captain Frederick Pabst mansion, the chapel in Forest Home Cemetery, St. John's Cathedral Tower, the Matthews and Steinmeyer Buildings, and numerous other fine commercial and residential jobs.

The winners were ready to begin work when the Common Council created another unexpected roadblock. The contract which it submitted for approval featured an architect's commission of what amounted to a little over 3%. Since the competition advertising clearly stated 5%, Ferry & Clas refused to sign. A resolution was introduced to raise the city's ordinary commission in this case and its good argument included this statement: "Beauty and dignity of design should be essential in a building which represents the best and highest ideals of modern life . . . Only men of a high degree of talent and of considerable experience are fit to be trusted with such a building . . . The only hope of attracting such men to the competition lay in offering a fee at least equal to that paid for other work of the kind."

The arguments fell on deaf ears and the Council defeated the resolution. A year was to pass until the city finally reached a compromise which was acceptable to the architects. In the meantime the city librarian complained, "The beautiful site on Grand Avenue stands vacant, a dumping ground for paving blocks,

surrounded by advertising boards, which, in such a place, are an offense to public taste." It was noted that the year's delay cost the city more than the amount saved in the commission percentage battle.

Ferry and Clas were finally forced to settle on 3½% commission and the work got underway. In March of 1895 final plans were submitted and by October the actual construction was begun. Milwaukeeans watched with great interest as the striking building started to rise from that shabby, long-neglected lot. After much deliberation its material had been changed from Berea sandstone to the one originally favored by the architect, blue Bedford limestone. And it was the bright and crisp effect of this stone which made such a favorable impact on the community. But it is the hand-carved ornament and detailing of this stone which is the true glory of the exterior.

The architects were taking no chances with the principal character-giving element of their design. In the published specifications book they required, "All carving shall be done by skilled artists, and if any carvers are employed who have not the proper ability to produce the quality of work desired on this building, they shall be dismissed if demanded. All carvers submitting proposals for this carving shall submit with their proposals, models they have made and photographs of work they have executed."

A further step was taken to ensure that no mistakes were made on the ornamentation. The masons' instructions demanded: "All carving shall be done after the stone is set in place at the building. For carved molding, the rough molding will be cut by the cut stone contractor, but for other work he will leave large square blocks that must be cut down by this contractor." What the masons left were crude stone blocks or roughly-shaped pieces which were then finished on the building by the carvers. In these days before modular steel scaffolding, the stage for the carvers was erected by lashing together a framework of timber poles with rope.

Passersby could hear the constant clinking sound of the carvers' chisels as they worked high above the street. For months the small limestone chips rained down through the scaffold as Corinthian capitals, wreaths, garlands, swags and decorative panels took shape. The only exceptions to the stone carving were the two gigantic eagles flanking the dome at the roofline. Their bodies were modeled in terra cotta and their wings were cast in bronze.

Left, one of the custom-cast brass push-plates with the Milwaukee "M" emblem. Above, the board room showing custom carved chairs, carved fireplace and Roman-type opus tesselatum mosaic floor.

The fine proportions and Renaissance detailing were carefully drawn into the interior. The entrance rotunda is a spectacular three story space which rises to a plaster coffered dome. One wall is illuminated by the windows of the front façade's central pavilion while the other three contain passageways at all levels and two major marble staircases.

Below the dome is one of the finest mosaic floors in the Midwest. Done in the pure tradition of a Roman opus tessellatum pavement, this masterpiece was hand laid by skilled Italians who had then recently settled in Milwaukee. The elaborate design is composed of countless tiny marble cubes in may colors. This fine floor treatment was extended widely throughout the corridors and public areas.

Another interesting, and now almost forgotten craft can be seen in the rotunda. While the handrails and turned balusters are cut from yellow Sienna marble, the tall matching columns are done in an imitation material called scagliola. This Italian technique, which employs colored plaster, is so effective that most people pass through the rotunda assuming that everything in sight is solid marble.

Hallways and public and staff rooms were tastefully related with carved oak, ornamental plaster detail, fine brass hardware and high-quality bronze and art-glass light fixtures. All hardwood was rubbed down with pumice stone and oil.

Today, after numerous changes, remodeling and additions, the building still serves the Milwaukee Public Library, but its original co-tenant, the Milwaukee Public Museum, has since moved to a new and larger building. Now, with the recently completed exterior restoration, Milwaukeeans can once again appreciate the beauty which had been concealed by bird droppings and the black stain of air pollution. This was one of the first American buildings to follow the powerful influence of the Chicago Fair, and it deserves its status as one of Milwaukee's most important landmarks. ●

Close-up of one of a pair of giant terra cotta eagles with cast bronze wings at the roof line.

BIBLIOGRAPHY

Architectural Glossaries and Architect Biographies

Adeline, Jules. *Adeline's Art Dictionary.* New York: D. Appleton & Company, 1891.

Audsley, William James and George Ashdown Audsley. *Popular Dictionary of Architecture and the Allied Arts.* New York: G. P. Putnam's Sons, 1881-1882.

Brees, S. C. *The Illustrated Glossary of Practical Architecture and Civil Engineering.* London: Savill and Edwards, 1852.

Clement, Clara Erskine. *A Handbook of Legendary and Mythological Art with Descriptive Illustrations.* New York: Houghton, Mifflin, Cambridge Riverside Press, 1890.

Davis, Richard S. *50 Years of Architecture.* Milwaukee: Eschweiler, 1943.

Fairholt, F. W. *A Dictionary of Terms in Art.* London: Virtue, Hall, & Virtue, 1854.

Nicholson, Peter. *Nicholson's Dictionary of the Science and Practice of Architecture, Building, Carpentry, etc.* 2 vol. London: The London Printing and Publishing Company, [1854].

Parker, John Henry. *A Glossary of Terms used in Grecian, Roman, Italian and Gothic Architecture.* 3rd ed., 2 vol. Oxford, 1840.

Placzek, Adolf K., ed. *Macmillan Encyclopedia of Architects.* 4 vols. New York: The Free Press, 1982.

Richards, J. M., ed. *Who's Who in Architecture: From 1400 to the Present.* New York: Holt, Rinehart & Winston, 1977.

Sturgis, Russell. *A Dictionary of Architecture and Building.* 3 vols. New York: Macmillan, 1905.

Withey, Henry F. and Elsie Rathburn Withey. *Biographical Dictionary of American Architects (Deceased).* Los Angeles: Hennessey & Ingalls Inc., 1970.

Architectural Histories

Fergusson, James, *A History of Architecture in All Countries.* 4 vols. London: John Murray, 1873-1876.

Fletcher, Banister, Sir. *A History of Architecture on the Comparative Method.* 17th ed. New York: Charles Scribner's Sons, 1967.

Gwilt, Joseph. *An Encyclopedia of Architecture: Historical, Theoretical & Practical.* London: Longmans, Green & Co., 1867.

Koehler, S. R. *Architecture, Sculpture, and the Industrial Arts.* Boston: L. Prange and Co., 1879,

Osborne, Charles Francis, ed. *Historic Houses and Their Gardens.* Philadelphia: The John C. Winston Company, 1908.

Raguenet, A. *Petits Edifices Historiques.* 3 vols. Paris: Morel, 1896.

Smith, G. E. Kidder. *A Pictorial History of Architecture in America.* New York: American Heritage Publishing Co., Inc., 1976

Thorp, William H. *An Architect's Sketch Book at Home and Abroad.* Leeds: R. Jackson, 1884.

Uhde, Constantin. *Die Konstruktionen und die Kunstformen der Architektur.* 4 vols. Berlin: Ernst Wasmuth, 1902-1911.

Architectural Pattern Books

Allen, Lewis Falley. *Rural Architecture.* New York: Orange Judd & Company, 1852.

Atwood, Daniel Topping. *Atwood's Country and Suburban Houses.* New York: Orange Judd & Company, 1871.

Baker, Z. *Modern House Builder* Boston: Higgins, Bradley, and Dayton, 1857.

Benjamin, Asher. *The Architect: or, Practical House Carpenter.* Boston: L. Coffin, 1843.

Bicknell (A. J.) & Co. *Specimen Book of One Hundred Architectural Designs.* New York: A. J. Bicknell & Co., 1878.

Brunner, Arnold William. *Cottages.* New York: William T. Comstock, 1884.

Cummings, (Marcus Fayette) and Miller, (Charles Crosby). *Architecture.* Troy, New York: A. J. Bicknell & Co., 1868.

Dwyer, Charles P. *The Economic Cottage Builder.* Buffalo: Wanzer, McKim & Co., 1856.

Gibson, Louis H. *Beautiful Houses.* New York: Thomas Y. Crowell & Co., (1895).

Holly, Henry Hudson. *Holly's Country Seats.* New York: D. Appleton & Co., 1863.

Hooper, Chas. Edw. *The Country House* Garden City, NY: Doubleday, Page and Co., 1906.

Jackson, Allen W. *The Half-Timber House.* New York: McBride, Nast & Company, 1912.

Jacques, Daniel Harrison. *The House: A Manual of Rural Architecture.* New York: G. E. & F. W. Woodward, 1866.

Kerr, Robert. *The Gentleman's House; or How to Plan English Residences, From the Parsonage to the Palace.* London: John Murray, 1871.

Kilham & Hopkins, Architects. *Garages, Country and Suburban.* New York: The American Architect, 1911.

Lafever, Minard. *The Beauties of Modern Architecture.* New York: D. Appleton & Co., 1835.

Lakeman, Albert. *Concrete Cottages, Bungalows, and Garages.* London: Concrete Publications, Ltd, c. 1924.

Lakey, Chas. D. *Lakey's Village and Country Houses.* New York: American Builder Publishing Co., 1875.

Loudon, John Claudius. *Cottage, Farm, and Villa Architecture and Furniture.* London: Frederick Warne and Co., (1869).

Maynard, Samuel T. *The Small Country Place.* Philadelphia: J.B. Lippincott Company, 1908.

Moore, Francis Cruger. *How to Build a Home: The House Practical.* New York: Doubleday & McClure Co., 1897.

Palliser, Palliser & Co., *Palliser's New Cottage Homes and Details.* New York: Palliser, Palliser & Co., 1887.

Reed, Samuel Burrage. *Dwelling for Village and Country.* New York: S. B. Reed, 1885.

Richardson, Charles James, *The Englishman's House.* London: Chatto & Windus, c. 1875.

Richardson, Charles James, *Picturesque Designs for Mansions, Villas, Lodges.* London: Atchley and Co., 1870.

Sloan, Samuel. *Sloan's Constructive Architecture.* Philadelphia: J. B. Lippincott & Co., 1859.

Sloan, Samuel. *Sloan's Homestead Architecture.* Philadelphia: J. B. Lippincott & Co., 1870.

Stevenson, J. J. *House Architecture.* 2 vols. London: Macmillan & Co., 1880.

Todd, Sereno Edwards. *Todd's Country Homes.* Philadelphia: J. C. McCurdy & Co., 1870.

Wheeler, Gervase. *The Choice of a Dwelling.* London: John Murray, 1872.

Woodward, George Evertson. *Woodward's National Architect.* New York: Geo. E. Woodward, 1869.

Architectural Trade Catalogs

Anaglypta; With Which is Incorporated the Best Selection in High Relief Designs of "Cordelova," "Cameoid" and "Salamander." London, 1926.

Architect's Standard Catalogues: Building & Decorative Materials, etc. 4 vols. London, 1933/1935.

Braun, (J. G.) Co. *Catalog No. 19: Illustrating Light Iron Pressed Rossettes, Cups, Husks, Leaves, Roses and Various Ornaments Used on Lamps and Light Fixtures.* Chicago and New York, c. 1919.

Corbin (P&F). *Hardware Catalogue & Supplement No. 2.* New Britain, Ct. 1885, 1890.

Christopher & Simpson. *Illustrated Catalogue of the Christopher & Simpson Architectural Iron and Foundry Co.* St. Louis: 1888.

Decorators Supply Co. *Catalog 105: Illustrated Catalog of Plastic Ornaments Made in Exterior Composition Plaster-Cement.* Chicago, 1917.

Electrical Supply Co., *Illustrated Catalogue of Electric Light and Power Supplies.* Chicago, 1892.

Fischer and Jirouch Co. *Catalog of Interior and Exterior Decorative Ornament.* Cleveland, c. 1910.

Fiske (J. W.) *Fiske Wrought Iron Railing Entrance Gates, Wire Fencing and Other Ornamental Utility Metal Work.* New York, c. 1925.

Fontaine et cie. *Album de Serrurerie Decorative (Hardware).* Paris, c. 1910.

Friedley-Voshart Co. *Manufacturers of Architectural Sheet Metal Ornaments Statuary Spun Work.* Chicago, 1925.

General Electric Company. *Edison Incandescent Lamps, Standard Special and Miniature, Number 1020.* Schenectady, 1900.

Gladding, McBean & Co. *Clay Products List No. 50.* San Francisco, 1923.

Gladding, McBean & Co. *Latin Tiles.* San Francisco, 1923.

Gross (Phillip) Hardware Co. *A Wholesale and Retail Builders' Hardware and Contractors' Supplies.* Milwaukee, c. 1910.

Hope (Henry) & Sons, Ltd. *Hope's Casements & Leaded Glass.* New York, 1919.

Hope (Henry) & Sons, Ltd. *Hope's Leadwork for the Garden.* New York, 1931.

International Casement Co., Inc. *Catalog No. 7: Casement and Composite Windows.* Jamestown, NY, 1922.

Jacobson & Company. *A Second Book of Old English Designs: Fifty-One Plates of Authentic English Ornament.* New York, 1928.

Jackson (Edwin A.), Inc. *Andirons & Fireplace Fittings, Catalog No. 10.* New York, 1927.

Kraus, Walchenbach & Peltzer. *Stolberger Zinkornamenten-Frabrik-Catalog.* Stolberg, 1889.

Livingston & Co. *Price List and Illustrated Catalogue of Builder's and Miscellaneous Hardware.* Allegheny City, PA, 1881.

MacFarlane (Walter) & Co., *Illustrated Catalog ... Architectural, Sanitary, and General Iron Founders.* Glasgow, c. 1890.

Maxwell Forbes & Stillman. *Architectural Ornaments in Exterior and Interior Composition, Wood, Cement, etc.* Milwaukee, 1909.

Milcor Steel Company. *Fireproof Building Products.* Milwaukee, 1942.

Morgan Company. *Artistic Grates, Fenders, Andirons, Fire Irons and Other Goods, for Fitting and Decoration of the Fireplace.* New York, 1882.

Mullins (W. H.) Co. *Catalogue of Architectural Ornaments and Statuary in Sheet Zinc, Brass or Copper.* Salem, OH, c. 1894.

Parker & Whipple Co. *Illustrated Catalogue: Door Locks, Knobs, and Hardware.* West Meridan, CT, 1880.

Pettingell-Andrews Co. *Exemplar Special Line Electric Lighting Fixtures.* Boston, c. 1915.

Pittsburgh Lamp, Brass and Glass Company. *Catalogue: Gas and Electrical Goods.* Pittsburgh, c. 1890.

Pittsburgh Plate Glass Co. *Glass, Paints, Varnishes and Brushes.* Pittsburgh, 1923.

Pritzlaff (John) Hardware Co. *Catalog #2.* Milwaukee, 1897.

Roberson (Charles) of London. *Craftsmanship in Woodwork and Carving.* New York, 1931.

Sanger, Rockwell & Co. *Sash, Doors, Blinds, Fine Interior Finishing.* Milwaukee, c. 1886.

Shapiro & Aronson. *Catalogue No. 11, Designers and Manufacturers of Gas, Electric and Combination Lighting Fixtures.* New York, c. 1913.

Stearns (A. T.) Lumber Co. *Catalog.* Boston, 1898.

Sweet's. *Catalogue of Building Construction.* New York, 1912.

Tiffany Studios. *Tiffany Studios Lamps.* T.A. Chapman Co., Milwaukee Imprint. New York, c. 1915.

Universal Moulding Book: Containing Latest Styles of Moulding and Architectural Designs of Exterior and Interior Finish in Great Variety. Chicago, 1887.

Weatherbest Stained Shingle Co., Inc. *The Construction of Thatch Straw Effect Roofs with Weatherbest Stained Shingles.* Tonawanda, NY, 1928.

Western Sand Blast Co. *Ornamental Glass, Railroad Pattern-sheet, Office Glass Pattersheet.* Chicago, c. 1880.

Yale & Towne Mfg. Co. *Catalogue No. 12.* Stamford, CT, 1889.

Young & Marten. *Illustrated General Catalog: Manufacturers, Merchants, Iron Founders & Shippers of Every Requisite for Building Construction.* London, 1903.

Milwaukee History

Anderson, W.J. & Julius Bleyer, eds. *Milwaukee's Great Industries.* Milwaukee: Association for the Advancement of Milwaukee, 1891.

Austin, H. Russell. *The Milwaukee Story.* Milwaukee: The Milwaukee Journal, 1946.

Bruce, William George. *A Short History of Milwaukee.* Milwaukee: The Bruce Publishing Co., 1936.

Bruce, William George, ed. *History of Milwaukee City and County.* 3 vols. Chicago: S.J. Clarke Publishing Co., 1922.

Buck, James S. *Milwaukee Under the Charter.* 2 vols. Milwaukee: Swain & Tate, Symes, Swain & Co., 1884-1886.

Buck, James S. *Pioneer History of Milwaukee.* 2 vols. Milwaukee: Milwaukee News Co., 1876-1881.

Cochran, Thomas C. *The Pabst Brewing Company: The History of an American Business.* New York: New York University Press, 1948.

Conard, Howard Louis. *History of Milwaukee from its First Settlement to the Year 1895.*

2 vols. Chicago and New York: American Biographical Publishing Company, 1895.

Flower, Frank A. *History of Milwaukee, Wisconsin.* Chicago: The Western Historical Co., 1881.

General Federation of Women's Clubs. *Milwaukee the Beautiful: Official Souvenir of the Biennial Meeting of the General Federation of Women's Clubs, June 4-10, 1900.* Milwaukee: Geo. H. Yenowine & Co. W.Peck Jr., 1900.

Gregory, John G. *History of Milwaukee, Wisconsin.* 4 vols. Chicago: S.J. Clarke, 1931.

Hooker, William F. *Bill Hooker's Old-Time Milwaukee.* Milwaukee: William F. Hooker, 1935.

Hooker, William F. *Glimpses of an Earlier Milwaukee.* Milwaukee: The Milwaukee Journal, 1929.

Illustrated News Annual: Milwaukee. Milwaukee: Geo. H. Yenowine, 1892-93.

The Industrial History of Milwaukee. Milwaukee: E.F. Barton, 1886.

Koss, Rudolph A. *Milwaukee.* Milwaukee: Schnellpressendruck des "Herold," 1871.

Metropolitan Milwaukee Association of Commerce. *Milwaukee: A Picturesque and Descriptive Account.* Milwaukee: Merchants and Manufacturers Assn., 1903.

Milwaukee Illustrated: Its Trade, Commerce, Manufacturing Interests, and Advantages as a Residence City. Milwaukee: W.H. Coleman, 1877.

The Milwaukee Monthly Magazine. Vol. viii, No. 48, Milwaukee: T. J. Gilmore, 1874.

Milwaukee of Today, the Cream City of the Lakes. Milwaukee and Chicago: Phoenix Publishing Co., (1892).

Milwaukee Press Club. *Commercial History of Wisconsin.* Milwaukee: Thompson H. Adams, 1910.

Milwaukee Sentinel. *An Illustrated Description of Milwaukee.* Milwaukee: The Milwaukee Sentinel, 1890.

Milwaukee Writers Project. *The History of Milwaukee County.* Milwaukee: Milwaukee Public Library, 1947.

Nordamerikanischer Sangerbund. *A Souvenir of the 24th Sangerfest.* Milwaukee: Casper and Zahn, 1886.

Ogden, Marion G. *Homes of Old Spring Street.* Milwaukee: Marion G. Ogden, 1944.

Old Settlers' Club. *Early Milwaukee: Papers from the Archives of the Old Settlers' Club of Milwaukee County.* Milwaukee: Old Settlers' Club, 1916.

Perrin, Richard W. E. *Milwaukee Landmarks.* 2nd rev. ed. Milwaukee: Milwaukee Public Museum, 1979.

Watrous, Jerome A., Lieut, Col. *Memoirs of Milwaukee County.* 2 vols. Madison, WI: Western Historical Assoc., 1909.

Watrous, Jerome A. Lieut,, Col. *Memoirs of Milwaukee County; Volume Deluxe: Biographical.* Madison, WI: Western Historical Assoc., 1909.

Wheeler, A. C. *The Chronicles of Milwaukee.* Milwaukee: Jermaine & Brightman, 1861.

Milwaukee Maps and View Books

Album of Milwaukee. Milwaukee: C.A. Rhode Co., 1896.

Baist, G. Wm. *Baist's Property Atlas of the City of Milwaukee and Vicinity.* Philadelphia: G. Wm. Baist, 1898.

Illustrated Historical Atlas of Milwaukee County, Wisconsin. Chicago: H. Belden & Co., 1876.

Insurance Maps of Milwaukee, Wisconsin. New York: Sanborn- Perris Map Company, 1888, 1894, 1910.

Map and Guide of the City of Milwaukee. Milwaukee: C.N. Caspar, 1892.

Milwaukee Illustrated: Photogravures. Milwaukee: C.N. Caspar Co., 1901.

Milwaukee - Indelible Photographs by the Albertype Co., NY Milwaukee: Schroeter & Thielecke, c. 1885.

Milwaukee Photogravures. Milwaukee: The Art Gravure & Etching Co., 1892.

Pictorial Milwaukee: Souvenir Album of the Cream City. Milwaukee: C. N. Caspar Co., 1902.

Rascher's Fire Insurance Atlas of the City of Milwaukee, Wis. Chicago: Western Fire Map Publishing Co., 1876.

Wauwatosa History

Daum, Mrs. Arthur J. & others. *The Wauwatosa Story.* Wauwatosa, WI: Board of Education, 1961.

Perry, Charles B. & others. *City of Wauwatosa: 100th Anniversary, 1835-1935.* Wauwatosa. WI: Wauwatosa Centennial Committee, 1935.

Watner, Emma Clapp. *Reminiscenses of Early Wauwatosa.* Wauwatosa, WI: Privately published, 1902.

Wheeler, Mrs. Leverett C. *Our Village: A Saga of Wauwatosa.* Wauwatosa, WI: Wawautosa Women's Club, 1947.

Wisconsin History

Aikens, Andrew J. & Proctor, Lewis A. *Men of Progress - Wisconsin.* Milwaukee: The Evening Wisconsin Co., 1897.

Gregory, John. *Industrial Resources of Wisconsin.* 2 vols. Milwaukee: Milwaukee See-Bote Job Print and Milwaukee News Company, 1870-1872.

Kohler, Ruth DeYoung. *The Story of Wisconsin Women.* Kohler, WI: The Committee on Wisconsin Women for the 1948 Wisconsin Centennial, 1948.

Lapham, Increase Allen. *Wisconsin: Its Geography and Topography. Milwaukee:* I. A. Hopkins, 1846.

Miller, F. A. Summer Homes in Wisconsin and Minnesota. Chicago: Chicago, Milwaukee & St. Paul Railway Co., 1909.

Perrin, Richard W. E. *Historic Wisconsin Buildings: A Survey in Pioneer Architecture 1835-1870.* 2nd ed. Milwaukee: Milwaukee Public Museum, 1981.

Tuttle, Charles R. *An Illustrated History of the State of Wisconsin . . . from its First Exploration down to 1875.* Boston: B.B. Russell, 1875.

Usher, Ellis B. & others. *The Evening Wisconsin Newspaper Reference Book.* Milwaukee: The Evening Wisconsin Company, 1914.

Usher, Ellis Baker. *Wisconsin: Its Story and Biography, 1848-1913.* 8 vols. Chicago and New York: The Lewis Publishing Co., 1914.

Walling, H. F. *Atlas of the State of Wisconsin, Including Statistics and Descriptions of Its History.* Boston and Detroit: Walling, Tackabury & Co., 1876.

Zimmermann, H. Russell *The Heritage Guidebook: Landmarks and Historical Sites in Southeastern Wisconsin.* Milwaukee: Heritage Banks, Inland Heritage Corp., 1976.

Newspapers and Magazines

Historical Messenger. Milwaukee: Milwaukee County Historical Society, 1941-1977.

Milwaukee Blue Books, Elite Registers and Social Registers, 1889-1911.

Milwaukee City Directories, 1947 to date.

Evening Wisconsin newspaper, 1868-1918.

Milwaukee Daily News newspaper, 1885-1918.

Milwaukee History. Milwaukee: Milwaukee County Historical Society, 1978 to date.

Milwaukee Journal, 1882 to date.

Milwaukee Sentinel, 1837 to date.

Wisconsin Magazine of History. Madison, WI: The State Historical Society of Wisconsin, 1917 to date.

Institutional Sources

Legislative Reference Bureau, Milwaukee City Hall 200 E. Wells St., Milwaukee, WI 53202

Milwaukee Building Inspection Department, Permit Files 841 N. Broadway, Milwaukee, WI 53202

Milwaukee Public Library, Local History Room and Marine Historical Collection. 814 W. Wisconsin Ave., Milwaukee, WI 53233

Milwaukee Public Museum Reference Library 800 W. Wells St., Milwaukee, WI 53233

Register of Deeds, Milwaukee County Courthouse. Plat books, deeds and mortgages. 901 N. 9th St., Milwaukee, WI 53233

State Historical Society of Wisconsin, library and iconographic collections. 816 State St., Madison, WI 53703

University of Wisconsin Milwaukee Library and Area Research Center 2311 E. Hartford Ave., Milwaukee, WI 53211

Wisconsin Architectural Archive (Milwaukee Public Library) 814 W. Wisconsin Ave., Milwaukee, WI 53233

Milwaukee County Historical Society 910 N. 3rd St., Milwaukee, WI 53203.

INDEX

266

269